THE PASTONS
AND
THEIR ENGLAND

Canto is a new imprint offering a range of
titles, classic and more recent, across a broad
spectrum of subject areas and interests.
History, literature, biography, archaeology,
politics, religion, psychology, philosophy and
science are all represented in Canto's specially
selected list of titles, which now offers some
of the best and most accessible of Cambridge
publishing to a wider readership.

THE PASTONS
AND
THEIR ENGLAND

STUDIES IN AN AGE OF TRANSITION

BY

H. S. BENNETT, F.B.A.

CAMBRIDGE
UNIVERSITY PRESS

Published by the Syndics of the Cambridge University Press
The Pitt Building, Trumpington Street, Cambridge CB2 1RP
40 West 20th Street, New York, NY 10011-4211, USA
10 Stamford Road, Oakleigh, Melbourne 3166, Australia

Library of Congress catalogue card number: 68–23175

First published 1922 in the series
Cambridge Studies in Medieval Life and Thought
Second edition 1932
Reprinted 1951 1968 1970 1975 1977
Canto edition 1990
Reprinted 1991 1995

ISBN 0 521 39826 6 paperback

Transferred to digital printing 2003

TO

MY FATHER

CONTENTS

v

CHAPTER XIII. LAWLESSNESS

CHAPTER XIV. RELIGION

CHAPTER XV. THE SECULAR CLERGY

CHAPTER XVI. THE REGULAR CLERGY

CHAPTER XVII. THE LIFE OF THE COUNTRYSIDE

APPENDIXES:

INDEX

PREFACE
TO THE FIRST EDITION

THE Paston Letters have long been known to students for their wealth of information on English life and manners in the fifteenth century. Dr Gairdner, in his Introduction, has emphasised their value to the constitutional historian. He sketched the political and constitutional history of the times in which the Pastons lived, and narrated the fortunes of the family and their part in public affairs. He could only devote a few pages to the social aspect of the times, and writes: "Indeed, to whatever length we should prolong these observations, we could not but leave an ample harvest of facts to be gathered by others." The present volume is an attempt to present, in a systematised form, the information this Correspondence gives us concerning everyday life in fifteenth-century England. This task has been enormously lightened by Dr Gairdner's great labours in collecting and arranging the Letters.

In order that the extracts from the Letters may be more easily read, it has been thought advisable to give them in modern English. Several letters in the original spelling will be found in Appendix IV, and one on page 247.

I have received help from many sources during the progress of this study which I gratefully acknowledge. I am especially indebted to Miss E. E. Power, late Director of Historical Studies at Girton College, Cambridge, for her interest and assistance; to Messrs Constable and Co. for kind permission to make very liberal extracts from the Letters; and to the Royal Historical Society for like permission to make use of the Stonor Letters. I desire also to thank Lt.-Col. G. Crosfield, D.S.O., for his generosity, the Syndics of the University Press for publishing this study, and Mr A. R. Waller for his kindly aid in many ways.

Finally, two names remain. Mr G. G. Coulton, the general editor of this series, first suggested this study, and he has given of his time, his thought and his learning unstintingly. In other directions I am almost equally indebted to my wife. To both of them I owe more than I can express here.

H. S. BENNETT.

CAMBRIDGE
1 *October* 1921

PREFACE TO THE SECOND EDITION

The publication of a second edition has made it possible to correct a number of minor errors pointed out by reviewers and correspondents, and also to insert some important alterations in the text where further study or the more recent work of others has made a change imperative.

H. S. B.

April 1932

NOTE TO 1968 IMPRESSION

This reprinting has enabled me to make a number of corrections to the manuscript references in Appendix IV, necessitated by the accession to the British Museum of Volumes I and II of Fenn's original edition.

H. S. B.

February 1968

ABBREVIATIONS AND AUTHORITIES

ABBREVIATIONS

Arch.	*Archaeologia.*
C.P.L.	*Calendar Papal Letters.*
C.S.	Camden Society Publications.
E.C.P.	*Early Chancery Proceedings.*
E.E.T.S.	Early English Text Society Publications.
Hist. MSS.	*Reports of the Historical MSS Commission,* 1874–
N.A.	*Norfolk Archaeology.*—Transactions of the Norfolk and Norwich Archaeological Society, 1846– .
P.L.	*Paston Letters,* ed. Gairdner, J. London, 1872–5. Supplement, 1901.
P.P.	*Piers Plowman,* ed. Skeat, W. W. Oxford, 1886.
P.P.C.	*Proceedings of the Privy Council.*
P.R.	*Patent Rolls.*
R.H.S.	*Royal Historical Society Transactions.*
R.P.	*Rotuli Parliamentorum.*
R.S.	Rolls Series.
S.E.	*Social England,* ed. Trail, H. D.
S.L.	*Stonor Letters,* ed. Kingsford, C. L. [R.H.S.] London, 1919.
S.S.	Selden Society Publications.
Sur. S.	Surtees Society Publications.

AUTHORITIES

Abram. *Social England in the 15th century.* Abram, A. London, 1909.

Arnold. *Select English Works of J. Wyclif.* Arnold, T. Oxford, 1869.

Berkeley, *Extracts.* Abstracts and extracts of Smyth's *Lives of the Berkeleys.* Fosbroke, T. D. London, 1821.

Blomefield. *History of Norfolk.* Blomefield, F. 1805. 12 vols.

Bury Wills. Wills and Inventories of the Register of Bury S. Edmunds, ed. Tymms, S. [C.S.] 1850.

Cely. The Cely Papers, ed. Malden, H. E. [R.H.S.] 1900.

Chanc. Pro. Select Cases in Chancery, ed. Baildon, W. P. [S.S.] 1896.

Col. Ang. Pre. Collectanea Anglo-Premonstratensia, ed. Gasquet, F. A. [R.H.S.] 1904.

Cor. Rolls. Select Coroners' Rolls, ed. Gross, C. [S.S.] 1896.

Cov. Leet. *The Coventry Leet Book*, ed. Harris, M. D. [E.E.T.S.] 1907–9.

Cutts. *Parish Priests and their People.* Cutts, E. L. London, 1898.

Denton. *England in the Fifteenth Century.* Denton, W. 1888.

Dom. Arch. *Domestic Architecture in England.* Turner, T. H. and Parker, J. H. London, 1859–77.

Early Wills. *The Fifty Earliest Wills*, ed. Furnivall, F. J. [E.E.T.S.] 1882.

Eliz. Engl. *Elizabeth's England*, ed. Withington, L. [Camelot Series.] 1890. [Extracts from Harrison.]

Exeter Regs. *The Exeter Registers*, ed. Hingeston-Randolph, F. C. London, 1889– .

Gasquet. *Parish Life in Medieval England.* Gasquet, F. A. London, 1906.

Gilds. *English Gilds*, ed. Toulmin Smith. [E.E.T.S.] 1870.

Henry IV. *History of England under Henry IV.* Wylie, J. H. London, 1884.

Hillen. *History of the Borough of King's Lynn.* Hillen, H. J. Norwich. 1907.

Hist. Eng. Law. *History of English Law.* Pollock, F. and Maitland, F. W. 1895.

Howard, i. *Accounts and Memoranda of Sir John Howard*, ed. Turner, T. H. 1842.

Howard, ii. *Household Books of John, Duke of Norfolk*, ed. Collier, J. P. 1844.

Ital. Rel. *The Italian Relation of England*, ed. Sneyd, C. A. [C.S.] 1847.

Jusserand. *Wayfaring Life in the Middle Ages.* Jusserand, J. J. 1899 edn.

La Tour Landry. *The Book of the Knight of La Tour Landry*, ed. Wright, T. (E.E.T.S.] 1868.

Libraries. *Old English Libraries.* Savage, E. A. London, 1911.

London Wills. *Calendar of Wills proved and enrolled in the Court of Husting, London*, 1258–1688, ed. Sharpe, R. R. London, 1889.

Meals and Manners. *Early English Meals and Manners etc.*, ed. Furnivall, F. J. [E.E.T.S.] 1868.

Memorials. *Memorials of London and London Life*, ed. Riley, H. T. London, 1868.

Mullinger. *The University of Cambridge from the earliest times to...* 1530. Mullinger. Cambridge, 1873.

Mun. Acad. *Munimenta Academica*, ed. Anstey, H. [R.S.] 1868.

Myrc. *Instructions for Parish Priests*, ed. Peacock, E. [E.E.T.S.] 1868.

North Country Wills, ed. Clay, J. [Sur. S.] 1908.

North Household Book. *The Northumberland Household Book*, ed. Percy, Bp. 1770.

Norwich Records. The Records of the City of Norwich, ed. Hudson, W. and Tingey, J. C. 1910.

Nottingham Records. Records of the Borough of Nottingham, vols. I and II, ed Stevenson, W. H. 1882–3.

Plum. Corr. The Plumpton Correspondence, ed. Stapleton, T. [C.S.] 1839.

Pollard. *Factors in Modern History.* Pollard, A. F. London, 1907.

Public Works. Public Works in Medieval Law, ed. Flower, C. T. [S.S.] 1915.

Rashdall. *Universities of Europe in the Middle Ages.* Rashdall, H. Oxford, 1895.

Redstone. *England during the Wars of the Roses.* Redstone, V. B. [R.H.S.] 1902.

Rogers, *Prices.* History of Agriculture and Prices in England, vols. III, IV. Rogers, J. E. T. 1866– .

Rogers, *Work.* Six Centuries of Work and Wages. Rogers, J. E. T. 1886.

Schools. *The schools of Medieval England.* Leach, A. F. London, 1915.

Scrope. *History of Castlecombe.* Scrope, G. P. 1852.

Shillingford. *Letters and papers of John Shillingford,* ed. Moore, S. A. [C.S.] 1871.

Statutes. The Statutes at Large, ed. Pickering, D. 1762.

Test. Ebor. Testamenta Eboracensia. [Sur. S.] 1836–1902.

Town Life. Town Life in the Fifteenth Century. Green, A. S. 1894.

Trevisa. *Bartholomew, de Proprietatibus Rerum.* London, 1535. [Trans. by Trevisa, J. 1398.]

Wilde. *Ingatestone, and the Essex Great Road.* Wilde, E. E. Oxford, 1913.

Wright. *The Homes of Other Days.* Wright, T. London, 1871.

INTRODUCTION

THE period of the Wars of the Roses has been studied and described very frequently. Its battles have been re-fought, its laws brought under close scrutiny, and its slow movement towards the more vigorous and more stable government of the Tudors explained and appreciated. The object of these pages is not to make yet another survey from any of these angles, but rather to examine in detail the life and activities of one Norfolk family and those of their friends. The history of any particular period is made by the mutual interactions of all sorts and conditions of men, and it is therefore illuminating to focus our attention upon a little group of people, and to try to see them as they were. For this purpose, we can scarcely have better material than that which lies before us in the Paston Letters. "Here is God's plenty," indeed, for this collection comprises over 1000 letters and documents of the fifteenth century, most of them written by, or to, the various members of one family.

Family letters of this nature are peculiarly important to the student of social history, for they enable him to view the life of the time from the inside. As he follows the fortunes of the writers, he sees what hopes and fears were theirs, how they lived and thought, and how their environment conditioned their actions. The Paston Letters give us all this, and represent the thought and activities of a typical English squire's family of the fifteenth century. The Pastons were not people of any peculiar genius, but ordinary well-to-do folk. They found, as did most of their neighbours, that if they wished to hold, or still more to increase what possessions they had, it was necessary to fight vigorously with every weapon law, use, experience or cunning could devise. Hence, a study of their many-sided activities allows us to form a clear idea of the conditions under which they lived, while the letters of their friends and many correspondents help to complete and to widen the view-point. They receive letters from Bishops or serving-men, prisoners or Dukes, priests or ribald companions; and all help us to reconstruct the social history and life of their times.

Yet even this method of reconstruction has obvious limitations, for the Pastons and their friends usually record only the things that concern or interest themselves and their correspondents. The bulk of this correspondence, therefore, deals with life as it was seen from a manor-house, and not with the very different and narrow view that was the only outlook of the peasant's cottage. It gives a distinct and true impression of the conditions of life in a stratum of English society; but it is only a stratum, and not the whole. The poor, and the labourer, figure incidentally in these letters, but almost always objectively, and as underlings. That is to say, we are able to learn the very secrets of the Paston's hearths and hearts, but only see Hodge and his friends as shadowy figures.

A more subtle, yet equally present difficulty must be noticed. As in numerous collections of letters, many of the most ordinary and everyday things of life go unrecorded. Just where we most desire to know every detail, we often lack not only detail, but also the main facts. For example, the whole negociations which preceded marriage are set out in full, but the actual ceremony is ignored in these letters. The difficulties of any long journey are not alluded to; the important part played by religion in everyday life, and the performance and arrangements for a thousand homely details of home-life almost escape notice. Such limitations are doubtless to be expected in any series of letters, but it is necessary constantly to beware of assuming that lack of information on any particular point means that the writers were uninterested or that the event seldom occurred. The opposite is probably far truer. The very frequency and commonplace nature of certain events is often the cause of their omission.

CHAPTER I

THE RISE OF THE PASTONS

THE PASTONS, as behoved any family with pretensions to gentility, claimed their descent from a Norman ancestor. It is not necessary for us to travel so far back into their obscure history, for it is probable that the family fortunes were not very extensive shortly before the end of the fourteenth century. About that time, their condition is thus described by one of their opponents:

A remembrance of the worshipful kin and ancestry of Paston, born in Paston in Gemyngham Soken.

First, There was one Clement Paston dwelling in Paston, and he was a good, plain husband[man], and lived upon his land that he had in Paston, and kept thereon a plough all times in the year, and sometimes in barlysell two ploughs. The said Clement yede [*i.e.* went] at one plough both winter and summer, and he rode to mill on the bare horseback with his corn under him, and brought home meal again under him, and also drove his cart with divers corns to Wynterton to sell, as a good husband[man] ought to do. Also, he had in Paston a five score or a six score acres of land at the most, and much thereof bond-land to Gemyngham Hall, with a little poor water mill running by the little river there, as it appeareth there of old time. Other livelode nor manors had he none there, nor in none other place.

And he wedded Geoffrey of Somerton [whose true surname is Goneld]'s sister, which was a bondwoman, to whom it is not unknown [to the prior of Bromholm and Bakton also, as it is said] if that men will enquire. And as for Geoffrey Somerton, he was bond also, to whom &c., he was both a pardoner and an attorney; and then was a good world, for he gathered many pence and half-pence, and therewith he made a fair chapel at Somerton, as it appeareth, &c.

Also, the said Clement had a son William, which that he set to school, and often he borrowed money to find him to school; and after that he yede to court with the help of Geoffrey Somerton, his uncle, and learned the law, and there begat he much good; and then he was made a serjeant, and afterwards made a justice, and a right cunning man in the law. And he purchased much land in Paston....[1]

[1] *P.L.* Intro. p. xxxv. *Note.* The references throughout are to *The Paston Letters, 1422–1509*, ed. by James Gairdner, 4 vols., London, 1901. The 1904 edition has been collated with this in Appendixes III. and IV

Whatever the fortunes of his fathers may have been, it is clear that Clement Paston was a careful, far-seeing man. He found means (even if by borrowed money and his father-in-law's help, as his enemies said) to send his son William to school, and later in life to London, where he was a student in one of the Inns of Court. Nor was this foresight without its reward, for young William Paston soon became a noted man, and his rise was rapid. He was early appointed Steward to the Bishop of Norwich, and the trust that was placed in him is seen by the number of families which appointed him as a trustee for their properties, or as an executor to their wills. In 1421 he became a serjeant of the Court of Common Pleas, and eight years later was raised to the bench, receiving a salary of 110 marks.[1]

Such are the main outlines of this remarkable man's public fortunes. His private life is equally interesting. He lost no opportunity of improving his position, and of increasing the family prosperity. He purchased land round about the family holdings in Paston, and so gradually made himself the chief landowner there. Then, acting in the accepted way, he looked about him for a suitable match, and finally chose Agnes, the daughter and heiress of Sir Edmund Berry of Harlingbury Hall in Hertfordshire. By the marriage settlement, Paston was to have the manor of East Tuddenham in Norfolk,[2] and, besides this, Agnes inherited much property from her father, including the manors of Marlingford, Stanstede, and Harlingbury.[3] Large purchases of land round about Paston had made the Justice lord of the greater part of the soil. It was possibly his wish to enclose his new property, and build a family residence there; for he obtained leave to divert a road which ran through his grounds on the south side of the house, on condition that he made a new road on the north side.[4] At the same time he enclosed the family property at Oxnede in much the same way.

This land at Oxnede was another of the Justice's recent purchases, and he dowered it on his wife Agnes.[5] It was to become one of the favourite homes of the family throughout the next fifty years; although, after the death of her husband, Agnes had

[1] Blomefield, v. p. 53; VI. p. 517; VII. pp. 217; X. p. 176, etc.
[2] P L. No. 2.   [3] Id. No. 556.
[4] Cal. Pat. Rolls, Henry VI [1441–46], p. 192.   [5] P.L. No. 556.

a hard fight to retain possession of it. Among other lands and properties, we find he obtained with Thomas Poye, "a grant of a market, fair and free warren in his manor of Shipden which had belonged to his father Clement before him,"[1] and also he bought the manor of Gresham. As we have already said, Agnes had some difficulty in keeping Oxnede, but an even fiercer struggle arose later over the rightful ownership of Gresham. William Paston was too strong a man for most people to quarrel with; for he grew more and more powerful, acquiring esteem and favour as well as wealth. After his death, a man complained that, owing to the fact that he was proceeding against the Pastons, he was unable to obtain the aid of counsel, so great was the respect of the Bar for the memory of the late Justice.[2]

Before he died, Justice Paston had succeeded in putting the family affairs on a very sound footing.[3] The Pastons were the owners of large estates and could not be disregarded, although naturally their rapid rise was not pleasing to all their neighbours. The Justice was as careful to find a suitable match for his son, as he had been in seeking an alliance for himself that would strengthen the family position. John Paston married Margaret, the daughter and heiress of John Mauteby of Mauteby, Norfolk; and by so doing increased the family fortunes still further, by the acquisition of the manors of Mauteby, Sparham and other properties.

This young man, John Paston, was little more than twenty-two or twenty-three when his father died; and he was suddenly called upon to take control of his father's large properties, and to uphold the newly gained family position in the County. It was a difficult task. The great Justice had naturally made many enemies by his judicial decisions. Also, the immense increase in the family fortunes in so short a while had caused envious eyes to be turned on their lands; and the knowledge that an inexperienced young man was now controlling the affairs of the family was an encouragement to their enemies. The task before John Paston is interesting to us, not chiefly for its own sake, but because it

---

[1] *Cal. Pat. Rolls*, Henry VI [1422–29], p. 346.
[2] *P.L.* No. 47.
[3] As evidence of his wealth in bullion and plate alone, we know he had £1460 in gold in London; £958 in gold at Norwich Priory; 24 lb. 11 oz. of gilt, and 92 lb. 2 oz. of ungilt plate. Blomefield, IV. p. 40.

exemplifies what was constantly happening in those days, when the breakdown of the Feudal System left the way open for the advance of ambitious and unscrupulous men. The Paston's story probably follows much the same lines as marked the rise of many other families. In the main the aims of the Pastons were the aims of all these struggling newcomers among the gentry. They desired to consolidate their possessions and to establish their position in the county. In order to do this, they were ready to protect their possessions by every means available; by the law, by the influence of patrons, by favourable marriages, and by placing their children in the houses of great landowners, or of the nobility.

Little time was lost after William Paston's death before the enemies began their attacks. In the first place, the Parson of Paston thought the time ripe for this purpose, and repudiated the agreement he had made with the Justice as to the new road at Paston. He pulled up the "doles" that were to have marked the new roadway, and threatened to cut a ditch right across its track.[1] Another neighbour presented his claim for a rent of 8s. from one of the Paston tenants, which had never been presented while the Justice lived. On being asked why he had never asked for payment during that time, the claimant replied, "He was a great man, and a wise man of the law, and that was the cause men would not ask him [for] the rent."[2]

William Paston had foreseen what must inevitably happen, and had warned his sons that in a thorough study of the law lay one of their chief means of salvation. Their father had been but a short while dead when Agnes wrote to her son Edmund, "I advise you to think once [a]... day of your father's counsel to learn the law, for he said many times that whosoever should dwell at Paston, should have need to know [how to] defend himself."[3] The right of Agnes to Oxnede was disputed by one John Hauteyn, although, having been a Carmelite Friar, he was legally unable to hold property. This difficulty he had overcome by obtaining from the Pope a dispensation to renounce the Order. Then he sued Agnes at common law. He obtained the Duke of Suffolk's favour, and was sanguine enough to noise it abroad in Norwich that through this help he would get possession

[1] *P.L.* No. 46.   [2] *Id.* No. 46.   [3] *Id.* No. 46.

of Oxnede.[1] His suit was still before the Courts when Suffolk was murdered. The loss of his patron seems to have disheartened him, and after a time he surrendered all claims to Agnes.[2]

The disputes over the manor of Gresham, another property of the Pastons, were not settled so simply. William Paston had bought the manor, and it was left to his heir John. Then Lord Molynes was persuaded by a certain John Heydon that he had a claim to the manor; and, then and there, Molynes went and took possession on 17th February, 1448. John Heydon was ever an enemy of the Pastons, and was usually associated with Sir Thomas Tuddenham. These two men were often behind the intrigues and oppressive measures that were fomenting discontent in Norfolk, and were well known in the county as Suffolk's tools. Now, while the Pastons had been able to grapple successfully with an ex-Carmelite Friar, it was not so simple a matter when it came to disputing with a nobleman who was the heir apparent to another barony, and the prospective heir of great properties. A young and comparatively unknown family such as the Pastons had to use great circumspection in trying to redress their wrongs. John Paston was well aware of this, and got William Waynflete, the Bishop of Winchester, to act as his friend. As a result of the Bishop's intervention, Lord Molynes agreed that his lawyers should go into the whole question of the title with those of Paston during the summer.[3] Meanwhile Molynes' officials lost no time in asserting their authority, and Margaret Paston wrote to tell her husband that ' the Lord Molynes man is collecting the rent at Gresham at a great pace."[4] After the whole matter had been gone into, Molynes' lawyers advised Paston to seek an interview with Lord Molynes personally. They practically admitted they had no case; and, during the autumn, John Paston went to Salisbury and other places, trying in vain to speak with Lord Molynes. Finding this useless, Paston seems to have resolved on bolder measures, and Lord Molynes' retainers at Gresham were kept on the alert throughout the summer, being "sore afraid that you would enter again upon them, and they have made great [defences] within the house."[5] Paston made his preparations, and on the 6th October,

[1] P.L. No. 66.   [2] Blomefield, VI. p. 479.   [3] P.L. No. 61.
[4] Id. No. 59.   [5] Id. No. 67.

1449, he took possession of "a mansion within the said town," and evidently established himself there. No further move was made until the 28th January, 1450. Then, while John Paston was absent in London, Lord Molynes sent a force a thousand strong to turn the Pastons out. This small army was fully armed; they had "curresse, brigaunders, jakks, salettes, gleyfes, bowes, arrows, etc.," besides implements of devastation such as "cromes" to pull down houses, picks, battering rams made of long poles, and "pannys with fier."[1] Margaret was only protected by a small force, there being but twelve persons with her, so that the swarms outside found it an easy task to drive out the garrison, and then to mine "down the wall of the chamber wherein [she] ... was." Then they "bore her out at the gates, and cut asunder the posts of the houses, and let them fall, etc."[2] The whole place was sacked and badly damaged, and Paston and some of his adherents were threatened with death if they should be caught.

Paston petitioned both the Parliament and the Lord Chancellor for redress, but the troubled days of 1450 were not an opportune moment for gaining a sympathetic hearing.[3] Lord Molynes put off the Chancellor with further assertions of the justice of his claim, and pleaded that he was too fully engaged on the King's business in Wiltshire to go to Norfolk for an enquiry.[3] What happened exactly during those troubled months we do not know, but the spring of 1451 found John Paston "entered peaceably in the manor of Gresham" once again. Threats were made by Molynes' agents, but no active measures were taken, despite the fact that Lord Molynes had been able to speak to the King personally about the matter.[4] Emboldened by this success, John Paston determined to pursue his advantage by bringing an action against Lord Molynes and his agents for forcible ejection. He saw quite clearly that if he could win such an action it would greatly improve his standing among the County gentry, and would also serve as a salutary warning to any others who proposed to attack his properties.

For this purpose, he obtained an indictment against Lord Molynes, and another against his men. Here, however, he had

---

[1] *P.L.* No. 77. "Brigandine," a coat of joined mail; "Jack," the same; "Salet," a steel head-piece.
[2] *Id.* Nos. 77 and 107.   [3] *Id.* No. 103.   [4] *Id.* No. 122.

miscalculated the forces against him, for Lord Molynes easily outwitted him by his personal influence at Court. Before any trial could be held, the Sheriff of Norfolk openly told Paston's friends "that he [had] writing from the King that he [should] make such a panel [as] to acquit the Lord Molynes."[1] Beaten here, Paston concentrated all his efforts upon winning his case against the retainers. He quite naturally resorted to the usual methods of his day, and set his friends to work to bribe the Sheriff to favour his interests. John Osbern, a friend of Paston's, wrote him a long and very illuminating letter, detailing his efforts to win over the Sheriff. Lord Molynes' friends were equally active, and the Duke of Norfolk and Lord Molynes had both written to the Sheriff, hinting that unless the men were acquitted, both the King and themselves would not fail to understand his partiality! The Sheriff bluntly told Paston his best hope was to get a letter from the King, such as Lord Molynes had obtained, "especially," he adds, "as you said a man should get such...for a noble."[2] There is no doubt that, despite the best offers the friends of John Paston could make, the Sheriff was aware that Lord Molynes was too powerful a man to offend. He could only say that he would be Paston's friend in any action but this one! We do not know specifically what happened, but it is obvious that there could only be one end to so grotesque a trial. For some reason, however, Lord Molynes seems to have withdrawn his claim, and the whole affair closes amidst negociations between the rival parties concerning the damage done at Gresham, and the terms upon which John Paston would be satisfied.[3]

It is clear from this episode that the Pastons were holding their own in the never ending struggle that was going on in fifteenth century England. The weakness of the central government gave such opportunities to unscrupulous and violent men, that litigation and forcible methods were both freely used to increase men's wealth and power. It is the greatest testimony to John Paston's ability, that his long struggle for Gresham should thus terminate amidst negociations, and not by another overwhelming display of force on Lord Molynes' part.

[1] P.L. No. 155.   [2] Id. No. 159. A noble was worth 6s. 8d.
[3] Id. Nos. 156 and 164.

Already there are not wanting indications that Justice Paston's policy was reaping its rewards. The damage done at Gresham, in household goods and buildings alone, was estimated by John Paston at £200—a large sum for those days; and the fact that he was prepared to offer a surety of £100 to the Sheriff shows how affluent the family was. His brother William, a few years later, reports a conversation among common friends which is interesting evidence of the family wealth, and also of their careful manner of living.

> That is the [way] of your countrymen, to spend all the goods they have on men and liveries, and horses and harness, and so bear it out for a while, and at last they are but beggars. . . . As for Paston, he is a squire of worship, and of great livelode, and I wot he will not spend all his goods at once, but he spares yearly an hundred marks or an hundred pounds. He may do his enemy a shrewd turn and never fare the worse in his household, nor [have] the less men about him.[1]

A family of whom this could be said in 1451 was certainly in a strong and thriving position.

But, however strong their position may seem to us, as we see it by the help of the meagre documents which remain, John Paston was by no means satisfied. He had come out of his first great ordeal successfully; but his shrewd common sense, and the teaching of his father, had convinced him that continuous exertions were necessary if he wished to retain, or increase, his inheritance. Throughout the years he was fighting with Lord Molynes and with lesser claimants, he was losing no opportunity of increasing his importance in the County. His strength of purpose and ability soon associated him with others, all eager to break the tyranny of a few men which was rapidly making life in Norfolk unbearable.[2] During the ten years following his father's death, he is to be seen as a strong public-spirited man working for the good of the County, yet all through these years never losing sight of his prime objects—the increase and firm establishment of the family fortunes, and as an aid to this, the favour of some great patron.

John Paston's growing importance in the County was undisputed. As early as 1450, he was advised to make an effort to be returned to Parliament,[3] and was one of the leaders of the

1 *P.L.* No. 211.   2 *E.g. Id.* No. 179.   3 *Id.* No. 113.

opposition to Tuddenham and Heydon, the malign spirits of the
County. He helped to rouse the gentry of Norfolk to issue a
complaint against the terrorism which was being exercised by
Charles Nowell and his band of ruffians.[1] Shortly after the
petition was presented to the Sheriff, John Paston was set upon,
outside Norwich Cathedral, by some of Nowell's gang, "as it
seemed, purposing there to have murdered the said Paston."[2]
It is doubtful whether Tuddenham and Heydon instigated this
affair, but they did all they could to harass Paston and his friends
in the Civil Courts.

Yet as we have said, John Paston was primarily a calculating,
shrewd man of affairs, and most probably only a servant of the
County, because he recognised that in the main the interests of
the County and his own were identical. His whole energies were
absorbed in the double adventure. The zeal and capacity he
showed were not wasted, for he early attracted the attention of
just such a man as his growing fortunes most needed. The records
are distressingly meagre here where we could wish for the fullest
information, but it is clear that, within a few years of his father's
death, John Paston was the intimate friend and confidant of Sir
John Fastolf. What first attracted Sir John we do not know,
but we can see he had a great respect for Paston's business
ability, and that alone would place him high in Fastolf's esteem.
Perhaps he was distantly related to the Pastons, for Margaret
once writes "I suppose Sir John Fastolf if he were spoken to,
would be gladder to let his kinsmen have part than strange men,"[3]
and he often speaks of John Paston as "cousin."[4] However this
may be, the old knight soon found that he was frequently seeking
the advice and local knowledge of Paston; and, the more use he
made of him, the more he grew to respect and trust his judgment.
His man of business Sir T. Howes again and again is ordered to
"speak to Paston about various matters,"[5] or to "deliver [writs]
in haste to the Sheriff by Paston's advice,"[6] or "to take Paston's
advice in proceeding."[7] As the years went on, Paston knew that
here was the man to whom he must cling. No man could outdo

[1] *P.L.* No. 174.   [2] *Id.* No. 179.   [3] *Id.* No. 183.
[4] *E.g. Id.* Nos. 123, 132, etc. This point cannot be pressed unduly, as
"cousin" was frequently used between people who had no blood relationship.
[5] *Id.* No. 129   [6] *Id.* No. 154   [7] *Id.* No. 169.

Paston in fighting for his rights, even against the most powerful opponents; but experience soon taught him that a rich and generous patron was a greater safeguard than the most undaunted pugnacity and perseverance.

It was a fortunate meeting for both parties, and mutual confidence begot friendship, so that by 1454 we find Sir John declaring to William Paston that John is "the heartiest kinsman and friend that he knows."[1] This feeling continued until Sir John's death in 1459. More and more, John Paston became indispensable to the old knight. His zeal and his knowledge of the law were unceasingly exercised on Fastolf's behalf, and in 1457 Sir John had made him one of the trustees of his immense properties in Norfolk and Suffolk. By this time, Fastolf's great mansion at Caister, near Yarmouth, was complete, and he had moved into it. There the Pastons were frequently with him. Even John Paston's continued absences in London, dealing with the unending legal business incident to great estates, did not weaken Fastolf's affections. Indeed his influence on the old knight seemed to increase, and Paston's friend Friar Brackley did everything possible to this end. When it was seen that Fastolf could not last much longer, Brackley wrote urging Paston to come down to be with the dying man. "Every day this five days he says, 'God send me soon my good cousin Paston, for I hold him a faithful man, and ever one man'."[2] Only two days before he died Sir John ordered a clause to be inserted in his will which ran:

And also the said Sir John said and declared that the said John Paston was the best friend and helper and supporter to the said Sir John, and that [it] was his will that the said John Paston should have and inherit the same manors, lands, and tenements and other [properties] after his decease, etc.[3]

On the morning after Sir John's death, John Paston was wealthy, and a landowner on a scale that would have surprised his father, even in his most sanguine mood. In a night, he was transformed from a mere country squire into the inheritor of the Fastolf lands in Norfolk and Suffolk. Sir John had been one of the richest men in England, and probably some portion of his money came directly to his chief executor, John Paston. The unceasing efforts of fifteen years were thus liberally rewarded, but

---

[1] *P.L.* No. 211.   [2] *Id.* No. 331.   [3] *Id.* No. 333, and cf. No. 469.

John Paston's position before Fastolf's death was distinctly
more secure than it had been when first he inherited the property.
During this period, as we have seen, he had gradually built up
a solid reputation and position amongst his Norfolk neighbours.
If the Fastolf lands had not fallen to him, he would probably
have passed his subsequent years in comparative ease. But his
newly gained possessions again made him an object of envy. The
men who would not trouble themselves to attack the properties
of a rising squire, found it quite another matter when the rich
lands left by Fastolf were the prize. All Paston's tactics at this
time show how well aware he was of this. A few days after
Fastolf's death, he dispatched his brother William to London,
to collect and sequestrate the dead man's goods, which were
distributed in various parts of the City. Besides this, William
was instructed to interview Bishop Waynflete, the Lord
Chancellor, who was one of the executors. From him it was
hoped to obtain the necessary writs of "diem clausit extremum."[1]
One of these writs had to be issued for every county in which
the deceased held lands; and, on the receipt of the writ, the
escheator of the county held an enquiry as to what lands belonged to the dead man, and who was to inherit them. Despite
all his efforts, William could not get the writs for Norfolk and
Suffolk. Within five days of Fastolf's death, the writs were
issued for Surrey and Essex, but in these counties the Pastons
had small interest. There were adverse forces at work, which prevented the issue of the writs they wanted until the following
May.[2] This delay gave time to many claimants, who hoped by
their audacity to win something for themselves. The Duke of
Exeter, for example, at once laid claim to Fastolf's house and
goods in Southwark, and a little later, the Earl of Wiltshire
actually entered this mansion, and lived there for a time. Gradually
Paston wore down the opposition, and the necessary inquisitions
were held, and Fastolf's trustees named as the controllers of
the property. Fastolf's last will, however, had given the administration of his estates into the hands of Paston and Sir
Thomas Howes, so that the effect of the inquisitions was to give
these two executors the active control of the Fastolf lands.

　　Paston's new position seems to have had almost instant re-

[1] *P.L.* No. 338.　　　[2] *Id.* Intro. pp. ccxxvii–iii.

sults, though his great labours in the County in previous years must not be forgotten. Within a year of Fastolf's death he was a Knight of the Shire, and when in 1461 Edward IV became King Paston was again returned to sit in the first Parliament.[1] The Mayor and Mayoress of Norwich showed their appreciation of the Pastons' new dignity by a quaint compliment of the time, whereby they sent out dinner to Margaret, and came and dined with her! Paston had now assumed complete possession of Fastolf's lands, and his agents were active in making new agreements, and letting the farms and mills on the properties.[2]

Clearly John Paston would need to exert all his energies, if he was to retain the great possessions he had won. Despite many anxious moments, he had managed so far to overcome all obstacles. But his experiences after his father's death had taught him the folly of hoping for any long cessation from attack, so that he was probably prepared for a struggle. The wild days that were the inevitable result of the deposition of Henry VI were peculiarly suited to the designs of determined and lawless men. Caister Castle had always been a desirable property in the eyes of the Duke of Norfolk, and he took advantage of the general unrest to seize the place. Fortunately for Paston, at this time he stood higher in the King's favour than ever after, and his suit for redress was not brushed aside, as it might well have been otherwise. The Duke's answer to the King's letter was to enter a plea that Paston was not the rightful owner; and further, that others had certain claims which they had surrendered to the Duke, who pleaded for time to prove all this. Paston's evidences were too strong, however, and Caister was restored to him.[3]

By this time, Paston had achieved two of his three great aims. He stood high in the esteem of his neighbours in the County, and he was the possessor of a great property. There yet remained the third and most vital of requirements,—the sure protection of a great patron. Without this, the very magnitude of his possessions could only be a constant source of trouble, and, as soon as Fastolf was dead, he bestirred himself to this end. By means of his friends, he seems to have been in the King's household itself for a while and, as we have seen, was in the King's

favour.[1] Although some years before he had paid a fine to avoid
being made a Knight,[2] it was rumoured that Edward IV proposed to confer this dignity upon Paston at the coming Coronation.[3]

Paston, however, had no ambition for distinctions of this kind;
he managed to get his eldest son knighted in place of himself.
Sir John,[4] as he now became, was recently of age, and his father
found the means to obtain a place for him as a member of the
King's household. He hoped the young man would make friends
among the young squires about the King, and possibly thus
form a means of checkmating impudent attempts on the family
lands. He also tried to consolidate his position in other quarters
by a similar plan. The Duke of Norfolk, who had held Caister
for a time, died, and was succeeded by his son, a youth of
seventeen. Now Paston's second son, also named John Paston,
was of much the same age as this youth, and his father obtained
a position for him in the household of the young Duke. Clearly
he hoped the boy might win favour with the Duke, and that
the Paston lands would benefit by the protection of so great a
noble. Furthermore, he was well aware that in the Duke's train
his son would continually come into contact with influential men
and friends of the King.

These manœuvres of Paston's were scrutinised very closely
by his enemies, who evidently saw the necessity of acting before
his position became too strong. Although in the first place he

---

[1] *P.L.* No. 393.   [2] *Id.* No. 321.   [3] *Id.* Nos. 391, 394.
[4] The reader may find some difficulty in keeping clear the several members
of the Paston family christened John. The following table shows their
relation one to another, and the reader will be further helped by remembering that the father (John I) died in 1466, and that his eldest son (John II)
was knighted, and became Sir John in 1463. Thus, after 1466, all references
to plain John Paston concern only the second son of John I, and brother of
John II.

Justice Paston = Agnes Berry
|
John Paston I = Margaret Mauteby
died 1466

John Paston II   John Paston III
knighted 1463

For instances of brothers of the same Christian name, alive at the same
time, see *Scottish Antiquary*, vol. XII. p. 168 (April 1898) and vol. XIII.
p. 20 (July 1898).

had been allowed to assume control over all the Norfolk and Suffolk properties of Fastolf, it was not long before this was strongly challenged. Two of his co-executors, Judge Yelverton and William Jenney, refused to admit Paston's rignt to act as the sole executive member, and gave point to their protest by taking possession of some manors of Fastolf's in Suffolk. Paston found it very difficult to protect his property from them; and, while he was in Norfolk doing so, he neglected to obey the King's command to come to him at London. This greatly angered the King, who said, "We have sent two privy seals to Paston by two yeomen of our chamber and he disobeys them; but we will send him another tomorrow, and, by God's mercy, if he come not then, he shall die for it."[1] When these words of the King reached Paston, he hurriedly abandoned his interests in the country and hastened to London, only to be thrown into the Fleet prison.[2] Paston's enemies had won a complete triumph, but it was very brief; for, as soon as the King learnt the whole facts of the case, he showed great fairness and ordered Paston's immediate release from prison. He also appointed an officer of his own household to be the new Sheriff of Norfolk, so that justice should be between Paston and his enemies in their quarrel. So the struggle went on, now in the Manor Courts, now at Norwich and now in the King's Courts at Westminster. For over a year the two parties used every means that medieval lawyers could employ to delay and confuse the issues, and Paston seemed no nearer a settlement. Indeed his friends warned him that, unless he changed his tactics, he would spend the rest of his days in the Courts. As we have seen, Paston knew only too well the need he had of a patron, and had made efforts to secure one. The Duke of Suffolk, he was told, would be a tower of strength to him. "Sundry folks have said to me that they think verily...while the world is as it is, you can never live in peace without you have his good-lordship."[3] No doubt Paston himself would have welcomed the protection of the Duke, but the proximity of their lands had already led the great noble to cast a covetous eye on the Paston properties at Drayton. So there was little to hope for in this direction.

The main attack on Paston's position, however, was not made

[1] P.L. No. 417.   [2] Id. No. 421.   [3] Id. No. 472.

by great lords desirous of increasing their properties. It was the efforts of some of his co-executors that gave Paston trouble and endless litigation for the rest of his days. Their attack was developed on two sides: first in the Ecclesiastical Courts, where they endeavoured to upset the will of Fastolf which gave such large powers to Paston and Sir Thos. Howes; and secondly in the local County Courts, where they brought various actions against him. This forced him into a very serious position. It was essential that he should be present in London to watch every step taken before the Ecclesiastical Courts, and at the same time, his absence from home could not have been more inopportune. His difficulties were complicated by the fact that he was on the point of concluding his negociations with the King for the foundation of the College of Priests at Caister, in accordance with Fastolf's wishes. While he was following the King to Marlborough and obtaining the license, his enemies were able to get him proclaimed an outlaw owing to his non-appearance at the County Courts, and soon after this he was again thrown into the Fleet.[1]

Meanwhile, Yelverton the other co-executor had started the proceedings against Paston and Sir T. Howes in the Ecclesiastical Court. For six months before his imprisonment, Paston was kept fully occupied in combating the determined attempts that were being made to impugn the validity of Fastolf's will. If Yelverton could have upset this, then Paston would have been only one of several executors, and would not have been entitled to the great possessions which the last will bestowed upon him. Yelverton's case was that this will was a forgery, and that Paston had no right to Caister or the manors of Drayton, Hellesdon, Cotton and all the other lands of Fastolf in Norfolk and Suffolk. It is obvious that Paston was bound to watch every step taken by his enemies in so vital a matter; and, however his affairs were prospering or suffering in Norfolk, he was often compelled to leave them to the care of his wife and sons, while he fought the gravest danger himself in Town. By the autumn of 1464, the family affairs had reached so serious a crisis, that a family council was held in London. Whatever the result of this may have been, the next year was not very old before a new and

---

[1] *P.L.* Nos. 491-4.

formidable enemy appeared in the person of the Duke of Suffolk. He claimed the manor of Drayton, and it was also rumoured that he had bought up the rights of a man who laid claim to the neighbouring manor at Hellesdon. Both of these manors Paston had inherited from Fastolf, and they lay on the opposite side of the river, facing the Duke's mansion of Costessey. For reasons unknown to us, Paston was unable to leave London during the greater part of 1465. In all probability this was due to the law-proceedings concerning the will, and also in part because he was again imprisoned in the Fleet. There can be no doubt that, however serious affairs seemed in Norfolk, Paston himself was in the centre of the whirlwind in London. The story of the Duke's early attacks on Drayton is told elsewhere[1]; but, after Margaret Paston's triumphant outwitting of her enemies in the first encounter, other forces took a hand. The great castle of Caister had already once been in other hands than the Pastons'. Once again Yelverton attacked them. Baffled in the Ecclesiastical Court, he now endeavoured to wrest away their lands at Caister and Cotton by playing on the cupidity of the Queen's brother Lord Scales. He was not very successful, for Lord Scales does not seem to have done anything beyond expressing his intention to come and take Caister.[2] Yelverton still had another string to his bow. He had instigated a friend of his to dispute the Paston's right to the manor of Cotton, and it was necessary for them to take strong action if they meant to protect their title. Evidently Margaret and her husband, consulting together in London in the summer of 1465, appreciated this. Consequently, on her way home, Margaret stayed at Cotton, sent a message to her younger son John to meet her there, and started collecting the rents. This naturally provoked the Yelverton nominee, who came to expel the intruders; but, by the good offices of the Duke of Norfolk, both parties agreed to a truce, so that the actual title deeds to the property might be examined. But this concentration of attention on one part of their property was exactly what the Duke of Suffolk had been waiting for. With no one to protect the Paston interests at Norwich, the Duke had made a friend of the new Mayor, and a species of armed terrorism set in against all who were Paston's friends. One high-handed

[1] See pp. 63 ff.   [2] P.L. No. 517.

action succeeded another, till finally, on the 15th October, the
Duke's men attacked the Pastons' house at Hellesdon. There
was no opposition to this, for the Pastons were almost wholly
unprotected, and the next two days saw the whole place pillaged.
The house itself was completely wrecked,—even its walls being
broken down,—the church was violated, and the tenants' houses
robbed. The flagrancy of the attack won much sympathy for
Paston. His wife wrote to say

> There cometh much people daily to wonder thereupon, both of
> Norwich and of other places, and they speak shamefully thereof.
> The duke had better than a thousand pound that it had never been
> done; and ye have the more good will of the people that it is so
> foully done.[1]

This was well enough in its way, but only small comfort to
John Paston. Another year had nearly passed, and throughout
the whole of it he had been entirely occupied by his efforts to
protect what Fastolf had left him. Yet all his efforts had not
availed to ward off some of the attacks of his enemies. The
Ecclesiastical Courts were still hearing evidence and counter
evidence concerning the will, although the case had now been
before them for nearly two years. Besides this his rights to the
manor of Cotton were in dispute and awaiting settlement, and
now his property at Drayton was taken, his possessions stolen,
and his friends and retainers ill-treated.

From the moment of Fastolf's death onwards, Paston had
had little rest; and, prematurely worn out by his exertions, he
died in London in May 1466. Three times imprisoned, continually detained in London when his interests imperatively
needed him in Norfolk, he must have found his inheritance a
heavy burden. Indeed the Bishop of Norwich, who knew all the
facts of the case, did not hesitate to declare to Margaret Paston
"that he would not abide the sorrow and trouble that [her
husband] had abiden, to win all Sir John Fastolf's goods."[2]

---

[1] *P.L.* No. 534, and see p. 167.   [2] *Id.* No. 503.

CHAPTER II

THE PASTON FORTUNES

THOSE who knew the family best must have wondered among themselves what would happen now that John Paston was dead. He may have had faults as a husband and a father, but no man could have laboured more strenuously to protect and to increase the family fortunes. Now he was succeeded by his son Sir John, whom everyone knew to be of a different calibre. He was known to his friends as "the best chooser of a gentlewoman" of their acquaintance, but they may be pardoned for doubting his ability to combat opponents whom his father's undoubted powers could not wholly subdue.

The attempts which were made to wrest his property from him follow very closely the methods adopted against his father, when first he succeeded to the Justice's estates. There is the same series of small men trying to bite away a piece here and there; and at the same time, the constant fear of attack by a more formidable foe. Within three or four years of his father's death, Sir John found that his manors at Hellesdon, at Caister and at Cotton were all being threatened by various people. Indeed, his mother was very fearful as to what would be the end of it all, and advised him "not to be too hasty to be married till you were more sure of your livelode."[1]

Although John Paston was dead, the negociations which he had begun, and the help he had craved from high quarters were not nullified, and within fifteen months of his death the lengthy litigation in the Ecclesiastical Court was terminated. A compromise was effected in the Court of Audience. Sir John and Bishop Waynflete, who was now acting as sole executor, agreed together to divide all the Fastolf lands in Essex, Surrey, Norfolk and Suffolk between them. They also agreed that Sir John should surrender the title deeds of all except Caister. The

---

[1] *P.L.* No. 601. "Livelode," "Lands and rents from which an income was derived." Gairdner.

question of establishing a college for priests at Caister still remained to be settled, as it was a specific instruction in Fastolf's will that a college was to be founded there. It was finally decided that, instead of founding the college at Caister, the money should be spent in providing for seven priests and seven poor scholars at Magdalen College, Oxford. Thus the great struggle for Fastolf's lands was ended; but the prolonged litigation had had its inevitable consequence, and the indenture setting forth the agreement definitely stated that by the "disputes...the property...has been much wasted."[1] Whether these terms would have been approved by John Paston is doubtful, but his son was much more a courtier and lover than a lawyer, and he was doubtless prepared to cut his losses, if only he could get a definite settlement. The agreement left the Pastons with only a small part of what John Paston had held on Fastolf's death.

Though it was small in comparison, yet it left the Pastons in possession of the magnificent Caister Castle, upon which Fastolf had lavished his wealth. William Worcester, an old servant of Fastolf and of the Pastons, describes it as "a rich jewel...at need, for all the country in time of war; and my master Fastolf would rather he had never builded it, than it should be in the governance of any sovereign that would oppress the country."[2] As we have seen, the Duke of Norfolk had before this occupied it for a time, and no doubt there were many others who wanted it besides a certain Fastolf of Cowhaw who was biding his time "with five score men ready, and...daily espies to understand what fellowship keep the place."[3] It was Caister, therefore, the last remnant of the Fastolf inheritance, that was the storm-centre of future attacks, and Sir John found he would have to fight hard if he wished to retain it. William Yelverton, an old enemy, had induced Sir Thomas Howes to join forces with him against the Pastons. Now Howes had been first Fastolf's confidential agent, and latterly chief co-executor with Paston, and a great friend of the family. However he was induced to join Yelverton's party, and the two soon took steps to declare the last will of Fastolf to be false, and to start negociations with the Duke of Norfolk for the sale of Caister.[4]

[1] P.L. No. 645.   [2] Id. No. 582.
[3] Id. No. 576.   [4] Id. Nos. 589, 590, 591.

Sir John was greatly alarmed at this, and at once sought the protection of his friends at Court.[1] Besides this, he very wisely set about collecting a garrison for Caister, until he was ordered to cease doing so, and to appear before the King at Westminster.[2] Consultations and attempts to compromise followed, but during the summer the whole situation was changed by the action of the Earl of Warwick, who overcame the King's forces, and took Edward himself prisoner. The disorder ensuing gave Norfolk his opportunity. In August 1469 he began his ordered attack upon Caister, and surrounded the place with 3000 men.[3] As Sir John was in London, the castle was defended by his brother, John Paston. Continuous negociations were conducted both at Caister and in London. Sir John never realised the actual position of the garrison, or the unscrupulous nature of his enemy. He hoped by means of his influence at Court to gain the day, never understanding that, in the troubled state of the country, the Duke of Norfolk could ignore any commands from the King's advisers in London. Indeed even when the Duke's own relatives had agreed to certain terms as being fair, the Duke absolutely rejected them, and continued his own plans.

Throughout the whole siege, John Paston in Caister put up a brave resistance, but he had a mere handful of men, and their victuals were scanty. Sir John failed to send food, or men, or to get a truce; and while he was still making plans for truces and imploring the help of great lords, the garrison had to yield. John Paston and his men were allowed to depart unharmed, with everything except their guns, crossbows and quarrels. He had made the best resistance possible, and had nothing to regret.[4] Margaret Paston, with her customary shrewdness and plain speaking, had summed up his brother's case:

Send word how ye will be demeaned, by as good advice as ye can get, and make no longer delay for they must needs have hasty succour that be in the place; for they be sore hurt and have none help. And if they have hasty help, it shall be the greatest worship that ever ye had. And if they be not holpen it shall be to you a great disworship; and look never to have favour of your neighbours and friends but if this speed well.[5]

Thus, in little more than three years after John Paston's death, his son had lost the greater part of the rich lands the family had inherited from Fastolf. Partly as a result of this, and partly through the ineffective and careless way in which Sir John dealt with his business affairs, the family was always in want of money. Nothing in the *Letters* is more striking than this change. Again and again, the problem of obtaining even a few pounds seems almost insurmountable to Margaret, or to those left in Norfolk to control the farms and estates. The story of the Pastons throughout Sir John's life is one of continuous effort to win back Caister, and to negociate loans and sales of land, in order to raise money.

John Paston had not been dead many months, when Margaret began to foresee the coming troubles. These arose very largely from the lack of interest Sir John displayed in his business affairs. He appears to have valued all his properties chiefly for what he could get out of them. His days were mostly passed in London, and the care of the Norfolk properties he left to his mother, or his brother, or the bailiffs. So long as the rents were forthcoming, he went on his own careless way. Hence, only six months after John Paston's death, Margaret writes to Sir John and tries to urge him to conclude all the outstanding business:

Speed your matters so this term, that we may be in rest hereafter...and remember the great cost and charge that we have had hither toward, and think verily it may not long endure. Ye know what ye left when ye were last at home, and wite it verily there is no more in this country to bear out no charge with.[1]

Other letters of this time show us how hardly pressed the family was for money. An effort was even made to gather rents from the tenants of some of the estates before it was due, but without avail.[2] A few weeks later a loan of £100 or 200 marks was promised for six months,[3] and Sir John's letters for the next few years are full of appeals for funds.[4] His condition seems constantly to have been that so graphically stated by his brother, who says "For this I ensure you, so God help me, he hath at this season not a penny in his purse, nor wots where to get any."[5]

Coupled with these continued requests for money, was the knowledge exasperating to Margaret and his brother John, that

Sir John was not devoting all his energies in London to main-
taining his claims. The money they so hardly gathered together
was being squandered by Sir John in making wagers,[1] or in in-
dulging his fancies as a courtier; not in fighting his enemies in
the Law Courts. He writes home to his brother a letter full of
enthusiasm for a recent tournament. "My hand was hurt at
the tourney at Eltham upon Wednesday last. I would that you
had been there and seen it, for it was the goodliest sight that was
seen in England this forty years."[2] John III, troubled by all
the worries in Norfolk which were rightly his brother's lot, replies drily:

> Whereas it pleaseth you to wish me at Eltham, at the tourney,
> for the good sight that was there, by truth I had rather see you once
> in Caister Hall than to see as many king's tourneys as might be
> between Eltham and London.[3]

As we have seen, this could have but one end, and Caister was
lost, as well as most of the Fastolf lands made over to Bishop
Waynflete. As a result, the Pastons were more in want of ready
money than ever, although the loss of Caister proved a salutary
shock to Sir John, who thereupon set about in earnest to get
back what he should never have lost. Margaret had spent all
she could raise on the garrison of Caister, and was so hard
pressed that she said, "I fear me I shall be obliged to borrow for
myself, or else to break up household, or both."[4] John III was
in the same plight, and tells his brother:

> If you send me word that I shall come to you to London for to
> common [talk over] with you of any matter, so God help me, I have
> neither money to come up with, nor for to tarry with you when
> I am there unless you send me some.[5]

Sir John saw that the position was rapidly becoming impossible,
and sold his manor of East Beckham and other lands for 100
marks.[6] At the same time, he began making enquiries to as-
certain the value of his woods at Sporle.[7] Besides this, he
was sacrificing the family plate, and we have three documents
showing he pawned twenty dishes and a saucer of silver on one
occasion,[8] "16 pottingers weighing 22 lb. 10½ oz. Troy weight

[1] P.L. No. 574.   [2] Id. No. 572.   [3] Id. No. 573.
[4] Id. No. 629.   [5] Id. No. 631.   [6] Id. No. 634.
[7] Id. No. 633.   [8] Id. No. 643.

for £40 till Whitsuntide" on another,[1] and two chargers and four pottingers weighing 11 lb. 1¾ oz. silver for £20 a few weeks later.[2] So their troubles went on. Money is the ever recurring topic in the letters of this period, Margaret, Sir John, and his brother were all equally penniless, and it is almost impossible from the few documents we have to piece together any ordered story of their financial plans, and the means they were forced to adopt to raise money. Sir John showed little ability in conducting his business. At one time in 1471 he made a release of some estates at Saxthorpe and Titchwell, without any intention of surrendering the property for ever. This was not made clear; and, early the next year, one William Gurney started to hold a Court at Saxthorpe in the name of the new lord of the manor. Young John Paston interrupted this Court by appearing with one of his men and ensured his brother's rights, by preventing the Court from sitting peacefully.[3] Again, several months later, he appeared at the critical moment, and was able to secure an adjournment of the Court until Gurney and Sir John had talked the matter over.[4] Unfortunately he was not in control; and, a few weeks later, Saxthorpe and Titchwell were sold over the Pastons' heads by the Bishop of Winchester, as sole executor of Fastolf's will. Sir John, apparently, had never recognised the Bishop's claim to the manors, and was taken unawares by the sale. But now the lands were gone, and it was not likely they could be recovered. Margaret writes in deep sorrow:

We beat the bushes and other men have the birds. My Lord hath false counsel and simple that adviseth him thereto; and as it is told me, Guton is like to go the same way in haste....What shall fall of the remnant God knoweth,—I trow as evil or worse.[5]

About this time Margaret announced that if Sir John sold any more lands, she would withdraw double their value from anything he should inherit from her.[6] Nothing daunted, Sir John set to work to get his woods at Sporle valued, so that the timber might be sold. Since he might not sell his lands without risking his mother's displeasure, he adopted the subterfuge of borrowing money on them on mortgage. This Margaret could

[1] P.L. No. 644.   [2] Id. No. 649.
[3] Id. No. 688, and see account on p. 256   [4] Id. No. 693.
[5] Id. No. 695.   [6] Id. No. 694.

not but consider as much the same thing; "for she says she knows well it shall never be pledged out."[1]

We might continue the story indefinitely. Sir John's letters until the time of his death are full of allusions to his plans for raising money. He borrowed as much as he could from his relatives, especially his uncle William, and was also very much in debt to Justice Townsend at various times.[2] When these sources failed, he pledged more of the family plate,[3] or negociated for the sale or leasing of his manors, or raised money upon mortgage.[4]

Yet, weak and careless as he was in most matters, Sir John was always most anxious to win back Caister. When he was staying at his mother's family mansion of Mauteby, the great Castle was only three miles distant, and the sight of it was a constant reminder of the loss of what Margaret called "the fairest flower in our garland." Sir John and his brother John did all they could to influence great personages on their behalf. Through his former position in the Duke's household, John III was able to approach the Duke's council at Framlingham. He persuaded the Council of the justice of the Paston's case, but the Duke would not hear of surrender, and the matter was at a deadlock.[5]

A little later a possible opportunity presented itself, and the Pastons resolved to make the most of it. After many years of married life, the Duchess was with child, and at the large and festive gathering at Framlingham consequent on the expected birth, the Pastons hoped to get a friendly hearing. John drew up a petition to the Duke, while Sir John got letters from the King to be presented to the Duke, the Duchess and also to the Council. It was all in vain. Neither the King's letters, nor the pleading of Bishop Waynflete who baptised the new-born infant, nor the general opinion of the countryside had any effect on the Duke.[6] Caister was too fair a possession to be abandoned lightly, and the Duke did not mean to give it back if he could help it. This was in the winter of 1472, and Sir John was destined to spend several more years in fruitless efforts to get it restored to

[1] *P.L.* No. 702.
[2] *Id.* No. 754.
[3] *Id.* No. 701.
[4] *Id.* Nos. 634, 702, 708, 745, 746, 755, 802.
[5] *Id.* Nos. 745, 802.
[6] *Id.* Nos. 704, 705, 706, 708, 714, 715.

him. His letters throughout this period show how determined he was, and also how his hopes were often raised to the highest pitch, only to be shattered at the last moment. He used every means in his power to bring pressure to bear on the Duke. He hoped at one time that Caister would be his by the Christmas of 1473,[1] and enquired whether Margaret wished to dwell there or not.[2] But these hopes did not materialise, and in the following February he could do no more than "trust to have good tidings thereof hastily."[3] Almost the whole of 1474 had passed, and Margaret had evidently grown impatient, for he wrote "As for Caister, it needeth not to spur nor prick me to do ought therein. I do [all] that I can with good will."[4] Then in 1475 he was in France most of the year, but he continued to press his suit by every possible means. His brother and his uncle William promised to see the Duke and Duchess again, and Sir John was greatly annoyed by the "slow Bishop of Winchester," who had not yet fulfilled a promise to do the same.[5] His hopes were roused by the active interest the King now showed in the matter, despite the fact that the Duke was reported to have said that "the King should as soon have his life as that place."[6]

Sir John saw the time was ripe for a great effort, and drew up a petition to the King. This set forth at length the whole story of the dispute, and stated that for four years the Duke had held the property unlawfully, all the while refusing to see Sir John, or to listen to his pleas.[7] Before Sir John had actually presented this petition, the Duke suddenly died. Sir John for once did the right thing. Without wasting more time he sent a messenger to Caister to assert his rights there. This action caused some trouble, for it was considered by some of the Duke's servants to show want of respect for their master. Sir John, however, showed much commonsense in his plea of justification and, having done this, at once set off to London to put in his claim. The Duchess was not so hostile as the Duke had been, and John III soon found there was a great possibility of the lands being restored. Sir John was warned not to do anything rash that might alienate the good-will of the Duchess, and his brother was careful to point out to the lady that although the moat was frozen, and

[1] P.L. No. 732.   [2] Id. No. 733.   [3] Id. No. 736.   [4] Id. No. 746.
[5] Id. No. 760.   [6] Id. No. 764.   [7] Id. No. 766.

Caister thus exposed to attack, Sir John had no intention of using force.[1] At length in May 1476, the matter was brought before the King's Council, and the Lords, Judges and Serjeants present all held the title of Sir John to be good. After seven years' exile he wrote to his mother the last words in the long strife. "Blessed be God, I have Caister at my will."[2]

Sir John was destined to live peacefully in his newly-recovered home but a few years, for he died in the autumn of 1479. Even during the interval between the recovery of Caister and his death, he was in constant difficulties. The Duke of Suffolk early in 1478 once again claimed Hellesdon and Drayton, and even went so far as to sell the woods to the Mayor of Norwich. The Mayor began forthwith to cut down the woods, and Sir John had to hasten to London to get his rights protected. While he was there, the Duke formally took possession of Hellesdon, dined at the manor house, and evidently held a manor court.[3] Although the Duke had not much influence at Court, he continued to oppress the Pastons, and the troubles between them were not quite settled when Sir John died.

His brother John, third of that name, at once took control of affairs. Certain properties of the family were in dispute between him and his uncle William, and John took all possible precautions to assert his own claim. Gradually these troubles were overcome. John was too able and too trustworthy a man to be ignored in the stirring days when Henry VII had newly gained the throne; and we may fitly take our leave of this chequered family history on the day he became Sheriff of Norfolk, "right well beloved councillor" of the Earl of Oxford,[4] and destined to be knighted before long for distinguished service at the battle of Stoke.[5]

[1] P.L. No. 772.   [2] Id. No. 779.
[3] Id. No. 817. For full details of the scene, see p. 257.
[4] Id. Nos. 887, 892.   [5] Id. Intro. p. ccclvii.

CHAPTER III

MARRIAGE

ONE morning in 1440, soon after Easter, Justice Paston received a letter from his wife Agnes, containing news of such interest that she had been unable to wait for a secretary, but had written it herself. Her letter announced the first meeting of their eldest son John with Margaret, daughter and heiress of John Mauteby, a neighbouring landowner. The Pastons, like very many others, were intent on increasing their lands and possessions, and a marriage such as this was all part of the plan by which the family hoped to take a prominent place among the Norfolk gentry. To this end it was essential that their children should marry well, and no doubt the Justice's well-known ability had been employed in arranging the match. His efforts had been successful, and his wife's pleasure reflects his own when she writes:

> And as for the first acquaintance between John Paston and the said gentlewoman, she made him gentle cheer in gentle wise, and said, he was verily your son. And so I hope there shall need no great treaty between them.[1]

It is a strange picture to modern eyes: the young girl brought over to the Pastons' home, and there paraded before the eldest son, while hard old Agnes Paston looked at her with eager eyes, not seeing a shrinking bewildered young woman, but the rich pastures and the manor of Mauteby which were to be her inheritance. The two young people were held fast by the hard circumstances of their age. Whatever their own desires, had they been free to choose, they both yielded to the parental arrangements, and soon afterwards were married.[2]

It is well this letter comes early in the correspondence, for its implications will prepare the reader to some extent for the frank business way in which marriage is treated throughout the rest of the *Letters*. The marriage of convenience was the rule—at least among the nobility and landed classes in fifteenth century

[1] *P.L.* No. 25.   [2] *Id.* No. 29.

England, and many readers will be heartily tired of, and repelled by, the insistence on financial and worldly matters shown by both men and women in discussing marriage proposals. The question of a marriage was considered on much the same lines as any other business proposition, and generally with little or no reference to the individuals concerned. Contemporary documents are full of cases in which such proceedings are set forth at length,[1] and the *Paston Letters* themselves provide a mass of interesting evidence. One or two cases may first be quoted to show the cold-blooded attitude often adopted by parents. William Molynes, who was a descendant of a well-known Norfolk family, had the option of purchasing the manor of Gresham, which eventually was owned by the Pastons. Apparently he was without the necessary funds to do so; and, finding he would lose the property unless he acted promptly, he took his wife's advice and entered into an agreement with T. Falconer, a London merchant. By this agreement, he sold his young son's marriage, and it was arranged the boy should marry the merchant's daughter as soon as they should come of age. Fortunately, Molynes broke his agreement, and the marriage never took place; but it affords a striking example of the lengths to which both men and women were ready to traffic in their flesh and blood to serve their own ends.[2]

In another case, John Paston bluntly told his brother Sir John that a neighbour of theirs had "bought Joan Walsham's part of her livelode, and married her to a knave."[3] The whole affair was so bad that John, who was far from being squeamish in these matters,[4] said he had fallen out "fowly" over it with his uncle William. Unfortunately we have no details whatever to enable us to see what was particularly bad in the affair. Bad enough, and cynical to a degree, was the attempt made by John Wyndham of Felbrigg to sell his child so that he might achieve his own ends. He had fallen in love with the widow of Sir John Heveningham, but unfortunately there remained unpaid 300 marks of her husband's debts, and these were very pressing. When Wyndham had exhausted every other means of ingratia-

[1] E.g. Plum. Corr. pp. xliii, lxiv, lxx; Berkeley, Extracts, p. 162; Essex Archaeolog. Trans. vol. II. p. 174; Cely, No. 123.
[2] P.L. No. 10.
[3] Id. No. 694. [4] See his own marriage affairs below.

ting himself with her friends, he played his master stroke by offering to pay off the debt at once if she would marry him. The lady seems to have been as cautious and business-like as many were at the time, and it was rumoured that, "if the large proffers may be performed,...she will have him."¹ Incredible as it sounds to modern ears, Wyndham proposed to raise the money to pay off this debt by the sale of his young son's marriage. For this he was to get 600 marks, so that there would be a goodly balance of 400 marks after paying his lady's debts. The future of his son never seems to have entered into the question, and the very matter of fact way in which Margaret Paston gives an account of the whole affair to her husband shows how commonplace such amazing transactions were to a fifteenth century society.

The Pastons seem to have indulged fully in the maze of negociation and enquiries that surrounded all medieval marriages. The details of the preliminaries of John Paston's own marriage we do not know, but there is no reticence throughout the *Letters* in discussing the efforts which were made from time to time to effect suitable marriages for various members of the family. From 1449 until 1459, there are continuous references to the negociations for the hand of John Paston's sister Elizabeth. During these years the Pastons were continually at work trying to find a suitable match for her. They first tried to marry her to Stephen Scrope, the son of Sir S. Scrope by his wife Millicent.² Scrope was the heir to considerable property, but cannot otherwise have been a very attractive man, for besides being nearly fifty and a widower, he himself tells us that he had "suffered a sickness that kept [me] a thirteen or fourteen years ensuing; whereby I am disfigured in my person and shall be whilst I live."³ Nevertheless, Agnes Paston had made up her mind that he offered a suitable match, and quotes approvingly her niece's statement that "it were a folly to forsake him unless you knew of another as good or better."⁴ The reservation is absolutely characteristic of the times. Already Agnes Paston had arranged that Scrope should "show the indentures made between the

¹ *P.L.* No. 190.
² Millicent afterwards became the wife of Sir J. Fastolf.
³ *History Castlecombe*, Scrope, G. P., pp. 264-83.   ⁴ *P.L.* No. 70.

knight that hath his daughter and him, whether that Scrope, if he were married and fortuned to have children, if the children should inherit his land, or his daughter the which is married."[1] The niece Elizabeth Clere also wrote:

> Meseemeth he were good for my cousin your sister, unless you might get her a better.... Cousin, it is told me there is a goodly man in your Inn [the Inner Temple] of the which the father died late, and if you think that he were better for her than Scrope, it would be laboured; and give Scrope a goodly answer that he be not put off till you be sure of a better.[2]

Elizabeth was undoubtedly moved by Elizabeth Paston's sad state and wished to help her all she could, and yet had no hesitation in advising her brother to offer her to the highest bidder.

Meanwhile what of the girl herself? Her mother told John Paston that she "found her never so willing to none as she is to him, if it be so that his land stand clear."[3] This sounds more like the mother than the girl speaking, and his cousin Elizabeth Clere's letter written at the same time gave Paston the truth of the matter. Agnes Paston was a hard determined woman, very suspicious and obstinate, as her letters show again and again.[4] She had made up her mind it was time her daughter was married, and she intended to carry out her own ideas.

To this end she had kept the girl shut up so that she could not see nor speak to any man, and was even suspicious of her conversing with the very servants in the house. As if this were not enough, she had attempted to break the girl's spirit by other means. Elizabeth had in all probability scorned the idea of marrying Scrope,—this old battered widower of nearly fifty, and she a girl of about twenty,—but her mother knew how to deal with such high spirits. Agnes applied her remedies with the result that Elizabeth "was never in so great sorrow as she is nowadays," and with good reason, for "She has since Easter [3 months ago] for the most part been beaten once in the week or twice, sometimes twice in one day, and her head broken in two or three places."[5] It is not surprising that in the end Elizabeth surrendered, and agreed to marry Scrope, if her brother was satisfied with his prospects and promises. Her cousin warned

[1] P.L. No. 71.   [2] Id. No. 71.   See Appendix IV for original.
[3] Id. No. 70.   [4] E.g. Id. Nos. 46, 415.   [5] Id. No. 71.

Paston, however, that he must be careful what action he took, "for sorrow oftentime causeth women to beset them otherwise than they should do, and if she were in that case, I wot well you would be sorry."[1]

It is quite clear that no attention whatever was paid to anything but the most material interests in this matter. The Pastons, mother, son and cousin all wanted to marry Elizabeth well, and were only concerned in giving her to the highest bidder. Scrope displayed his "endentures," and told them of his "livelode" with an air of assurance that, after all, these were the things that mattered; and poor Elizabeth, rendered desperate, decided for him, "notwithstanding it is told her his person is simple." She also—though with more reason than the others—insisted on her brother making sure that her "children and her may inherit, and she have reasonable jointure." Fortunately, after all these negociations, this monstrous wooing was unsuccessful for some unknown reason, and Elizabeth was saved the melancholy satisfaction of knowing that men would praise her because she was willing "to rule her to him as she ought to do..., notwithstanding his person is simple."[2]

The relief however was only temporary. Throughout the next ten years, her marriage was ever in the mind of her family, and in 1453 Margaret Paston told her husband that his mother "prayeth you to remember my sister, and to do your part faithfully ere you come home to help to get her a good marriage." Not to waste time she adds,

It was told her that Knyvet the heir is for to marry; both his wife and child be dead, as it was told here. Wherefore she would that you should enquire whether it be so or no, and what his livelode is, and if you think that it be [wise] for to do, to let him be spoken to thereof.[3]

Life at home must have been very miserable for Elizabeth. Apparently she was quite unwanted there, and Margaret was forced to tell her husband that "it seemeth by my mother's language that she would never so fain to have been delivered of her as she will now."[4] As the weary months dragged on and brought no marriage, Dame Agnes' tongue grew more and more bitter; and she used "such language to her [daughter] that she

[1] P.L. No. 71.   [2] Id. No. 71.   [3] Id. No. 185.   [4] Id. No. 185.

thinketh right strange and so that she is right weary thereof."[1]
The most Elizabeth could hope for was that her brother would
do his best for her, and he was told "she sayeth her full trust is
in you; and, as ye do therein, she will agree her thereto."[2]

About this time John Paston was negociating with a certain
Sir William Oldhall for her hand. Elizabeth was willing to
accept him, being convinced it would be "for her worship and
profit." Her mother gave a grudging consent, saying, "I feel
your sister well willed thereto"--but this consent was condi-
tional on it being quite certain that "his land stands clear."[3]
Again the marriage was abandoned at a later stage; but undaunted the Pastons still persevered. John Clopton, a country
squire, next engaged their attention.[4] He was evidently pleased
at the prospect of marrying Elizabeth, and a draft marriage
settlement was drawn up. The Pastons probably did not think
him rich enough, and no more is heard of the affair.[5]

The next effort was made by others than the Pastons. Lord
Grey of Hastings wrote to John Paston saying,

> If your sister be not yet married, I trust to God I know where
> she may be married to a gentleman of 400 marks of livelode, the
> which is a great gentleman born and of good blood; and if you think
> that I shall labour any further therein, I pray you send me word
> by the bringer of this letter, for I have spoken with the parties, and
> they have granted me that they will proceed no further therein till
> I speak with them again.[6]

John Paston, however, had a very shrewd idea of what would
be considered his sister's "market value"; and acknowledging
this letter said:

> Forsooth my Lord, she is not married, nor ensured [engaged] to
> no man; there is and hath been, divers times and late, communica-
> tion of such marriages with divers gentlemen not determined as yet,
> and whether the gentleman that your Lordship means be one of
> them or not I doubt.[7]

After a little polite flattery, he promises his sister shall not be
married, or engaged, within the next two months; and asks
bluntly for "certain information of the said gentleman's name
and of the place and country where his livelode lieth, and
whether he hath any children."[8]

[1] *P.L.* No. 196.   [2] *Id.* No. 196.   [3] *Id.* Nos. 196-7.
[4] *Id.* No. 202.   [5] *Id.* No. 203.   [6] *Id.* No. 209.
[7] *Id.* No. 210.   [8] *Id.* No. 210. Country, *i.e.* county.

A little later John Paston discovered the motive which had
actuated Lord Grey in trying to arrange this marriage. It appeared that the "great gentleman" was a ward of his own whom
he was anxious to get married to Elizabeth, so that her 400 marks
of dowry should come into his coffers. However pleased Lord
Grey might have been by this, his young ward could not appreciate the humour of being married thus, in order to provide
money for his guardian. The young man declared that if he
married the girl he wanted her dowry himself, whereupon Lord
Grey's interest in the marriage vanished, and he declared "he
shall marry himself for me."[1] So another failure had to be
added to the growing list. Her brother William was frankly
displeased at all this waste of time and said "At the reverence
of God, draw to some conclusion; it is time."[2]

At length, however, their persistence was rewarded. Elizabeth
was married to Robert Poynings, who had been sword-bearer
and carver to John Cade, and who was instrumental in saving
the life of Fastolf's servant John Payne during the insurrection.[3]
From the artless phrases of the first extant letter she wrote to
her mother after her marriage, it is difficult to judge whether or
no she had at last found happiness. She writes:

> As for my master, my best beloved that you call, and I must
> needs call him so now, for I find no other cause, and as I trust to
> Jesu, none shall; for he is full kind to me, and is as busy as he can
> to make me sure of my jointure.[4]

Margaret Paston did not learn a great deal from the varied
fortunes of her sister-in-law. Her own children were treated
with considerable severity, and the harsh genius of Agnes still
dominated the Pastons' ideas of the education of children. They
continued to make use of the common medieval practice of
boarding them out (of which more will be said later).[5] Anne
Paston had been put out with her cousins the Calthorpes. Late
in 1470 Calthorpe decided that he must reduce his household,
and asked Margaret to arrange for Anne to return to her home.
He added "She waxeth high, and it were time to purvey her a
marriage."[6] Margaret did not fail to notice her cousin's advice,

---

[1] *P.L.* No. 216.   [2] *Id.* No. 216.   [3] *Id.* Nos. 99 and 252.
[4] *Id.* No. 322, and see *Id.* Nos. 357, 395 and 687 for her subsequent
married life.
[5] See pp. 82–6.   [6] *Id.* No. 660.

and within eighteen months, besides having received an offer from a Norfolk family of reputation, Anne was pledged to William Yelverton, a grandson of the well-known Justice.[1] Nothing more is heard of the match in the *Letters* until November 1473 when Sir John, having heard his sister was ill, expressed surprise that she was not married. Such ignorance on his part is very extraordinary, the more so as he went on to say, "As for Yelverton, he said but late that he would have her if she had her money, and else not; wherefore me thinketh that they be not very sure."[2] Evidently Sir John had done all he meant to do in the matter, and had not even concerned himself to know whether or not the marriage had taken place. What Anne's real feelings were may be seen from her brother's closing words. "Among all other things, I pray you beware that the old love of Pampyng renew not. He is now from me. I wot not what he will do."[3] The bartering away of his sister, so long as it was to a man of some social position, was not a matter to worry him; but he was greatly concerned that care should be taken lest she should throw herself away by entertaining foolish ideas of love for an inferior. When Sir John wrote again three days later he did not mention the marriage, but the fear of this catastrophe was still in his mind, and he warned his brother to "take good heed to my sister Anne, lest the old love between her and Pamping renew."[4] As we shall see later, the Pastons had already had one experience of a daughter of their house marrying a servant of the family, and they had not yet recovered from the shock.[5]

For unknown reasons, the engagement dragged on year after year, until the Pastons began to fear Yelverton never meant to marry Anne. Sir John was offered a good marriage for her to a Lincoln gentleman,[6] but at last Yelverton and Anne were married in the summer of 1477, and thereafter practically disappear from the *Letters*.[7]

This question of matrimony was not less important to the men of the family. Wrecks of their matrimonial plans, both for themselves and for one another, strew the pages of the *Correspon-*

[1] *P.L.* No. 695.   [2] *Id.* No 732.
[3] *Id.* No. 732.   [4] *Id.* No. 733.
[5] *Id.* Nos. 607, 609, 617, 632, and see pp. 42 ff. for the details.
[6] *Id.* No. 771.   [7] *Id.* But see Nos. 787, 799.

dence; and we can only say that, although Sir John may have been in later life "the best chooser of a gentlewoman," he certainly had acquired the art by dint of long practice. His brother John was even more determined in seeking out a good match for himself, and it is only our knowledge of his many sterling qualities that reconciles us to his good fortune in finally winning Margery Brews.

The problem of arranging a marriage for one or another of the family seems seldom to have left the minds of the elder members, yet almost always, apparently, without any direct reference to the person concerned! News of a possible match would at once be sent on to Norfolk, as speed was all important in these preliminary investigations. So we find the Love Chase being started by some such information as:

"I heard while I was in London where was a goodly young woman to marry,...and she shall have £200 in money to her marriage etc.,.... and ere I departed out of London....I spake with some of the maid's friends, and have got their good wills to have her married to my brother Edmund"[1]; or "I understand that Mistress Fytzwater hath a sister, a maid to marry. I trow if ye entreated [Fitzwater] she might come into Christian men's hands."[2]

In the same way they wasted no time on hearing of people left widowed, but hastened forthwith to interview the bereaved party in the hope of negociating a good business marriage. So Edmund Paston writes:

Here is lately fallen [become] a widow in Worsted, who was wife to one Bolt, a worsted merchant, and worth a thousand pounds:... She is called a fair gentlewoman. I will for your sake see her.... This gentlewoman is about 30 years, and has but two children, which shall be to the deed's charge: she was his wife only 5 years. If she be any better than I write, take it in truth I show the least.[3]

Throughout it is evident that the monetary value of the marriage was all-important; and more, the terms used in speaking of possible marriages are those of business. The reader will look almost in vain for any of the sentiment and romance that goes so largely to the making of the books of the middle ages. Such things were all very well in the bower, and perhaps after a good day's hunting to be recited in the hall; but they did not come into the sphere of actual practical life. There, marriage was a

[1] *P.L.* No. 812.   [2] *Id.* No. 777 and cf. Nos. 739, 789, 858, etc.
[3] *Id.* No. 858, and cf. No. 71.

matter of business, and so they talk of "dealing,"[1] of "inspecting evidences,"[2] of making certain the property involved "stands clear"[3]; or they draw up indentures setting out in every detail the dowry and lands to be given by either side.[4]

By a strange irony of fate, Sir John Paston in the very centre of all this maze of marriage-making lived and died unmarried himself. The whole story of his loves cannot be written from our inadequate materials, but there can be little doubt that he remained single of his own deliberate choice. Fastidious and "the best chooser of a gentlewoman" known to his friends, he was at the same time a great favourite with womenfolk. He gives his brother the fruit of his garnered wisdom when he advises him in pursuing a match, to "bear yourself as lowly to the mother as you list, but to the maid not too lowly, nor that you be too glad to speed, nor too sorry to fail."[5]

While he was in Calais about 1468 Sir John became acquainted with Anne Haute, an English lady who was a relative of Lord Scales. She seems to have lived long abroad, and may even have been born there. In his first letter to her Sir John says, "I am proud that you can read English"; and the depth of his early passion for her may be gauged by the fact that he makes his eager protestations even before any financial details have been discussed.[6] He had had other love affairs, but thenceforth his relationship to Anne Haute became the central matrimonial prospect of his life; although towards the end of their engagement we learn that he had a mistress by whom he left a natural daughter. There is little that is pleasing in the story of Sir John and Anne Haute; for, except in these early days of their acquaintance, there is a lack of love or of any deep feeling in the whole affair.

Strangely enough, Sir John does not seem to have troubled to tell his mother of his engagement. Margaret however heard of it from other sources and, as was her wont, could not forbear reading him a little homily:

I have no certain knowledge of your engagement, but if you are

[1] *P.L.* Nos. 747, 739.   [2] *Id.* No. 71.
[3] *Id.* No. 197, and cf. *Cely*, Nos. 53, 89.
[4] *Id.* No. 203, and cf. *E.C.P.* 15/340, 40/144, etc.; *Plum. Corr.* pp. lxx–lxxii.
[5] *Id.* No. 570.   [6] *Id.* No. 588.

engaged I pray God send you joy and worship together, and so I trust you shall have, if it be as is reported of her.

She goes on to warn him of the sacred and binding nature of an engagement. For fear his raptures should transport him beyond the realms of commonsense, she seeks to bring him to earth by the very practical advice:

Also I would that you should not be too hasty to be married till you be more sure of your livelode, for you must remember what expenses you shall have, and if you have not [enough] to maintain it, it will be great rebuke; and therefore labour that you may have release of the lands and be in more surety of your land, ere that you are married.[1]

That he was engaged is clear enough, for we have two letters of Lord Scales, written on Paston's behalf to the Council of the Duke of Norfolk and to some unknown people, in which he definitely says, "A marriage is fully concluded between Sir John Paston and my right near kinswoman Haute."[2] There was something wanting, however; and, in the following spring of 1470, Paston was still uncertain about the match. Indeed, from his words, the engagement itself does not seem very clear. "As for my good speed, I hope well. I am offered yet to have Mistress Anne Haute, and I shall have help now as some say."[3] There is nothing definite extant to elucidate this mystery. We may perhaps be allowed to surmise that Sir John's irresolute conduct, his known impecuniosity, or his partisanship for Henry VI were not well received by Anne's relatives, who were kinsfolk of Edward IV's queen. In the autumn of 1471 matters were still very unsatisfactory, and Sir John saw he must take definite action. Evidently he wished to terminate the matter one way or the other, but had not the necessary courage to force a decision at once. Characteristically enough he is sure he can settle it in the near future, and writes home, "I had almost spoken with Mistress Ann Haute, but I did not; nevertheless this next term I hope to take one way with her or other; she is agreed to speak with me, and she hopes to do me ease as she sayeth."[4] It is evident that the supposed lovers were not very frequently together, and had no strong affection for one another. Hence it is not surprising that a few weeks later we find the friends of

[1] P.L. No. 601.
[2] Id. No. 637.
[3] Id. Nos. 603, 604.
[4] Id. No. 675.

both parties were more concerned over questions of dignity than of the personal issues involved.[1]

Probably by this time all expectation of a marriage had been abandoned, and the parties were only concerned as to how to end the whole affair. When Paston next met the lady in February 1472, not much seems to have been accomplished, for he writes:

> I have spoken with Mistress Anne Haute at a pretty leisure, and, blessed be God, we be as far forth as we were heretofore, and so I hope we shall continue; and I promised her that at the next leisure that I could find thereto that I would come again and see her.[2]

They cannot be charged with undue haste, for the next recorded meeting was over a year later. Too much required to be settled however, and Sir John apparently had little leisure to devote to this, so we find him writing:

> As for me, if I had six days' leisure more than I had, and others also, I would have hoped to have been delivered of Mistress Anne Haute. Her friends the Queen and Atclif agreed to "common" [talk] and conclude with me, if I can find the means to discharge her conscience, which I trust to God to do.[3]

Here we get the first hint of what was the proposed solution. The discharge of her conscience meant an application to Rome for a dispensation of the espousal. Remembering the chronic shortage of money which ever afflicted Sir John, his reluctance to carry the matter to Rome is easily explained by a reference to the cost of such a proceeding. An application to Rome confirmed his worst fears, and when his brother wrote asking how the affair was progressing he replied:

> I have answer again from Rome that there is the well of grace and salve sufficient for such a sore, and that I may be dispensed with; nevertheless my proctor there asketh a thousand ducats, as he deemeth. But Master Lacy, another Rome runner here, which knoweth my said proctor there, as he sayeth as well as Bernard knew his shield, sayeth that he meaneth but an 100 ducats or 200 at the most; wherefore after this cometh more. He wrote to me also that the Pope does this nowadays very frequently.[4]

Again the progress of the whole affair is obscure for about four years, save for a remark of his mother's wishing he were well delivered of Anne, "and then I would trust that you should

[1] *P.L.* No. 678.   [2] *Id.* No. 690.   [3] *Id.* No. 722.
[4] *Id.* No. 732. See *C.P.L.* vols. v.–vii. *passim.*

do the better."[1] Clearly, although we have no other evidence, Sir John was still giving much attention to procuring his release. The tedious affair dragged on until 1477 when the end seemed in sight at last for Sir John writes, "This day (14th February, 1477), the matter between Mistress Anne Haute and me has been sore broken, both to the Cardinal, to my Lord Chamberlain and to myself; and I am in good hope."[2] The months following did not belie his hopes, and in August he learnt that "the matter between Anne Haute and me shall, with God's grace, this term be at a perfect end." He also makes a rueful statement that the cost of the dispensation "will charge me further than I have money as yet, or am like to have before that time, of my own."[3] There must have been good reason for his hopes, for we hear no more of the lady Anne Haute; and so, with a sigh for its costliness, this nine-year old matrimonial venture is at an end.

Sir John was important enough, despite all this, to have another marriage offered to him in the following year "right nigh to the Queen's blood."[4] His mother was full of hope for the success of this plan, chiefly because through it she saw a prospect of their recovering much of their property and of getting peace in Norfolk. During the next year, however, Sir John died before anything definite had been done.

It is in the matrimonial affairs of John Paston the youngest that we get the fullest and most open account of medieval marriage-making. He was a full-blooded young man, who loved being outdoors and riding about the Norfolk properties. Never in his early life does he seem to have thought of love in connection with marriage. His outlook may be guessed from his appeal to his brother to "get us a wife somewhere for 'Melius est enim nubere quam uri'."[5]

His first recorded venture was for the hand of Lady Boleyn's daughter. Lady Boleyn was not at all in favour of his suit,[6] and evidently John did not prosecute it with any great eagerness,[7] so that it is not surprising if, after a while, no more is heard of it. After this early attempt three years pass before the letters give any hint of his further adventures. Then he became

[1] *P.L.* No. 752. [2] *Id.* No. 786. [3] *Id.* No. 802.
[4] *Id.* No. 818. [5] *Id.* No. LXXXII. See I Cor. vii. 9.
[6] *Id.* No. 570. [7] *Id.* No. 573.

a suitor for Mistress Katherine Dudley. This young lady had much the same light-hearted nature as his own; and, although not displeased with his proffered love, she says frankly that "she rekketh not how many gentlemen love her; she is full of love...she will none this two year, and I believe her; for I think she hath the life that she can hold her content with."[1] John Paston had no desire to wait so long. His cry was "I pray get us a wife somewhere," and he continued his searches for a suitable mate. The next year saw him still unmarried, but zealously wooing the Lady Elizabeth Bouchier. Here his eagerness was too excessive, and his more cultured brother warned him that his behaviour had in some way "a little chafed it, but I can not tell how."[2]

Evidently John had more than "a little chafed it," and the Lady Elizabeth passed to join the other lost chances. John was learning wisdom, and began to bring more finesse to his task. When his next venture seemed ripe for definite action, he did not trust his own impetuous ways, but made use of his brother. Sir John was never unwilling to see a pretty lady, nor to forward his brother's affairs. He was asked to see a certain Mrs Eberton, a London draper's wife.[3] His brother had been negociating for an engagement and thought it time to force a decision. So Sir John went to see Mrs Eberton and told her his brother had received an offer of marriage worth more than 600 marks, but such was his "fantazy" for her daughter, that he would be content to marry her even with a lesser dowry. The worthy draper and his wife do not seem to have been as impressed as he hoped, and a few months later he admits "As for Eberton's daughter...he heard never more speech thereof."[4]

At this time, besides the offer of a 600 mark marriage, John Paston had learned of a widow living at Blackfriars and was making eager enquiries concerning her. It is uncertain whether this is the woman he wished his brother to go and see at the same time he was negociating with Mrs Eberton. Then he asked Sir John to "understand how the matter at the Blackfriars doth, and that ye will see and speak with the thing yourself, and with her father and mother, ere ye depart."[5] The "thing,"

[1] *P.L.* No. 637.   [2] *Id.* No. 675   [3] *Id.* No. 739.
[4] *Id.* No. 747.   [5] *Id.* No. 739

however, was not to be won so easily, for a few months later she married a certain Skerne. Her tale that Master Paston had once come with twenty men, determined to carry her away, was probably only an attempt on her part to increase her importance in her listeners' minds.[1] His general attitude towards women, and more particularly the slighting allusion to her by John Paston, do not support her story. At the same time, his chances of marrying the draper's daughter grew less and less, and negociations ceased.[2]

Nothing daunted he continued the eager quest, and Sir John worked with great zeal to promote his brother's suit to Lady Walgrave. He tried to persuade her to take his brother's ring, but she refused, and told him she meant to keep to the answer she had personally given John Paston.[3] Afterwards she did hold out the slightest hope, but he realised it was of the slightest, and again he had failed. Continued rebuffs made him desperate, and he resolved to marry anyone with a suitable fortune, even "some old thrifty draff-wife" in London. "Thomas Brampton at the Black Friars, with such others as he and I appointed, will help you to espy one for me."[4] This was said in irritation perhaps; he was too experienced by now to be so easily pleased. Two more attempts have to be recorded before the long list is closed. A short while after his plea for a thrifty old "draff-wyff," he learnt that a friend had a marriageable sister. At once he wrote "I pray you speak with Master Fitzwalter of that matter for me. I trow, if ye entreated him, she might come into Christian men's hands."[5] Again he failed, and then comes his last attempt, —perhaps the most pathetic of all. Sir John as usual acts as investigator, and he report:

As for this matter of Mistress Barley, I hold it but a bare thing. I saw her for your sake. She is a little one; she may be a woman hereafter, if she be not old now. Her person seemeth thirteen years of age; her years men say be full eighteen.[6]

But by this time John Paston's fortunes, as we shall see later, had taken an unexpected and happy turn. The long Love Chase was at an end.[7]

[1] *P.L.* No. 747.   [2] *Id.* No. 747.   [3] *Id.* No. 749.
[4] *Id.* No. 772.   [5] *Id.* No. 777.   [6] *Id.* No. 789.
[7] See p. 46.

CHAPTER IV

LOVE

It is refreshing to leave this atmosphere of intrigue and bargaining to come among the few love marriages reported in these *Letters*. Despite the hard mercenary nature of the times, it was not always possible for parents or guardians to enforce their views upon the young. So it is that, amidst the enquiries and sordid grasping that prelude most medieval marriages, here and there the authentic accents of true love survive in all their freshness.

The love story of Margery Paston and Richard Calle is one of the fairest things in this *Correspondence*. It would be easy to be lyrical over this beautiful episode among the sorry matrimonial struggles of those days; but a bare recital of the actual facts will show clearly enough its pathos and strength. It is the story of two people so deeply in love that they could successfully challenge and overthrow all the obstacles that their age and environment placed in their course. Margery was the youngest sister of Sir John, and as such no doubt had been marked down as a suitable match by various guardians and squires; while her own mother was looking about to find a husband for her before she was more than a girl.[1] Her brother received various offers for her hand,[2] and when she was in London, her mother had taken her to the Rood at the North door of St Paul's, and also to St Saviour's Abbey, Bermondsey, "to pray to them that she may have a good husband."[3]

Several years after this she was still unmarried, though her affections were not unengaged, and suddenly Sir John was startled by the news that she had pledged herself to Richard Calle, his chief bailiff! Sir John was quite incapable of dealing with such a situation, and he worked off some of his anger by writing home to say how surprised he was to hear his brother John approved of the affair. This was too much for brother John, who was as outraged as any of the family, and he replied with

---

[1] *P.L.* No. 479.   [2] *E.g. Id.* No. 567.   [3] *Id.* No. 526.

spirit giving a full account of the whole proceedings. Calle had evidently made use of a friend to make some enquiries as to how the land lay. This man had casually asked John Paston if a marriage had been arranged between Margery and Calle, adding that if nothing was settled, he knew of a good match for her. John quickly disabused him,

> I answered him, that if my father whom God pardon, were alive and had consented thereto, and my mother, and ye both, he should never have my good will for to make my sister to sell candle and mustard in Framlingham. And this with more, which were too long to write to you.[1]

The scenes following on this avowal may be imagined. There was no one in the household to say a good word for Margery. Her mother was violently angry; her brother's emphatic disapproval we know, and the chaplain Sir J. Gloys was equally hostile. She had known too well how bitter and unsympathetic everyone would be, and for long had hesitated to break the news to them. There are few letters in this *Correspondence* showing such deep feelings of tenderness and devotion as Richard Calle's letter to Margery, imploring her to announce their betrothal and so cut the knot of all their difficulties by one bold stroke. The Pastons had become suspicious, and had tried by various means to get definite evidence as to the relations between them. At one time Margery seems to have been so cowed that she allowed them to see some of Calle's letters. He countered this by ceasing to write for about two years, and it is the strongest testimony to their devotion that it remained undiminished, although they met only at intervals when his business brought him near to her. Calle, however, saw that nothing was to be gained by writing. He knew the Pastons would never consent to their bailiff marrying their daughter.

Calle's great comfort lay in the fact that Margery had already betrothed herself to him. The plighting of troth between two people at this time was absolutely binding.[2] No witnesses were required, and no ceremony other than the actual plighting of the two lovers. "The whole world was one vast Gretna Green," and although the Church discouraged such secret engagements,

---

[1] *P.L.* No. 607.
[2] Pollock and Maitland, vol. II. p. 372; *Borough Customs*, vol. II. pp. 135-6.

she was bound to uphold them when made, and to consider them
as binding as marriage itself.[1] Indeed Calle refers to their betrothal as "the great bond of matrimony that is made between
us," and remarks, "I marvel much that they should take this
matter so seriously, as I understand they do, remembering it is
in such case as it cannot be remedied." Since it was so binding
he cannot but exclaim at being kept from his love, "Alas, alas!
good lady, full little remember they what they do that keep us
asunder; four times a year are they accursed who hinder matrimony."[2] Margaret herself had once written to Sir John:

> If ye be engaged, I pray God send you joy and worship together...
> and before God, you are as greatly bound to her as [if] you were
> married, and therefore I charge you upon my blessing, that ye be
> as true to her as [if] she were married to you.[3]

There is no doubt then that the binding force of an engagement was fully recognised by them; but evidently they were
hoping against hope that Margery had not definitely pledged
herself, and so they continued to ignore Calle's appeals:

> "This is a painful life that we lead," he writes, "I suppose they
> think we be not betrothed together, and if they do so I marvel, for
> then they are not well advised, remembering the plainness that I
> broke [the matter] to my mistress at the beginning, and I suppose
> by you as well if you did as you ought to do of very right. If you
> have done the contrary, as I have been informed you have done, you
> did neither in keeping with your conscience nor to the pleasure of
> God, unless you did it for fear, and to please for the time such as
> were about you. If you did it for this, it was a reasonable cause,
> considering the great and importunate calling upon that you had,
> and many an untrue tale was made to you of me, which God knows
> I was never guilty of." He goes on, "I suppose if you tell them plainly
> the truth, they would not damm their souls for us. Though I tell
> them the truth they will not believe me as well as they will you,
> and therefore good lady, at the reverence of God be plain to them and
> tell the truth.[4]

Margery finally yielded to Calle's judgment, and made it quite
clear to her mother that she was pledged to him; and the storm
broke about her. Having made her announcement, she stood
by it. Threats, cajoleries, promises, were of no avail; and at
last the Pastons were forced to admit partial defeat. They were

[1] *Concilia*, Wilkins, vol. II. p. 135.
[2] See Myrc, p. 66.   [3] *P.L.* No. 601.
[4] *Id.* No. 609.

by no means content to leave the matter in this state, but at once set to work to get the betrothal annulled. After a time, the whole matter was laid before the Bishop of Norwich. He sent for Margery and for Richard Calle, and examined them both separately. Margery's courage was still high, and after the Bishop had put before her all the drawbacks, the shame to her kindred, the disapproval of her friends, etc., he asked her to repeat the words she had used in pledging herself to Calle so that he might see if they were sufficient and binding. This she did, and "if those words made it not sure, she said boldly that she would make it sure ere she went thence, for she thought in her conscience she was bound whatsoever the words were."[1] The examination of Calle only confirmed what Margery had said; and the Bishop, not knowing how to continue, said he would reserve his judgment until the week after Michaelmas, in case any other impediments might arise. The lovers demurred at this delay, but the Bishop was firm and they had to be content.

Margaret Paston, fearing how the proceedings in the Bishop's Court might go, had given orders that the girl was not to be allowed to return under her roof. So after the Court rose and Margery returned home, she was met by Sir J. Gloys who told her that never again would her mother, or her mother's friends, receive her. The poor girl had to return to Norwich, and the Bishop eventually found a lodging for her. Margaret had rooted her out of her heart, and was able to write to her son:

I pray you and require you that ye take it not pensively, for I know well it goeth right near your heart, and so it doth to mine and to others. But remember you, and so do I, that we have lost of her but a worthless person, and set it the less to heart,...for if he [Calle] were dead at this hour, she should never be at my heart as she was.[2]

It was clear that the matter had arrived at such a pass that further opposition was almost useless. The Bishop had no case against them; and, although in the first flush of his anger Sir John proposed getting the betrothal annulled,[3] on calmer reflection he found it wiser to leave things alone. Indeed, when he wrote a few months later, his only comment was to express a wish that the marriage should not take place before Christmas.[4]

[1] P.L. No. 617.   [2] Id. No. 617.
[3] Id. No. 617.   [4] Id. No. 632.

Calle throughout had acted honourably and openly, and he had accounted for his stewardship of the Paston lands in so satisfactory a way that he won the grudging approval of his enemy John Paston the youngest. Calle and Margery were at this time staying at Blackborough nunnery near Lynn awaiting the time of their marriage. In spite of all that had happened Calle was still faithful to the Pastons, and had again put his services at the disposal of the family before he offered them to others.[1] Sir John evidently swallowed his pride and kept his good man of business, for in later years we find Calle still his bailiff.[2] It is probable however that he was never received into the family, although we may be allowed to believe there was some sort of reconciliation between Margery and her mother. At any rate when Margaret died she left the sum of £20 to Margery's eldest child.[3]

After his very numerous attempts to secure a suitable marriage, John Paston the youngest met with better fortune than most modern readers will think he deserved. He met, fell in love with, and finally married one of the most charming women who pass through these pages,—one Margery Brews. The story of their love-making is a slight, if beautiful thing when we remember the deep emotions and prolonged sufferings that were experienced by Margery Paston and Richard Calle. In this case, there was little to hinder the match except a certain amount of wrangling by the parents over the financial details. The whole romance went forward with a sweep and assurance that makes any discussion of the hard practicalities almost needless. John had met his fate,—the days when he talked of viewing "the thyng," or of choosing an "old thryffty draff wyff," or of "dealing" with a prospective mother-in-law were over. He loved, and was loved; and from the outset this pair of lovers move forward with a serene confidence and mutual trust which overcome all obstacles.

John had heard originally of Margery "by many and diverse persons, and especially by my right trusty friend Richard Stratton." This friend had so sung the lady's praises, that John, unemotional and hard as he has seemed in his previous adventures, began to feel more than interested. It is evident that he plied

[1] *P.L.* No. 633. [2] *Id. e.g.* Nos. 732, 758, 938, etc. [3] *Id.* No. 861.

his friend with questions concerning her, until before they met he could write, "I have oftentimes heard say that ye can, and will, take everything well that is well meant." So he declared the devotion of his "poor heart that sometime was at my rule, which now is at yours."[1]

Things moved rapidly, and early in 1477 the girl's mother Elizabeth Brews wrote most sympathetically to him. She was a warm-hearted woman in whom the love of romance overcame the common worldly wisdom of her class. The Paston women, as we have seen, were made of a harder fibre; but Elizabeth was "ful plesaunt and amyable of port," and her "tendre herte" was quite unable to resist the blandishments of her daughter.[2] John seems to have won her heart as easily as he gained her daughter's, and though she boasts that Margery is "a witty gentlewoman, and if I say it, both good and virtuous," yet she is the first to admit that, "I trust you so much, that I would think her well bestowed upon you."[3] To further the match, in February 1477 she wrote to John reminding him that the coming Friday was "Saint Valentine's Day, and every bird chooseth him a mate." She invited him to come on Thursday and stay till Monday so that he might have plenty of time to discuss the whole affair with her husband. "Remember," she adds, "it is but a simple oak, that [is] cut down at the first stroke." John had pledged his word that he would not speak definitely to Margery, until the details were settled, but this arrangement was made without considering the maiden's ideas on the matter. She was deeply in love with John; and, although he had given his promise, perhaps she had understood his message though it was unspoken, and "Sometimes from his eyes...did receive fair speechless messages." So she played upon her mother, as she best knew how, until Elizabeth declared to John, "Ye have made her such an advocate for you, that I may never have rest night or day for [her] crying and calling upon [me] to bring the same matter to effect."[4]

Margery was under no interdict apparently, and wrote to John calling him her "right well-beloved Valentine." The monetary considerations that weighed with her father seemed

---

[1] P.L. No. 774. [2] Id. No. 782.
[3] Id. No. 781. [4] Id. No. 782.

slight, when balanced against the volume of her love. In the whole-hearted surrender of herself to John she could not imagine that anything else mattered, and appealed to him thus:

My mother hath laboured the matter to my father full diligently, but she can get no more [dowry] than ye know of—for the which God knoweth I am full sorry. But if ye love me, as I trust verily that ye do, ye will not leave me therefore; for if that ye had not half the livelode that ye have, for to do the greatest labour that any women alive might, I would not forsake you.[1]

The rumour that her father's persistence might cause John to postpone any further efforts, caused her "heart to be full heavy, and if you do come, and the matter take no effect, then should I be much more sorry and full of heaviness." She concludes her letter with a passage so loving, so tender in its simple appeal, that even in those days it could scarcely have been read unmoved. She writes:

Wherefore, if ye could be content with that good and my poor person, I would be the merriest maiden on ground; and if ye think not yourself so satisfied, or that ye might have much more good, as I have understood by you before; good, true and loving Valentine, that ye take no such labour upon you as to come [any] more for that matter, but let it pass, and never more be spoken of as I may be your true lover and bedewoman during my life.[2]

She did not appeal to him in vain. John worked to win this girl as he had never striven before. No difficulty was too great for him. He met the objections of his brother, or the claims of Sir Thomas, or the doubts of his mother with equal adroitness. Within a month he was so near a settlement that he wrote to his mother, "The matter is in a reasonable good way,...for I trow there is not a kinder woman living than I shall have for my mother-in-law, if the matter take."[3] At some date after this the negociations proceeded less smoothly. Sir John gave little help, and indeed assumed so unfavourable an attitude that Sir Thomas was alarmed, and possibly this was the cause of the delay. However that may be, John had so impressed even his calm sagacious mother with his earnestness that she made a further endeavour to bring about the marriage. In the middle of June she wrote to Elizabeth Brews and invited her and her husband to meet with the Pastons at Norwich, to see if a settle-

[1] *P.L.* No. 783. [2] *Id.* No. 784. [3] *Id.* No. 787.

ment could not be made "considering that it is so far spoken."[1]
The determined labours of John Paston were beginning to bear
fruit, and after this meeting, by dint of perseverance and a
measure of diplomacy, he gained his bride.[2] We have no letter
by which we may determine the exact date, but we know they
must have been married late in the summer of 1477, less than
a year after the preliminary overtures had been made.[3]

The further scanty references to love matches of the family may
be briefly dealt with. While still at Eton, and barely nineteen
years of age, William Paston fell in love with a young girl he met
at a wedding. He gives his brother an account of it all, and invites
him to call and see the family so that he may make enquiries as
to their wealth for himself. Of the maiden the youthful lover
writes, "As for her beauty, judge you that when you see her,
if so be you take the trouble, and especially behold her hands,
for if it be as it is told me, she is disposed to be thick."[4] Such
clear-sighted definition of his beloved's defects could have but
one end, and we hear no more of her.

Outside the Paston family, a most interesting love match is
recorded between Thomas Denyes and a lady of Norfolk whose
Christian name was Agnes. Denyes was a trusted servant of
the Earl of Oxford, but whilst in Norfolk had fallen violently in
love with Agnes, who was an acquaintance of the Pastons. So
great was his attachment, that the Earl was moved to act on
his behalf. He accordingly wrote to John Paston:

As you well know yourself, we have and long time have had the
service of Thomas Denyes, by continuance whereof we thought to
have had his attendance at our pleasure; nevertheless we have so
strictly examined his demeaning that we feel, and plainly conceive
that the love and affection which he has to a gentlewoman not far
from you...causeth him always to desire towards your country,
rather than towards such occupation as is suitable unto us.[5]

He goes on to ask Paston to do everything possible to promote
the match. While we cannot assume that the lady felt as strongly
as Denyes himself, yet the influence of the Earl, and Paston's
advocacy of Denyes' cause won her consent.[6] Poor Denyes was

---

[1] P.L. No. 799.   [2] Id. No. 501.   [3] Id. No. 809.
[4] Id. No. 827. "Sche is dysposyd to be thyke" =She is likely to grow fat.
[5] Id. No. 97.
[6] Id. Nos. 98 and 199. For Denyes' subsequent tragic career see Nos.
204. 389. 396, 397, 399, 403 and p. 225.

not left long in enjoyment of his treasure. He was thrown into the Fleet prison for inciting hired men to violence in defence of his wife's property. His enemies were not satisfied by this, but threw his wife into the Counter and afterwards to Newgate, although she was then with child. Denyes' regret and sorrow for his wife's misery when they were both imprisoned were the heaviest burden he had to bear. He writes to John Paston from prison, "But ever I beseech your mastership of continuance, and that you like to do my wife help and comfort in her disease.... And truly I have no thought, nor sorrow, but for her."[1]

With Denyes' despairing cry in our ears, we take our leave of the lovers in the *Paston Letters*. During the fifteenth century, as at all times, true love had often to overcome difficulties. But the very detailed evidence we may glean from this *Correspondence* shows that, even in an age when mercenary motives actuated most men in seeking wives, there were some who put love before convention and could gain their ends, despite hostility from all sides.

[1] *P.L.* No. XLIX.

CHAPTER V
WOMEN'S LIFE

THE life of the average fifteenth century woman of Margaret Paston's rank is remarkable to the modern reader in two respects at least; first, the complete identification of the wife's interests with those of her husband, and secondly, the comparatively small importance attached to the claims of the children on their mother's care and love. The treatment and education of children will be discussed later, but here it is necessary to dwell on the first of these two considerations. The medieval marriage, as we have seen, was very much a matter of business, and the question may fairly be asked, "What happiness was to be expected of such unions?" The answer very largely depends on our right understanding of the position occupied by women in those days. It is evident from a brief survey of contemporary documents, that no woman was expected to remain long unmarried, and both legislation and local custom assumed marriage as the natural state for everyone of mature age. Since in all feudal society the superiority of men was unquestioned, and popular opinion recognised marriage as inevitable, women very easily came to look on matrimony as part of the scheme of things. Probably the idea that a woman had a right to remain single, unless she entered the cloister and became the bride of Christ, or to select her own husband, was unthinkable at that time. So marriages were arranged in the way we have seen; and then came the real crux of the whole affair; for it was only after marriage that "courtship" began. Certainly the constraining hand of custom and the plastic acquiescence of average humanity, were powerful factors making for agreement, and even content, in many cases. The newly-married couples were not in a very different position from that in which thousands of young French men and women find themselves after marriage even now. In spite of the great risks of incompatibility, in very many cases it proved itself to be a comfortable, satisfactory arrangement. Unromantic though it be, contemporary evidence supports the

impression that many of these marriages were quite as successful
as those contracted under modern ideas of freedom.[1] It must
be remembered, however, that we are here only speaking of one
part of the community. The loves and sorrows of the poor,
especially in medieval times, usually remained unrecorded.
"Only men of humble birth were at liberty to choose their own
wives," we are told, and doubtless rustic courtships have continued much the same throughout the centuries.[2] The same
passions and the same environment which inspired Hodge in
those far-off days, inspire him still to-day.

For the rich as well as the poor, a wife was essentially a housewife. Her real function was the ordering and proper manage-
ment of the house. Devotion to her husband in medieval thought
necessarily implied that she would be concerned for his well-
being and comfort, and anxious that everything in his house
should be well ordered. It is obvious how necessary this was in
a ruder state of society than ours. The interior economy of a
household is in all grades of life primarily the wife's concern,
but until modern times this had an essential importance we are
apt to forget. For it was not only necessary to arrange and see
that the house was kept clean, according to medieval ideas of
cleanliness, and to provide the necessary meals, but also the
housewife had to arrange for her supplies. In this matter she
was far more dependent on her own efforts than are modern
women. A lack of forethought on her part to-day might very
well mean lack of food for her family several months hence.
Most housewives therefore had to think ahead, and to preserve,
and store, and spin, in order to have ever ready to hand the
means of life.

If we want to see the medieval woman rightly, it is in her
home we must view her. All other things in her life were sub-
servient to her housekeeping. Margaret Paston, as well as all
women of a humbler station of life, was obliged to scheme and
plan in order to keep her kitchen and pantry well supplied.
Many farm houses of the present day, hidden away in the countryside remote from towns, still preserve some characteristics of

[1] E.g. Marg. Paston's own marriage, Richard II and his Queen.
[2] But see Court Rolls of Hales, ed. Amphlett, J. [Worc. Hist. Soc.] I,
pp. 119–126.

the everyday medieval life. Here in these farms, where often the very buildings have little altered for centuries, many of Margaret Paston's occupations are still the occupations of the farmer's wife. Bread-making, the preserving of fruits, the preparation of homely country wines, the smoking of hams and bacon and the like, are all household duties carried on from very early times. The dairy, the poultry and the pigs are still as inevitable a part of every farm as they were five hundred years ago. Margaret Paston must often have experienced all the trials and anxieties inseparable from these things. She had also many other matters to fill up her hours, for it was very much more necessary then for each household to be more or less self-contained.

Every reader of medieval romances will remember how frequently the good wife and her daughters and maids are spoken of as sitting at their spinning wheels, or at their weaving and allied occupations. By the middle of the fifteenth century weaving and spinning were still important, but the industry was becoming organised under capitalist clothiers, who employed workers to perform the various processes of the industry in their own homes, providing the raw materials and taking away the finished cloth. Spinning was thus essentially a bye industry as well as a purely domestic occupation.[1] Not only spinning and weaving, but the actual cutting out and making-up of garments and household gear must have occupied much time. The needs of growing families kept most mothers fully engaged in sewing and needlework of all kinds. Margaret Paston apologises in one of her letters because she has had no time to get some material made up into shirts for her son. She says, "I should have got them made here, but that should have been too long ere you should have had them. Your aunt, or some other good woman will do...them."[2] It must be remembered that, even when the material was not home-woven, it would be bought in a piece and made up at home. Ready-made garments were not usual. The housewife was therefore constantly occupied in making garments of all kinds, and also in keeping up her stock of household linen, and any inventory of the time will give the reader an idea of how much there was to be done. Dame Elizabeth Browne for example, whom we have met as a

[1] *Bury Wills*, pp. 3, 4, 7.   [2] *P.L.* No. LXXXIII.

young girl whose head was broken once or twice a week, left in
her will a great many articles such as fine sheets, tablecloths,
napkins, towels, etc. all of which were probably made and kept in
good repair by herself and her maidens.[1]

Besides all these things, which no doubt people could either
make for themselves from start to finish, or else could make up
from material they purchased, there were others for which the
medieval wife had constantly to be worrying her relatives or
friends in the great towns. If the *Paston Letters* may be relied
on as typical examples, it was only in London that a really wide
choice was offered. Again and again, Margaret Paston asks
someone to get things for her from London, because of the poor-
ness of choice, or complete lack of what she wanted, even in so
important a town as Norwich. So she writes to her husband:

> I pray you that you will...buy some frieze to make your child's
> gowns. You shall have best cheap and best choice of Huy's wife
> as it is told me. And that you will buy a yard of broad-cloth of black
> for an hood for me at 3/8 or 4/- a yard, for there is neither good
> cloth nor good frieze in this town [Norwich]. As for the child's gowns,
> if I have [the stuff], I will get them made.[2]

At another time, when her husband was anxious to get cloth
for liveries for his retainers, she reports:

> As touching your liveries, there can none be got here of the colour
> that you would have, neither murrey, nor blue, nor good russets,
> below 3/- a yd at the lowest price, and even so there is not enough
> of one cloth and colour to serve you. And as for [the possibility] to
> be purveyed [bought] in Suffolk, it will not be purveyed now in time
> without they had had warning at Michaelmas, as I am informed.[3]

The last words are noticeable, and remind us that it was not
so simple a matter for the housewife to get her materials as it
is to-day. Weaving was still a home industry, and it took time
to produce sufficient cloth to provide large orders such as John
Paston's seems to have been. Margaret, therefore, had always
to look ahead, and give her orders in good time, or else she found
she was kept waiting.[4] In addition to her worries in making
arrangements for all these kinds of linen and cloth, the housewife
had to think of such things as hats, girdles or hose. These could

---

[1] See p. 30. Probably girls who were "boarded out" assisted in work
of this kind. *P.L.* No. 988.
[2] *Id.* No. 67. Frieze—a coarse woollen stuff.
[3] *Id.* No. 260.   [4] *Id.* See Nos. 472, 528, 529.

not be made at home with any great success, and so we find in
Margaret's letters constant requests and enquiries concerning
the price and quality of materials used for articles of this nature.
Any member of the family who happened to be in London was
continually worried by cries from Norfolk for new hats, or gowns,
or laces. The unfortunate man would be instructed to

buy me three yards of purple schamlet price to the yard 4/-; a
bonnet of deep murrey, price 2/4; a hose-cloth of yellow carsey of an
ell, I trow it will cost 2/-; a girdle of plunket ribbon, price 6*d*.;
4 laces of silk, two of one colour, and two of another, price 8*d*.;
3 dozen points with red and yellow, price 6*d*.; three pair of pattens...
I was wont to pay but 2½*d*. for a pair, but I pray you let them not
be left behind though I pay more. They must be low pattens; let
them be long enough and broad upon the heel.[1]

Important as all this was, the really urgent duty for ever con-
fronting all women was the necessity of providing food. As soon
as we examine the plan of any large fifteenth century house, we
notice that provision is made for a brewhouse, a bakehouse, a
dairy and other buildings of like nature.[2] The reason for this is
obvious. No medieval family could sit down to a single meal
without eating and drinking things either made in the house, or
prepared for food by the housewife and her servants. Latimer,
in his First Sermon before King Edward [VI], mentions that his
mother milked thirty cows, and no doubt much of this milk
was used in various ways in her own household. But we can
see the actual daily food provided at the time, by looking at the
items in the *Northumberland Household Book*. After allowance
has been made for the station of some of the recipients, and the
style of living custom ordained as necessary in great households,
we can still gain much information which will help us to understand the kind of meals Margaret Paston had to provide for
her family. Omitting the more luxurious meals provided for the
Earl and his family, we read

This is the ordre of all such Braikfastis as shal be allowid daily
in my Lordis hous Every Lent....And what they shall have at

[1] *P.L.* No. LXXXV, and see Caxton's *Dialogues in French and English*
[E.E.T.S. Extra Series 1900], p. 14, for a vivid account of the bargaining
and talk that went to the buying of a piece of cloth. "Murrey," a purple-
red tint, very much favoured especially for liveries; "Carsey" or "kersey,"
a coarse ribbed cloth; "Plunket," a blue tint; "Points," tagged points
or laces; "Pattens," wooden shoes, clogs, or thick-soled shoes.
[2] *E.g. P.L.* No. 336; *S.L.* No. 140; and see p. 90 for details.

theire Braikfasts.... Braikfast for the Nurcy for my Lady Margaret and Maister Ingeram Percy. Item a Manchet a Quarte of Bere a Dysch of Butter a Pece of Saltfisch a Dysch of Sproitts or iij White Herryng. Braikfast for my Ladis Gentyllwomen. Item a Loof of Brede a Pottell of Bere a Pece of Saltfisch or iij White Herryng.

On flesh days instead of fish, three or four "Mutton Bonys or ells a Pece of Beif boiled" was substituted.[1] The provision of a meal of this nature meant careful planning by the housewife. Clearly much of it came day by day from the household store, whilst such things as beer, butter and bread were very frequently all made in the house. Hence it was highly necessary that the good wife should look ahead and make arrangements so that her various stores were never exhausted.

Now and again in the *Paston Letters* we can actually see Margaret making bargains and arrangements to this end. In Lent, as the above breakfast items show, it was necessary to have stores of dried fish available for certain days in place of meat. One year, for some unexplained reason, Margaret had not been able to purchase her Lenten supply until late in the season, but eventually was able to write to her husband, "As for herring, I have bought an horse-load for 4/6. I can get no eels yet."[2] Another time, the bailiff writes to her offering good advice, when he says:

Mistress, it were good to remember your stuff of herring now this fishing time. I have got me a friend in Lowestoft to help to buy me seven or eight barrel, and [they] shall not cost me above 6/8 a barrel. ...You shall do more now [Autumn] with 40 shillings, than you shall at Christmas with 5 marks [66/8].[3]

Provision was also made of other things, especially of meat for the winter months. The bailiff writes to Paston and tells him that he has been able to lay in sufficient beef for the Paston household to last from the late autumn till Lent.[4] This was salted down, and used from time to time when necessary.

Margaret had to supervise and arrange for all this, but unfortunately she seldom thought it worth while to trouble her husband with any details. In one letter, however, she does tell him that she has been from Caister into Norwich to buy such

---

[1] *North. Household Book*, pp. 73, 75.
[2] *P.L.* No. 149. [3] *Id.* No. 839.
[4] *Id.* No. 425, and cf. Tusser's "For Easter, at Martilmas (Nov. 11) hange up a biefe." *Book of Good Husbandry*, ed. W. Mavor, 1812, p. 49.

things as she needed for the coming winter.[1] Whether these
necessaries were clothes, or food-stuffs, we do not know. Among
the Stonor papers we find documents which confirm these impressions of the varied duties of the housewife. In an account
book of Elizabeth Stonor, we find that she ordered large quantities of herrings and also dried salt-cod early in 1479. Other
entries show payments for poultry, meat and fish throughout
the year.[2] Her London cloth-mercer forwards her his bill for
goods she has ordered, with an engaging apology for the price
of some cloth which has a very modern ring. He writes:

> Madame, the sarcenet is very fine. I think [it] most profitable and
> most worshipful for you and shall [last] you your life and your child's
> after you, whereas the harlatry of forty or forty-four pence a yard
> would not endure two seasons with you. Therefore, for a little more
> cost, me thinketh most wisdom to take of the best.[3]

Most of these things escape notice in the *Paston Letters* because of their very frequency. For the most part stores came from
the surrounding countryside, or from near towns like Norwich
or Yarmouth. Those things which were not obtainable in this
way caused the housewife more trouble. Foreign goods of all
kinds seem to have come very largely from London. The cooks
of the fifteenth century made great use of many spices and
flavourings, and there are constant requests in the *Letters* for
goods of this nature. Indeed, the list of such overseas products
is a bewilderingly large one. In one letter Margaret asks her son
to let her know the price of pepper, cloves, mace, ginger, cyna-
mon, almonds, rice, saffron, "raysonys of Corons," and ganingal.[4]
Applications for sugar loaves are frequent. Margaret would
write, "I pray you that you will vouchsafe to send me another
sugar loaf, for my old [one] is done"[5]; and much the same kind
of message is to be found in the *Cely Papers* about this time.[6]
Treacle (a medicinal electuary) was another luxury often sent
from town. Margaret told her husband:

> I have sent my uncle Berney the pot of treacle that you did buy
> for him. Also I pray you heartily that you will send me a pot with
> treacle in haste for I have been right evil at ease, and your daughter

[1] *P.L.* No. 479.   [2] *S.L.* No. 233.
[3] *Id.* No. 252, and cf. No. 95. "Sarcenet," a very soft silk; "Harlatry,"
meretricious or attractive looking inferior stuff. [Kingsford.]
[4] *P.L.* No. 681.   [5] *Id.* No. 178, and cf. Nos. 681, 689, LXIII, LXXXVI.
[6] *Cely,* No. 22.

both, since you rode hence, and one of the tallest young men in this
parish lieth sick and has a great myrr.[1]

When Sir John sent home three pots of treacle of Genoa he
made a great business of it, explaining to his mother which of
the three pots was likely to be the best.[2] Dates and oranges were
also frequently asked for,[3] and seem to have been greatly desired by women approaching confinement.[4] Indeed the youngest
John Paston thought it necessary to apologise in asking for some
to be sent to Elizabeth Calthorpe who "longed for oranges,
though she be not with child."[5] Probably all these things may
have been obtainable in so important a city as Norwich, although
the supply was small and prices were high. Margaret Paston
was careful enough a housewife to want to get good value for
her money, as she often admits. She tells her son to "send me
word what price a pound [are various things specified].[6] If that
it be better cheap in London than it is here, I shall send you
money to buy...such stuff as I will have."[7]

Now that we have seen the medieval wife at work in her
household, it is time to consider her relation to her husband.
The correct attitude of a wife towards her husband, the Good Wife
taught her daughter, was this:

> That man that schal thee wedde bifor god with a ryng
> Love thou him and honoure moost of ertheli thing;
> Meekely thou him answere, And not as an attirling,
> And so maist thou slake his mood, And ben his dere derlynge
> A fair worde and a meeke dooth wrathe slake,
>   Mi leve child.[8]

The Knight of La Tour Landry gives much good advice on this
subject, and since he tells us that his own married life was one
of idyllic happiness and beauty, it gives the greater emphasis to
his remarks. At the beginning of his book he describes how he
had

a wyff...that was bothe faire and good...and y delited me so moche
in her that y made for her love songges, balades, rondelles, viralles,

---

[1] *P.L.* No. 167. "Myrr," a heavy cold.
[2] *Id.* No. 563, and cf. No. 841.
[3] *Id.* Nos. 62, 637, 681, 689, 719, 812, etc.
[4] *Id.* Nos. 719, 812, LXXXII.
[5] *Id.* No. LXXXII. Cf. Webster's *The Duchess of Malfi*, Act II, scene 1,
ll. 140 ff.
[6] See list above.   [7] *Id.* No. 681, and see No. 67.
[8] *Meals and Manners*, p. 38, ll. 39–45. "Attirling," venomous thing.

and diuerse nwe thinges in the best wise that y couthe. But deth, that
on all makithe werre, toke her from me, the whiche hathe made me
have mani a sorufull thought and gret hevinesse. And so it is more
than xx yeere that I have ben for her ful of gret sorugh. For a true
loveris hert forgetith never the woman that enis he hathe truly
loved.[1]

Yet he tells stories in which refractory wives are beaten with
staves, or are struck by their husbands' fists, or are used in de-
grading ways; evidently accepting the conventional ideas that
such was the correct and necessary punishment for women who
did not humbly reverence and obey their husbands.[2]

Yet it would be foolish to assume that all husbands maltreated
their wives, or subjected them to harsh discipline. Much may
be learned concerning the happy relations often existing between
husband and wife by turning over the pages of collections of
medieval wills. Frequently the whole of a man's estate is left
to his wife to dispose of as she wishes.[3] One man plainly speaks
of his wife as "my most trusty frende," while another says "I
beqwethe all maner of godis to my wyf...and she for to do me
like as she wolde I dede for her in the same case."[4] After making
sundry bequests, many wills go on to say the residue is left "to
my entirely beloved wife," or "my right dere and welbeloved
wife."[5] One man makes his profession of love and faith as
follows:

All the residue of my goodes I give all holye to Margaret my saide
welbelovyd wif, whome I make my sole executrice of my goodes,
she to dispoase as she shall thinke for the wealthe of my soule as my
speciall and high truste is in hir above all other lyvinge.[6]

The married life of John and Margaret Paston illustrates what
a medieval marriage could be. It was undoubtedly a carefully
planned step in the "climbing" of the Paston family. They
wished to unite the manor and possessions of Mauteby with
their own; and Margaret's feelings do not seem to have been
considered very much. Once the marriage had taken place, and
Margaret had come to live in the Paston household, she and her
husband began to take each other's measure, and to seek for

---

[1] *La Tour Landry*, pp. 1, 2, and cf. p. 23.   [2] See p. 80.
[3] *North Country Wills*, Sur. Soc. vol. cxvi. 1908, pp. 86, 98-9.
[4] *Early Wills*, pp. 48, 83.   [5] *North Country Wills*, pp. 51, 65, 87, 136
[6] *Id.* p. 154, and cf. pp. 51, 68, 99.

points of contact. The formality of phrase which overlies the letters of women of this period must be duly discounted. Both Margaret Paston, and later on her daughter-in-law Margery, were punctilious in making use of strictly formal openings to their letters. They would begin, "Right reverend and worshipful sir, in my most humble voice I recommend me to you," or with some equally cold and humble phrases. These would be followed by ordinary news, and it is only in odd phrases, here and there as a rule, that the real woman reveals herself. Margery writes a perfectly formal letter to her husband, and signs herself "Your servant and bedewoman," but after this follows a postscript that tells all the truth, "Sir, I pray you, if you tarry long at London, that it will please [you] to send for me, for I think [it] long since I lay in your arms."[1] The appeal is as fresh in its simple lovingness to-day, as it was 450 years ago.

In the same way, Margaret Paston's love for her husband could not always be contained within set forms, and bursts out how it will. Her letter to him, written only three years after their marriage, shows how her love had rapidly ripened, and written, as it was, at a crisis reveals her more clearly than she ever shows herself to us again. She writes:

Right worshipful husband, I recommend me to you, desiring heartily to hear of your welfare, thanking God of your amending of the great disease that you have had. And I thank you for the letter that you sent me, for by my troth, my mother and I were nought in heart's ease from the time that we knew of your sickness till we knew truly of your amending. My mother promised another image of wax of the weight of you to Our Lady of Walshingham, and she sent four nobles [26/8] to the four Orders of Friars at Norwich to pray for you, and I have promised to go on pilgrimage to Walshingham and to S. Leonard's [Priory, Norwich] for you. By my troth, I had never so heavy a season as I had from the time that I knew of your sickness till I knew of your amending, and yet my heart is in no great ease, nor shall be, till I know that ye be really well....I pray you heartily that [you] will vouchsafe to send me a letter as hastily as you may, if writing be no dis-ease to you, and that you will vouchsafe to send me word how your sore doeth. If I might have had my will, I should have seen you ere this time. I would you were at home, if it were to your ease, and your sore might be as well looked to here as it is there [where] you are now, rather than a gown of scarlet. I pray you if your sore be whole, and so that you may

endure to ride...that you will ask leave, and come home..., for I
hope you should be kept as tenderly here as ye be at London. I may
no leisure have to write half a quarter so much as I should say to
you if I might speak with you. I shall send you another letter as
hastily as I may. Almighty God have you in his keeping, and send
you health.[1]

Despite her husband's frequent absences, and somewhat reserved disposition, Margaret's love for him remained unchanged.
Once when he was kept from home longer than he expected,
she was torn with anxiety concerning him. "If I had known
that you should not have been at home before this time, I
should have sent some man to you, for I think it right long till
I have some good tidings from you," she writes.[2] Even after
twenty years of married life she could say, "I thank you heartily
for your letter, for it was to me a great comfort to hear from
you."[3] Again and again she tells him she can never have ease
until he writes, and that he cannot write too often.[4] She urges
him, "Be not strange of writing letters to me betwixt this and
[the time] that you come home. If I might, I would have one
every day from you."[5] Fortunately, her husband loved her as
deeply as his nature would allow him to love anyone. To him
she is "my own dear sovereign lady," and her illness makes
him protest:

John Hobbs tells me that you are sickly, which melikes not to
hear. Praying you heartily that you take what may do you ease
and spare not; and in anywise, take no thought nor too much labour
for these matters, [of business enclosed] nor set it not so to your
heart [so] that you fare the worse for it.[6]

There were other outlets for a wife's devotion to her husband,
besides the ordinary details of domestic life. The medieval wife
was very frequently an active agent on her husband's behalf.
Women, as we have seen, were brought up for the most part in
a hardy school, which provided an admirable training for dealing
with the ordinary affairs of daily life. The fifteenth century
husband so identified his wife with his interests, that she shared
his joys and sorrows to an amazing degree. Judging from the
Paston Letters, whatever his interests were, and however detailed his affairs, they were not so numerous or so varied as to

[1] *P.L.* No. 36.	[2] *Id.* No. 134.	[3] *Id.* No. 422.
[4] *Id. e.g.* Nos. 435, 465, 502.	[5] *Id.* No. 185.	[6] *Id.* No. 514.

escape the understanding scrutiny of his wife. We find this impression supported by an examination of other contemporary evidence. Unfortunately we have nothing in the *Paston Letters* to equal the complacency and authority of the Lady Isabel Berkeley. While she was in London, conducting some law business on her husband's behalf, she wrote home to him, "keep well all about you till I come home, and treat not without me, and then all things shall be well."[1] The Celys, who were Merchants of the Staple, and whose business required their frequent absence from home, were often obliged to rely on the business powers of their wives. The other fifteenth century correspondence tells a similar story, for we find Elizabeth Stonor acting on her husband's behalf, and showing a great deal of knowledge of his affairs.[2]

There can be little doubt that the women of the Paston family —especially Agnes and Margaret Paston—were quite capable of carrying on any business affairs. Whether they were negociating for a marriage, or paying debts, or arranging the details of a new tenant's agreement, they were equally at home. No side of the complicated legal and territorial struggles which surrounded them for so long was too difficult for Margaret to understand and to deal with. Both she and Agnes Paston must often have had to make crucial decisions, owing to the absence in London of the head of the family. Margaret, indeed, grew so accustomed to bearing the responsibility of doing this, that her husband frequently left her in charge with the greatest confidence that all would be well.

Agnes Paston throughout her long life paid the closest attention to her own business affairs. She seems to have been quite capable of managing her own lands and moneys without much help from her son, although from time to time she arranged with him to collect rents from outlying properties for her. Even then, her letters give us an admirable idea of the exactness of her knowledge of how matters stood between her and her tenants. She writes to her son:

I pray you, forget not to bring me my money from Harlingbury, as you come from London—either all, or a great part. The debt was due at Christmas last past...and at this Midsummer it is £5 more;

---

[1] Berkeley, *Extracts*, pp. 152–3.   [2] *E.g. S.L.* No. 226.

and though I allow him all his asking, it is but twentysix and sixpence less, but I am not so advised yet.[1]

Other letters of hers show such a grasp of the multifarious duties of administering a medieval estate, as could only have been the result of continuous attention to the matter.[2]

Margaret Paston was equally capable. Whether she inherited this capability, or whether the Pastons instructed her we cannot say, but she showed singular ability in her conduct of the family affairs. Gairdner says:

> It was she who negociated with the farmers, receiving overtures for leases and threats of lawsuits, and reported to her husband everything that might affect his interests, with the news of the country generally. Nor were threats always the worst thing she had to encounter on his account. For even domestic life, in those days, was not always exempt from violence.[3]

John Paston's own words in his petition to the King will show what treatment Margaret had to endure, while acting as her husband's agent:

> The 28th day of January last past, the said Lord [Molynes] sent to the said mansion a riotous people to the number of a thousand persons,...arrayed in manner of war, with cuirasses, coats of mail, steel helmets, glaives, bows, arrows, large shields, guns, "pannys with fier," long cromes to draw down houses, ladders, and picks with which they mined down the walls, and long trees with which they broke up gates and doors, and so came into the said mansion, the wife of your beseecher at that time being therein, and twelve persons with her,—the which persons they drove out of the said mansion, and mined down the walls of the chamber wherein the wife of your said beseecher was, and bare her out at the gates and cut asunder the posts of the houses, and let them fall, and broke up all the chambers and coffers in the said mansion, and rifled...and bare away stuff, array and money...to the value of £200.[4]

The best way to see Margaret's quality is to watch her in action in one of the many crises of the family. Early in 1465, he Duke of Suffolk set up a claim to the manor of Drayton, which the Pastons had inherited from Sir John Fastolf. Whatever rights the Duke had—and they seem to have been small—his agent began to assert his claim and took a horse from one of the Paston's tenants while the man was going out to plough.

[1] *P.L.* No. 70.   [2] *Id.* No. 183, and cf. No. 426.
[3] *P.L.* Intro. p. xlviii and note *P.L.* No. 189.
[4] *Id.* No. 77. £200 = £2000 to £2500 of modern (pre-1914) money.

Margaret wrote to her husband from Caister to say that she was
going at once to the troubled parts to reassert his rights. To this
end she proposed to collect all the rents due, and "if you will,
I will...keep a court at Drayton."[1] Her men had little trouble
in collecting the rents, as most of the tenants were favourable
to the Pastons. One man, Piers Warin, was hostile, and they
took two of his mares as a surety for his good conduct. Piers at
once went to the Duke's bailiff, who retaliated by coming with
some 160 men fully armed and taking away some horses from
the parson and another tenant named Thomas Stermyn. The
bailiff told them both that if they wished for redress they must
first appear at Drayton on the following Tuesday to answer
certain charges which would be brought against them. Later in
the day they made a further application, but were told they
would not get their horses until Piers Warin had his returned
to him. Both the parson and Stermyn were pressed by Richard
Calle to take legal action against the bailiff, but they refused.
The parson put the ordinary man's point of view in refusing to
prosecute when he said, "he had rather lose his cattle, for he
knew well if he did so, he would be indicted, and so vexed by
them that he should never have rest."[2]

At this point Margaret took charge of the proceedings. She
saw Stermyn herself, and persuaded him to prosecute. She was
her husband's wife, however, even in this, for she tells John
Paston with obvious pride that Stermyn "is bound to you in an
obligation of £10 single without conditions, that he shall abide
by such actions as shall be taken by your advice in his name."[3]
Having done so much, she asked the advice of a neighbour, who
counselled agreement with the bailiff. Margaret would none of
this, and so she went to another friend who advised her to put
the whole matter in writing before her husband, so that he could
get a writ against the bailiff.

A state of armed readiness set in, as the Pastons' men settled
down on their side of the river that divided the properties to
watch the Duke's forces gathered on the other. Margaret,
possibly instructed by John Paston to whom she had written,
sent her servants to Drayton to drive home seventy-seven head
of neat. This caused great excitement. "First on the same

¹ *P.L.* No. 500.   ² *Id.* No. 502.   ³ *Id.* No. 502.

Saturday the tenants followed upon, and desired to have their
cattle again. I answered them, [that] if they would...pay such
debts as they ought...to pay to you, that then they should have
their cattle delivered again."[1] In the afternoon, Harleston, an
officer of the Duke's, saw the tenants and warned them that if
they paid any money to the Pastons they would be turned out
of their holdings. Next he saw Margaret, but it was wasted
labour, for she refused to move from the position she had taken
up. Early the following Monday morning, Harleston tried a
new plan. He served Margaret with a writ for the restitution of
the cattle [replevin] on the ground that the beasts were taken,
not on Paston's land at all, but on the Duke's fee. Margaret
was not so easily deceived; after making enquiries, she found
the beasts were not taken from the duchy fee, and again refused
to surrender them. Finally Harleston got a "replevin" from the
Sheriff of Norfolk, which Margaret dared not disobey, and so
the beasts were surrendered.

During many weeks of the summer of 1465, this duel went on
between the rival parties, both sides using force, or invoking
the law, as opportunity served. Margaret had to bear the brunt
of it all until she was almost worn out; she writes to her husband:

Right worshipful husband, I recommend me to you, praying you
heartily that you will seek means that your servants may be in
peace, for they be daily in fear of their lives....It were well done that
you should speak with the Justices ere they come here. If you will
that I complain to them, or to any other, if God fortune me life and
health, I will do as you advise, for in good faith...what with sickness,
and trouble that I have had, I am brought right low and weak, but
to my power I will do as I can or may in your matters.[2]

Shortly after this, her husband was thrown into the Fleet Prison,
and Margaret had to shoulder the whole responsibility. Her
son, Sir John, had succeeded in holding Drayton successfully,
and now she saw that if she could get a Court held at Drayton
it would greatly strengthen their case. How perilous a business
this was is shown by the lack of volunteers,—only Thos. Bond
and her own domestic chaplain being ready to run the risk. The
Duke's party, some sixty or more strong, were there before them,
and as soon as Paston's men said they had come to hold a Court,

---

the Duke's officers arrested Bond, "and bound his arms behind him with whipcord like a thief."[1] Again Margaret's personality and ability were conspicuous. Early the next morning, before the Judges left for the Shire House, she obtained an interview with them. There in the presence of many of the chief men of the County she laid the whole matter before the judges, who at once gave the Duke's bailiff "a passing great rebuke," and commanded the Sheriff to see what forces had been gathered on either side. On his report, they over-rode all demands against the Pastons, ordered Thos. Bond to be set free, and severely censured the Duke's officers. Margaret was so delighted that, in her excitement when writing to her husband, she describes the scene before the Judges twice over![2]

We have now looked at some of the numerous duties which filled up many of the waking hours of women such as Margaret Paston, and we have also seen how women were frequently closely associated with their husbands in business matters. Heavy as these labours undoubtedly often were, they did not always occupy the whole of the day, and it is interesting to see how women spent their more leisured hours. Even the hard, shrewd nature of Margaret Paston craved for rest and refreshment at times, when the troubles of her husband's affairs, or Sir John's behaviour had taxed her endurance to the uttermost. Although the *Paston Letters* do not give very full details of how she spent her leisure, contemporary documents will help us to fill the gaps.

Undoubtedly, for many women, religion and the services of the Church offered an ever-welcome respite from domestic cares. Especially after the death of John Paston, his widow found more and more solace in her religious duties and occupations. Sir James Gloys, who was her domestic chaplain, became her chief friend, and no doubt was often able to help Margaret to pass away a leisure hour. It is not difficult to picture Sir James sitting by the fireside, when his work was done, reading aloud from one of his own books of theology, or else from *The Temple of Glass*, or some other book of the Pastons', while Margaret and the other women sewed or embroidered. Even so pleasant and harmless an occupation may not have commended itself

[1] *P.L.* No. 518, and see p. 230 for details. [2] *Id.* No. 518.

to Margaret's frugal mind, and she may have agreed with a later writer, who condemned sitting up by candlelight. He wrote:

One thinge I wyl advise the to remembre, and specially in wynter-tyme, whan thou sytteste by the fyre, and hast supped, to consyder in thy mynde, whether the warkes, that thou, thy wyfe, and thy servantes shall do, be more avauntage to the than the fyre, and candell-lyghte, meate and drynke that they shall spende, and if it be more avantage, than syt styll: and if it be not, than go to thy bedde and slepe, and be uppe betyme, and breake thy faste before day, that thou mayste be all the shorte wynters day about thy busynes.[1]

But probably, then as now, women found most pleasure and recreation in the society and companionship of other women. This was not easy in the lonely country houses, but in towns no doubt friends often met and gossiped together. It is clear from her letters that Margaret Paston was frequently living in Norwich, or near by at Hellesdon; and, while there, she was able to see her friends and to entertain them. Now and again, she mentions in writing to her husband that Elizabeth Clere or some other friend has been to dine with her, or else she has been to see friends and to spend a pleasant day with them.[2] Once while Margaret of Anjou, Queen of Henry VI was staying at Norwich, Margaret had to borrow jewelry from her cousin so that she might look well among the brilliant crowd, "for I durst not for shame go with my beads among so many fresh gentle-women as were here at that time." The plea of "Nothing to wear!" is an old cry; and John Paston was entreated to send his wife "something for her neck," so that she might mix un-abashed among her friends.[3]

Again it is necessary to emphasise the fact that, while all this is true of a certain class, there lived and laboured unceasingly the great mass of women, to whom the day's work was all-embracing and left little leisure for such amenities. Always in the background of our picture there remain the humble people, who dwelt silent in their hovels, and plodded on day by day at their unending labours, till death brought relief. It is this class, or rather the worst elements in this class, that supply the material for the mass of sarcastic and amusing verse, story and play, so common in the middle ages. The ducking stool, the stories of

---

[1] *Book of Husbandry*, Fitzherbert, A , ed. Skeat, 1882, p. 101.
[2] *E g. P.L.* No. 167.   [3] *Id.* No. 187.

shrews and scolds and the tavern scene in *Piers Plowman* are
all evidences of the conditions of life these folk endured. Life
was a hard school for them, and was apt to produce women of a
rough hardy type, racy of the soil which bore them. Incessant
toil, and the rudest surroundings, made them snatch at any
momentary respite from the daily routine. Hence, instead of
the ceremonious visitings and dinings which helped to fill Margaret Paston's leisure, these folk gathered at a favourite ale-
house, and there tried to forget their troubles in a friendly
carouse.[1]

For women of Margaret Paston's position, besides the daily
pleasures of meeting friends, and of quiet talks by the fire, there
was always the possible excitement of travel. It is a well-known
economic fact that great lords and landowners were bound to
move about from manor to manor. This was the cheapest and
easiest way of living in days when the produce of land was the
chief source of wealth. When the stores and supplies of one
manorial demesne were exhausted, the proprietor and his family
would move on to another manor. The Pastons were not great
enough people to do this to any large extent, but they certainly
had various scattered properties in Norfolk, and from time to
time we find them moving from one place to another. Women
such as Margaret Paston were accustomed to riding, and probably found little inconvenience in taking short journeys. Margaret moved between Hellesdon and Norwich, or even Caister
and Norwich without concern, and she writes to her husband,
"I pray you that you will send me word whether you will that
I shall remove from hence, for it beginneth to wax cold abiding
here."[2]

Even long journeys were undertaken by women. Indeed the
second extant letter from Margaret Paston to her husband is full
of her distress because she has not been allowed to come from
Norfolk to London to visit him in his illness. We shall see in a
later chapter something of the difficulties and dangers of travel,
but these did not dismay her. "If I might have had my will,
I should have seen you ere this time," is her only comment
upon them. Generally speaking, however, it is not likely that
women were frequent travellers, and only urgent affairs took

[1] Wright, pp. 444–5.   [2] *P.L.* No. 421.

them on long journeys. Even the most careful precautions could not have greatly lessened the discomforts and risks every medieval traveller had to endure. Throughout Margaret Paston's life, we have only one reference to her journeying as far as London, although her husband and her sons frequently went to and fro. The numerous references to this proposed visit of Margaret's, and the preparations she had to make before setting out, help us to understand how difficult it was for a woman to leave her household to the care of others. She writes just before setting out to go to her husband:

> As for my coming to you, if it please you that I come, I hope I shall purvey so for all things ere I come that it shall be safe enough, by the grace of God till I come again. But at the reverence of God, if you may, purvey the means that you may come home yourself.[1]

Yet all the dangers and inconveniences of travel were frequently ignored by women when they went on pilgrimage. Year by year, crowds of people made their way to such famous shrines as those of Canterbury and Walsingham, although not all of them were actuated solely by religious motives. Many folk by the fifteenth century had discovered that going on pilgrimage could be a very pleasant affair, especially as it was customary to travel in small parties for mutual society and protection. Hence the easy-going man or woman of the world was found side by side with the fervent believer, and the tedium of the way was lessened by a constant interchange of stories, reminiscences and ideas.

As we know, among the twenty-nine immortal Canterbury Pilgrims of Chaucer, there rode the Prioress and her fellow nun, beside that incorrigible pilgrim, the Wife of Bath. The pictures in the Ellesmere MS. remind us also, that riding astride had not at that time quite gone out of use for women. The prioress, as we might expect from so well-bred a lady, followed the new custom and rode side-saddle. Not so the wife of Bath, who had "on her feet a paire of spores sharpe," and rode astride. Some pilgrims, in their religious ardour, scorned all such aids, and made their pilgrimage on foot.

Margaret Paston, in common with most women of her age, went on pilgrimage. In her anxiety for her husband during a

[1] *P.L.* No. 523.

severe illness, she promised to go "on pilgrimage to Walsingham, and to S. Leonard's" [Priory, Norwich] to return thanks for his recovery.[1] Again late in life we find her going along the well-worn road that led many thousands of pilgrims yearly to the famous shrine at Walsingham.[2] Many other instances might be quoted from these letters to show how women would make long journeys

> The hooly blisful marter for to seke,
> That hem hath holpen whan that they were seeke.[3]

[1] *P.L.* No. 36.   [2] *Id.* No. 859.
[3] *Id.* Nos. 610, 675, 696, 757, 866, 907, etc.

CHAPTER VI
PARENTS AND CHILDREN

ONE of the most remarkable sides of medieval family life **was** the relation between parents and children. When we read the stilted and carefully chosen language in which children wrote to their parents, we see at once the wide difference between their conception of the relation and our own. Children were brought up to regard their parents, and especially their fathers, with such awe that familiarity became unthinkable.[1] The old ideas resulting from the dominance of the Feudal System in England were still powerful. The various grades of society were so carefully and strongly differentiated, that the controlling power of a superior, whether in a family or in a territorial sense, was scarcely ever questioned.

All contemporary books of instruction for children emphasise this. In his *Booke of Nurture and Schoole of good manners for man and for Chylde*,[2] written in the sixteenth century, Hugh Rhodes says:

> Reuerence to thy parents deare, so duety doth thee bynde:
> Such children as vertue delight, be gentle meeke, and kynde.
> Agaynst thy Parentes multiplye no wordes, but be demure:
> It will redowne unto thy prayse, and to thy friends pleasure.
> ll. 41–8.

He returns again later on to this necessity of reverencing parents:

> When that thy parents come in syght, doe to them reuerence:
> Ask them blessing if they haue bene long out of presence.
> ll. 93–6.

If we turn to another of these strange compilations, we find in *Symon's Lesson of Wysedome for all Maner Chyldryn*,[3] the following instructions for the young boy or girl of those times:

> And, chyld, wyrshep thy fader and thy moder,
> And loke that thou greve nother or ne other,
> But ever among thou shalt knele adowne,
> And aske here blessyng and here benesowne. ll. 35–8.

---

[1] Cf. in modern times, *The Way of All Flesh*, S. Butler.
[2] *Meals and Manners*, pp. 61 ff.   [3] *Id.* pp. 399 ff.

Amid repressive influences, the young folk of the better class families of the fifteenth century had to endure life as best they might. The spontaneity and joy in life common to all healthy youth was kept well in hand by the iron conventions of the time.[1] Doubtless there was a certain amount of variation, and it is impossible to imagine growing children always sitting quietly under such repression; but generally all had to conform. Even after they had grown up and were men and women, the same deference was paid to the parents, "for daughters, grown women, and sons, gentlemen of thirty and forty years old, might not sit in their presence without leave, but stood like mutes bareheaded before them."[2] Chaucer's young squire too, for all his strength and service

> In Flaunders, in Artoys and Pycardie,

and his courtier's accomplishments, was glad to show all due respect to his father, and

> Curteis he was, lowely and servysable,
> And carf biforn his fader at the table.

The *Paston Letters* throw considerable light on all this. When writing to their father, the two sons both invariably use the most respectful and deferential language. When John Paston the eldest is writing, he usually begins his letter "Most reverent and worshipful father I recommend me heartily and submit me lowly to your good fatherhood, beseeching you for charity of your daily blessing,"[3] or "Right reverent and worshipful father, I recommend me unto you, beseeching you of your blessing and good fatherhood."[4] His younger brother uses much the same words[5] when he has to write letters to his father, although they were both grown men by this time.

The Pastons are equally deferential when writing to their mother. John Paston the younger addresses his letter "To my mistress Margaret Paston," and begins, "After all humble and most due recommendation, as lowly as I can, I beseech you of your blessing."[6] In a less formal letter some years later he writes,

---

[1] *S.L.* p. xxiv, and cf. p. xliii.
[2] *Ital. Rel.* note 38, p. 77, quoting Antiquarian Repertory.
[3] *P.L.* No. 410.   [4] *Id.* No. 442, and cf. Nos. 323, 531.
[5] *Id.* Nos. 463, 486.
[6] *Id.* No. 526, and cf. Nos. 654, 670, 757, 787, 801, 812, etc.

"Right reverend and worshipful mother, I recommend me to you as humbly as I can think, desiring most heartily to hear of your welfare and heart's ease, which I pray God send you as hastily as my heart can think."[1]

In examining other correspondence we find that much of this is merely "common form." William Stonor, a contemporary of the Pastons, uses almost identical language when he writes, "My right reverent and worshipful father, I recommend me unto your good fatherhood in the most humble wise that I can or may, meekly beseeching your good fatherhood of your daily blessing."[2] We must beware, however, of jumping to the conclusion that because this and similar openings are "common form" they are merely conventional and therefore worthless as evidence.[3] While they cannot be accepted at their full face value, yet they do indicate the orthodox point of view, which all well-brought up children were expected to adopt.

We need hardly say that parents for their part confidently expected absolute obedience and respect from their children. When John Paston died, his son Sir John became head of the family, and as such assumed his father's authority. Hence his brother John—not the most deferential of men—is careful henceforth to address him as "Right worshipful sir."[4] Also, as we have seen, Sir John either conducted all the negociations for the marriage of members of the family, or else the final decision was left to him. Earlier in life, Sir John had had very clear experience of the power of this convention. In 1459, he had in some way deeply offended his father and was consequently in disgrace. Before any reconciliation had taken place, his father had gone away to London, and Margaret was left to deal with the situation. Evidently it was not long before the young man was forced to recognise the impossibility of holding out against his father unless he was prepared to make a total break with him. His letter of surrender and apology is full of interest. He writes:

May it please your fatherhood to remember and consider the pain and heaviness that it has been to me, since your departing out of

---

[1] *P.L.* No. 585.
[2] *S.L.* No. 127, and cf. Nos. 122 and 136, and also *Plum. Corr.* pp. 202–3.
[3] Note, for example, how Margaret Paston rebukes her son when he drops the "common form" openings. See Nos. 797, 802, 803.
[4] *P.L.* No. 631, and cf. Nos. 696, 739, etc.

this country. I am here abiding till the time that by report my
demeaning be to your pleasing.... Wherefore I beseech you of your
fatherly pity to tender the more [kindly] this simple writing, as I
shall out of doubt hereafter do that [which] shall please you, to the
uttermost of my power and labour. And if there be any service that
I may do, if it please you to command me, and if I may understand
it, I will be as glad to do it as any thing on earth, if it were anything
that might be to your pleasing.[1]

John Paston was not the man to be easily placated by a few
professions of eagerness to do him service; consequently he did
not show any alacrity to forgive. He gave no sign until about
six weeks later, when his wife sent tidings which confirmed the
young man's own statements. She reports:

As for his demeaning since you departed, in good faith it has been
right good, and lowly and diligent in oversight of your servants and
other things, the which I hope you would be pleased with, if you
had been at home. I hope he will be well demeaned to please you
hereafter. He desired Albaster to petition to you for him, and was
right heavy of his behaviour to you, as I sent you word by Albaster.
I beseech you heartily that you vouchsafe to be his good father, for
I hope he is chastised, and will be worthier hereafter.[2]

Apparently this satisfied John Paston, and the too-froward lad
was forgiven.

The lesson was not so impressive as he had hoped, for four
years later his son left home without knowledge or permission.
Although he was now a full grown man, and had recently been
knighted, he was still under paternal control. The father was the
more angry, because he suspected that a woman's natural fond-
ness for her son had made his wife a party to the going. Poor
Margaret was much distressed, and could only write hastily to
her son imploring him to spare no efforts in trying to obtain
forgiveness. Her shrewd understanding of her husband did not
fail her even in her distress. Although her son had already once
written to his father imploring forgiveness, she advised a second
letter, and not to

spare to write to him again as lowly as you can, beseeching him to be
your good father;...and that you [be]ware of your expenses better
than you have been before this time. I hope he will be your good father
hereafter, if you behave well, and do as you owe to do to him.[3]

Here the evidence fails us, but as Sir John was living at home

[1] P.L. No. 323.   [2] Id. No. 325.   [3] Id. No. 480.

with the rest of the family when next we hear of him, it seems probable that his persistent letters had had the result his mother anticipated.[1]

John Paston and his eldest son could not get on together, and little more than a year later the young man was again in disgrace. Unfortunately we are once more in the dark as to the cause of offence, but his father seems to have exiled him from his house for a year. His mother as usual pleads for him:

> For God's sake Sir, have pity on him. Remember you it has been a long time since he had ought of you to help him with, and he has obeyed you and will do [so] at all times, and will do what he can or may to have your good fatherhood....And I hope he shall ever know himself the better hereafter and be the more wary to eschew such things as should displease you, to take heed of that [which] shall please you.[2]

So the father relented and his son was allowed to return. Even so, his stay in his old home was to be strictly supervised, and word sent to his father from time to time of his behaviour. Margaret writes:

> Your son shall come home tomorrow, as I trow, and as he behaves himself hereafter I shall let you have knowledge. I pray you think not of me that I will support him or favour him in any lewdness for I will not. As I find him hereafter, so I will let you have knowledge.[3]

Not all parents were fortunate enough to retain this hold on their children when they grew up. In many cases, the children felt very bitterly towards their parents, on account of the hardships of their childhood. Scrope, to whom Sir J. Fastolf stood "in loco parentis," speaks very feelingly of the old knight's methods, for as he says, "He bought me and sold me, as a beast."[4] Many other children were equally rebellious when they were of age; and the *Early Chancery Proceedings* yield many cases of law suits between parents and children.[5] The *Paston Letters* contain an interesting case in which is set forth at length a father's death-bed account of his troubles with his son:

> William Pickering, son of the said Nicholas Pickering reckoned with his father for twenty quarters of barley, that the said William

---

[1] *P.L.* No. 483.   [2] *Id.* No. 499.
[3] *Id.* No. 500, and see No. lix for Paston's clear-eyed view of his son.
[4] *Id.* Intro. p. clxxv.
[5] *E.C.P. e.g.* 60/153, 65/153, 42/20; and cf. *Plum. Corr.* pp. xxvi and cxxiii, for children charging aged parents for board, etc.

claimed of his father's gift to his marriage, and [also] for seven day's carriage of corn in harvest, and for a thousand wattles that his father had from William's wife's place—the which reckoning grieved Nicholas his father who said, "Thou comest in with many back reckonings. Remember thee, that thou hast been the costliest child that ever I had, and how I gave you ten acres of free land and a place in marriage, and many other things that are much better than all thy back reckonings. And I have now given thee another ten acres of free land after my decease:....If thou trouble thy brother John, or any of my executors, or claim any more lands or goods that ever were mine, I shall give you God's curse and mine, for thou has ever been froward with me."[1]

It has been necessary to dwell at some length on the relation between parents and children, not only because it is the clue to much which follows, but also because it is a basic principle of medieval family life. We have seen that Margaret Paston was greatly troubled by the fact that her husband thought she was supporting their insubordinate son. Such an action in the fifteenth century was against all the prevailing ideas, for the relation between husband and wife was the all-important thing. The more modern insistence on the place and importance of children in married life was little understood, and still less the question of their significance in the life of the nation. As we have noticed, medieval marriages followed the conventions implied by the feudal system. How these worked in practice is told by Portia at the moment of her surrender. She says:

> But now I was the lord
> Of this fair mansion, master of my servants,
> Queen o'er myself; and even now, but now,
> This house, these servants, and this same myself,
> Are yours, my lord: I give them with this ring.[2]

The surrender of self and possessions, prompted by love in Portia's case, was expected of women in medieval times. The greater part of a woman's affection and her personality had to sink itself to satisfy her husband's expectations. Contemporary literature has many examples of this. We need only think of Chaucer's superb story of patient Griselda,—although even then the times were changing, and Chaucer is careful to remark that "Griselde is deed, and eek hire pacience." Yet something of this same quality of mind existed in the fifteenth century woman,

[1] *P.L.* No. 522.
[2] *Merchant of Venice*, Act III, scene II.

and in too many cases they were little more than willing servants obeying their husband's commands.

Hence it is not surprising to find a certain coldness and want of consideration when they are dealing with their children. Necessarily the constraining hand of a custom which so belittled parenthood made demonstrations of affection almost impossible. Spontaneous affection there must have been. Nothing can overcome the love of women for their children, especially while they are still young. But as the complete dependence and intimacy of babyhood drew to a close, and the children became noisy human beings, then slowly but inevitably the repressive influences of the age did their work. Nevertheless, here and there in the *Paston Letters*, we find glimpses of maternal love.[1] Dour old Agnes Paston herself felt some affection for her son John, although she is careful to hide it as much as possible. In one letter, however, we can detect as much feeling as she was ever likely to show, as she gives him

that blessing which I prayed your father to give you the last day that ever he spake, and the blessing of all saints under heaven, and mine might come to you [at] all days and times. Think verily that none other but you have it, and shall have it.[2]

Margaret Paston was of softer stuff, but it is only now and then that we can see motherly love prompting her actions towards her children. Her eldest son evidently relied on her affection when in trouble. Several times she acted as mediator between him and her husband, and was even induced to keep material facts from John Paston, in order to help her son. Altogether she showed far more affection towards her children than did her husband, and they were very well aware that she could sometimes be cajoled into helping them, when to approach their father would have been useless. So it was that she lent the youngest John Paston six marks, pledging him to return it as soon as possible and with great secrecy, lest his father should suspect.[3] John Paston was not easily deceived, and no doubt at times he reproached her with what would seem to him her overfondness for her children; for on several occasions she has to

---

[1] And cf. *S.L.* Intro. p. xliii.
[2] *P.L.* No. 312, but cf. No. 502 end, which shows Agnes as a vigorous champion of her own rights against fancied or real infringements of them by John.   [3] *Id.* No. LXV.

assure him that her love and faithfulness to him are ever paramount.[1]

John Paston the youngest seems always to have been eager to keep his mother's affection. Although the part played by the "prowd peevish preste," Sir James Gloys, sadly frustrated his desires,[2] yet his words to his mother shortly before her death have a note of sincerity in them, and they show the relation which did sometimes exist at that time between mother and son:

> Mother...there needs [to be] no ambassadors nor means betwixt you and me; for there is neither wife nor other friend shall make me to do that [which] your commandment shall make me to do, if I may have knowledge of it....I am right glad that my wife is [in] anything [in] your favour or trust; but I am right sorry that my wife, or any other child or servant of yours, shall be in better favour or trust with you than myself.[3]

It was Walter, however, destined to die on the threshold of manhood, who was Margaret's favourite. When the final plans for his going up to Oxford were almost complete, his mother's pathetic words " I were loth to lose him, for I trust to have more joy of him than I have [had] of them that be older,"[4] show how dear he was to her, and also suggest her disillusionment regarding Sir John and his other brothers.

Unfortunately, although a certain amount of affection sometimes penetrates the conventional forms, the *Paston Letters* and other contemporary evidence show that the common attitude of parents towards their children was astonishingly cold. The stern isolation in which John Paston dwelt has already been noted. He can never have been regarded by his children, except with feelings of awe and even terror. He shows himself hard and almost implacable towards their errors. The idea that children themselves had any natural rights was almost impossible to a medieval mind. Children were just chattels, and therefore entirely at the direction and disposal of their fathers. We must understand this point of view before we can grasp their conception of fatherhood. Since the father was the head of the family, it followed, according to feudal ideas, that he had absolute control over all the members of it. The children were his, to deal with as he thought best; and his own ideas and needs

---

[1] *P.L.* See Nos. 480, 500.   [2] See p. 227.
[3] *Id.* No. 862.   [4] *Id.* No. 716.

were the sole directing factors. This lies at the back of all the negociating and unpleasantness of medieval matchmaking. The business of marriage, from the parents' point of view, was a business of bargaining and good terms. The feelings and desires of the children concerned, and the tragic possibilities they were challenging, did not concern them; and indeed, probably were scarcely thought of. This point of view enabled men to sell the marriages of their children:

> For covetise of chattels and cunning chapmen;
> Of kin, nor of kinsmen account men but little.[1]

The whole medieval coldness of parental love seems to be summed up in Scrope's words "For very need I was fain to sell a little daughter I have," followed by his complaint about the whole transaction "for much less than I should have done by possibility."[2]

Both Agnes and Margaret are seen in their worst light in their dealings with their daughters. Agnes was never a genial woman, but her treatment of Elizabeth exhibits the state of unhappiness that probably prevailed in many homes.[3] The Paston women seem to have been unable to tolerate the presence of their own daughters in the house, and were never so happy as when they had sent them away to live with some relative, or in the house of some important personage. After failing to marry her daughter Elizabeth to Scrope, Agnes seems to have become more impossible than ever, and Margaret writes to her husband, "It seems by my mother's language that she would never so gladly ...be delivered of her as she will now."[4] Her harsh treatment of the girl did not cease, so that Elizabeth was ready in the end to marry anyone her brother could find for her, and so win relief. "For her mother...has such language to her that she thinks right strange, and so that she is right weary thereof."[5] Margaret herself, in later years, showed a similar dislike for the company of her own daughters at home. She was constantly urging their brother to find homes for them in other families, and is quite honest with him about the cause. Writing to her son, concerning her younger daughter Margery, she asks him to find some "worshipful place" for her, "for we either of us weary

[1] *P.P.* c. xi. ll. 257–8.   [2] *P.L.* Intro. p. clxxvi.   [3] See pp. 29 ff.
[4] *Id.* No. 185.   [5] *Id.* No. 196.

of the other. I shall tell you more when I speak with you."[1]
The news that her eldest daughter may have to return to live
at home does not please her at all; and she tells Sir John he is
to do all he can to arrange it otherwise:

for I shall be loth to send for her, and with me she shall only lose
her time. Unless she will be the better occupied she will oftentimes
move me, and put me in great unquietness.[2]

Her impatience was not lessened by the presence in the house of
Sir J. Gloys, their domestic chaplain. Far from acting as a
peacemaker, and striving for a kindly relation between all in
the house, it is clear that too often he was a fomenter of discord
and petty jealousy.[3]

This want of affection went to greater lengths than mere ex-
pressions of distaste and occasional family quarrels. "The men
who bought their wives like chattels were only too likely to
treat them accordingly"; and the beating of both wives and
children was all too common. Contemporary literature affords
many instances. We may recall the racy account given by the
Wife of Bath concerning her several husbands, and of how the
last, when she angered him:

> He up starte as dooth a wood leoun
> And with his fest he smoot me on the heed,
> And in the floor I lay as I were deed.[4]

The Knight of La Tour Landry also recounts for his daughters'
instruction several cases of very violent assaults made by husbands on their wives. The matter-of-fact way in which he speaks
of these barbarous deeds is evidence in itself of their frequency.
One of his stories concerns three merchants, who laid a wager
as to whose wife was most obedient.[5] The first told his wife to
leap into a basin, and she asked "Why?" "For no thinge her
husbond coulde do she wolde not do it. So her husbonde up
with his fust, and gaue her two or three gret strokes." The second
also told his wife to leap into a basin and she refused, so "he
toke a staffe, and al tobete her." The third was obedient, and
won the wager for her husband. The good knight is not concerned particularly with the fate of the two wives who were

---

[1] *P.L.* No. 601.   [2] *Id.* No. 660.   [3] See above, p. 45.
[4] *Wife of Bath's Tale*, Prologue, ll. 794–7.
[5] Cf. *Taming of Shrew*, Act V, scene 11.

beaten. He advises his daughters to be obedient, or else the same fate will be theirs, but he does not see anything unusual in it.[1] The current feeling is well shown in an incident in the *Paston Letters* when a man was fined at Sporle Manor Court for chastising a servant of his, who was a bondman of John Paston's. He was indignant at this curtailment of his imagined rights, and in his anger expressed fear lest the day should come when "a man might not beat his own wife."[2] It was at those times one of the privileges and customs of many husbands.

Naturally this harsh treatment meted out to wives was also bestowed upon the children in full measure. Lady Jane Grey has left us a vivid and pathetic account of the methods adopted by her parents for her domestic education. She says:

One of the greatest benefites that God ever gave me, is, that he sent me so sharpe and severe Parentes.... For when I am in presence either of father or mother, whether I speke, kepe silence, sit, stand, or go, eate, drinke, be merie or sad, be sewyng, plaiyng, dauncyng, or doing anie thing els, I must do it, as it were, in soch weight, mesure, and number, even so perfitelie as God made the world, else I am so sharpelie taunted, so cruelie threatened, yea presentlie some tymes with pinches, nippes, and bobbes, and other waies which I will not name for the honor I beare them...that I thinke myself in hell.[3]

What a picture! This tender, sweet natured girl, is so treated that she thinks herself in hell, and dare not name the cruelties practised on her, and yet so disciplined that she calls it "one of the greatest benefites that God ever gave me"! The books of instruction of the time are all of a piece with this beating and baiting of children. Their cry for the unsparing use of the birch is as monotonous as it is brutal. One writes:

As a sharppe spore makyth an hors to renne
Under a man that shold werre wynne,
Ryght so a yerde maye make a chyld
To lerne welle hys lesson, and to be myld.

.   .   .   .

And therfor, chyldere, loke that ye do well,
And no harde betyng shall ye befalle.[4]

---

[1] *La Tour Landry*, pp. 26–7, and cf. pp. 25, 81, 95.
[2] *P.L.* No. 112, and cf. Blackstone, IV. p. 182. "Where a master is moderately correcting his servant, and happens to occasion his death, it is misadventure."
[3] Ascham, *The Scholemaster*, ed. E. Arber, 1870, p. 47.
[4] *Meals and Manners*, p. 402, and cf. pp. 93, 403–4.

4

Another of these preceptors says "If any stryfe or debate bee among them of thy house, at nighte charytably call them together, and wyth wordes or strypes make them alle to agree in one."[1]

The Pastons certainly acted on these precepts. We know how cruelly Agnes beat Elizabeth when she was in disgrace,[2] and the old woman showed equal zest when enquiring about the progress and behaviour of her son Clement. Her messenger to London was ordered to go and see his master Greenfield and ask him

to send...word, by writing how Clement Paston has done his duty in learning. And if he has not done well, nor will not amend, pray him that he will truly belash him till he will amend. So did his last master...the best that he ever had at Cambridge. And tell Greenfield [his master] that if he will take upon him[self] to bring him into good rule and learning, and that I may verily know he does his duty, I will give him ten marks for his labour, for I had rather he were fairly buried than lost for default [of correction].[3]

Such harsh treatment was the common lot of schoolboys at this time[4]; and it is suggestive that when a man became a Master of Grammar at the University he was given two important insignia of office—namely a palmer, and a birch. To emphasise his duties, he there and then, before the assembly, publicly birched a boy.

One of the most important results of the medieval relations between parents and children was noticed by the author of the *Italian Relation*. He was greatly struck by the presence of strangers in the homes of almost every family, and wrote:

The want of affection in the English is strongly manifested towards their children; for after having kept them at home till they arrive at the age of 7 or 9 years at the utmost, they put them out, both males and females, to hard service in the houses of other people... and few are born who are exempted from this fate, for every one, however rich he may be, sends away his children into the houses of others, whilst he, in return, receives those of strangers into his own. And on enquiring the reason for the severity, they answered that they did it in order that their children might learn better manners.[5]

When we recall the severe training most houses provided, and the importance attached to obedience and respect, it is evident

---

[1] *Meals and Manners*, p. 65.   [2] *P.L.* No. 71.   [3] *Id.* No. 311.
[4] *Meals and Manners*, pp. vii–viii.   [5] *Ital. Rel.* p. 24.

there was in reality little need for them to go outside their own homes for the alleged "better manners." Unquestionably, in many cases, the real motive was the hope that some material benefit might be gained therefrom. If parents could get children domiciled in the house of a great lord, or of some rich patron, their chances of advancement or of a profitable marriage were greatly enhanced. This was what the Pastons succeeded in doing with their second son John Paston III when they placed him in the household of the young Duke of Norfolk. As we have seen, they hoped by this means to gain the Duke's friendship and protection, and thus to strengthen their hold on Caister and other properties.[1] So young John Paston went down to Holt Castle in Wales with the Duke, and became conversant with the life and customs of a great house. The movements of his master from time to time brought the young Squire into contact with influential men, who might conceivably befriend him in later life.[2] Here are the actual instructions given by a father to his son when entering such a service:

You shall in all Things reverence, honour and obey my Ld Bp of Norwich, as you would do any of your Parents, esteeminge whatsoever He shall tell or Command you, as if your Grandmother... your Mother, or myself should say it.[3]

The Pastons' eldest son, who was knighted when he was 21, was not so successful. For a time his father had managed to get him attached to the King's household. Unfortunately Sir John was not energetic enough to make the best of his opportunities. Instead of shouldering a place for himself among the courtiers, he was timid and too easily abashed by the vigorous life around him. His uncle Clement was greatly dismayed and wrote concerning him:

I feel by W. Pecock that my nephew is not yet verily acquainted with the King's house....Also he is not acquainted with any body but Weeks [an usher in the King's Chamber] wherefore it were best for him to take his leave and come home, until you have spoken with somebody to help him forth, for he is not bold enough to put himself forth.[4]

After a while he returned home, and seems to have been idling about there so long that the neighbouring county folk began to

---

[1] See p. 13.   [2] *P.L.* Nos. 463–464.
[3] *Meals and Manners*, p. ix.   [4] *P.L.* No. 411.

talk. They could not understand why a young man should be left to waste his days in his father's home, instead of being attached to some worthy lord's retinue. A candid friend writes to Paston, "At the reverence of God, eschewing common language, see that he may worshipfully be sent for, either in the King's service, or in marriage."[1]

It is the girls, however, who provide most information concerning these "boarding out" projects, for neither Agnes nor Margaret wanted to have their grown-up daughters at home with them. A contemporary letter gives some light on what might be expected of an unfortunate girl sent out to another home by her parents. A knight's lady was left without any female attendants, and so enquiry was made if a girl could be found to help—but she was to be strong and worth her pay. The letter runs:

If there be any goodly yong woman, that is a good woman of her body and pay, twenty four [years] or more, (and I would have one of my own kin if there were any)...and ye or any for you can espy, I beseech you to get her for me.[2]

It is not pleasant to think of any unwanted girl being ousted from home by her parents to serve under such conditions. In too many cases misery must have been the result. Without pressing the point unduly, we must note it at least as significant that the three letters in this Paston correspondence which give any definite evidence on the point, all speak of the unhappiness felt by girls in others' houses. Elizabeth Paston was almost as wretched away, as her mother had made her at home.[3] Alice Crane, a friend of Margaret Paston's, writing from her mistress's house, concludes her letter by thanking Margaret for her recent kind hospitality "for I had never greater need than I have now, and if I had leisure and space, I would write to you the cause."[4] There can be little doubt that she too was not happy. In the third case Margaret was asked to take a girl into her household, "for she is at Robert Lethum's, and there as she is, she is not well at her ease."[5] Parents evidently were not surprised to get complaints from their children concerning their hardships and misfortunes while away from home. Perhaps they even wel-

[1] P L. No. 478.   [2] Plum. Corr. p. xxxix.   [3] P.L. No 311.
[4] Id. No. 251.   [5] Id. No. 157, and cf. Plum. Corr. pp. 202-3.

comed them as an outward sign that better manners were not
without growing-pains. At all events they seem to have been
unperturbed. Agnes Paston's only reply to her daughter's
complaints was to remind her "she must accustom herself to
work readily, as other gentlewomen do, and somewhat to help
herself therewith."[1] Another unhappy girl, Dorothy Plumpton,
got equally little sympathy or help from home. She had written
asking for her father "to send for me to come home to you,
and as yet I had no answere again." All her efforts were un-
availing; and she says sadly:

> I have sent you diverse messages and writings, and I had never
> answer again. Wherefore, it is thought in these parts...that you
> have little favour unto me; the which error you may now quench,
> if it will like you to be so good and kind a father unto me.[2]

No lack of care was exercised in making arrangements for
daughters, as well as sons, to be received into influential or
aristocratic households. In the case of girls it was even more
important, for their hopes of good marriages depended to a
considerable extent on their ability to attract the attention of
young men of good social standing. Hence Margaret was always
anxious to obtain all possible information concerning the importance and possibilities of the families into which her daughters
were to be introduced. Little as she wanted them at home, she
had no intention of allowing them to go to live with nobodies.
Her directions on these points are frequent and explicit. At
one time she wrote to her son:

> I greet you well, letting you know that as for your sister being
> with my Lady, if your father will agree thereto, I hold me right
> well pleased. For I would be right glad that she should do her
> service before any other—if she could do what should please my
> Lady's good grace. Wherefore, I would that you should speak to
> your father thereof, and let him know that I am pleased that she
> should be there if he would; for I would be right glad if she might
> be preferred by marriage, or by service—so that it be to her worship
> and profit.[3]

The important thing to be remembered, according to Margaret,
is the girl's ultimate preferment—which may result equally well
from finding a good mistress as a good husband! A few years
later she is urgently seeking for a mistress for her young daughter

[1] *P.L.* No. 311.   [2] *Plum. Corr.* p. 202.   [3] *P.L.* No. LXV.

Margery, so that her unfortunate attachment to Richard Calle might be forgotten. Even then, her zeal and anxiety do not outrun her discretion. She is careful to say that she is willing for her "to be with my Lady of Oxford, or with my Lady of Bedford, or in some other worshipful place, where...you think best."[1]

There can be little doubt that the treatment of children, as described above, is fairly representative. Whether we refer to writers of books of instruction, or to contemporary illustrations in manuscripts, or to the manuscripts themselves, the picture they give is the one we can draw for ourselves from the *Paston Letters*.

[1] *P.L.* No. 601.

CHAPTER VII

HOUSES AND FURNITURE

THERE are few things more difficult for the present-day reader to appreciate than the surroundings and home-conditions of medieval people. Most readers on being questioned would find that their impressions were that everyone then lived in a rough and rude style, seldom washed, and managed to live with little comfort; but few would be able to describe clearly the furniture and appearance of a parlour or living room, or to give an account of the bedroom furniture of that time. Yet to understand men and women rightly, we want to see them in their homes among their household goods, so that we may know what things they had about them, and what were lacking. Fortunately, fairly complete inventories have survived in wills and other documents, so that from these we can reconstruct a moderately accurate picture of the kind of home occupied by people of the same status as the Pastons.

The paucity and ruggedness of the furniture in a fifteenth century house would be very obvious to a modern observer. The standard of comfort rose rapidly during Tudor times apparently, for in 1577 Harrison could write:

> The furniture of our houses...is growne in maner even to passing delicacie: and herein I doo not speake of the nobilitie and gentrie onelie, but likewise of the lowest sort in most places of our south countrie, that have any thing at all to take to. Certes, in noble mens houses it is not rare to see abundance of Arras, rich hangings of tapestrie, silver vessell, and so much other plate, as may furnish sundrie cupbords, to the summe oftentimes of a thousand or two thousand pounds at the least. Likewise in the houses of knights, gentlemen, merchantmen, and some other wealthie citizens....But as herein all these sorts doo far exceed their elders and predecessors, and in neatness and curiositie, the merchant all other; so in time past, the costlie furniture staied there, whereas now it is descended yet lower, even unto the inferiour artificers and manie farmers, who by vertue of their old and not of their new leases have for the most part learned also to garnish their cupbords with plate, their joined

beds with tapestrie and silke hangings, and their tables with carpets and fine naperie.[1]

This, as he says, indicates a standard of luxury and comfort far higher than that of a hundred years earlier. His further remarks help us to appreciate what had been the standard in the fifteenth century, making some allowance for exaggeration.

"Our fathers and we ourselves," he writes, "have lyen full oft upon straw pallettes, covered only with a sheet, under coverlets made of dogswain or hop-harlots (I use, says he, the very words of the old men, from whom I received the accounts) and a good round logge under their heades, insteade of a boulster. If it were so that our fathers or the good man of the house had...a matteres or flock bed, and thereto a sacke of chafe to rest hys heade upon, he thought himself to be as well lodged as the lorde of the towne, so well were they contented. Pillowes, sayde they, were thought mete only for women in childe bed. As for servants, if they had any sheete above them, it was well, for seldome had they any under their bodies, to keepe them from the pricking straws, that ranne oft thorow the canvas, and rased their hardened hides.[2]

All but the very wealthy had to be content with little furniture, and that probably of a rough and unfinished nature. The inventory of the contents of a farmer's house in 1425 will give us a detailed picture of what might equally well have been found in any farm-house upon the Pastons' estates, and, with the addition of a few refinements, in the house of the Pastons themselves. The main room in this farm-house is described as the parlour, and it contained one long table with a pair of trestles; one small table with a pair of trestles; two forms; one iron plate to hold the candle; one hanging, and one piece of tapestry covering to throw over a bench.[3] This is the whole of the furniture said to be in the room, which was the living room of the farmer and his family. It will be noticed that tables with trestles were still in use, and not yet superseded by the "joined" table, the "table dormant" of Chaucer's time, which was slowly coming into favour in this century.[4] The trestle table, indeed, was used right on into the sixteenth century and beyond. They

[1] *Eliz. Engl.* p. 118.   [2] *Id.* p. 119.
[3] *S.L.* No. 50.
[4] See Wright, p. 475, for a good illustration of the "table dormant."
For trestle table, see *Dom. Arch.* III. p. 171.

were trestle tables that stood in old Capulet's hall when he
cried to his servants:

A hall, a hall! give room! and foot it girls
More light, you knaves, and turn the tables up.[1]

These trestle tables were extremely useful in the days when the
hall or parlour was the living room of the family; for, as soon
as the meal was over, the tables could be taken down, and
stacked against the wall.

From the inventory of the Stonor farmer's house it appears
that the only seats provided were the long forms, much the
same as those used in College halls at the present day. Outside
this farmer's parlour, in the passage leading to the kitchen, was
a long table of beechwood and another form. These, no doubt,
were brought into the parlour when needed. Chairs were still
a great luxury. Pictures in MSS. show them to have been mostly
of a very elaborate and ceremonial type, looking more like
modern ecclesiastical furniture than anything we are accustomed
to see in our houses. Usually they were reserved for the master
of the house, his wife and the chief guests, especially when
sitting at meat. Such chairs were expensive, and made for the
rich only. One of the Stonor servants writes to inform his
master that the new "chair for the mistress is made after your
device"[2]; which seems to suggest that detailed instructions
were given to the carpenter as to how the chair was to look
when finished.

Ordinary folk had very much rougher chairs, forms, or small
joint-stools. Every house possessed some of these stools, which
were very handy and inexpensive. They were to be found in
some of the chambers of Caister Castle for instance; while
among Dame Elizabeth Browne's goods we find she left seven
large and five small stools.[3] Usually near the fireplace of the
room there would stand forms or benches, either with or without
some kind of back. The benches with a back, or wainscot-
benches as they were called, were possibly the most comfortable
seats people then possessed.[4] People increased their comfort,
to some extent, by the use of cushions. At this time seats of

---

[1] *Romeo and Juliet*, Act I, scene v, ll. 30–1.
[2] *S.L.* No. 64. See fig. in *Dom. Arch.* III. p. 166.
[3] *P.L.* Nos. 336, 988.
[4] See figs. in *Dom. Arch.* III. pp. 112, 114.

all descriptions were not upholstered in any way, and consequently most inventories include cushions among the list of
requirements for hall or parlour. In 1474 an inventory of the
Stonors' hall shows them to have had there two cushions covered
with grey skin, two covered with red worsted, and two covered
with tapestry.[1] Caister Castle and Dame Elizabeth Browne's
house were also well supplied with cushions in various rooms.[2]
These could be used on forms or benches, or laid on the floor
by the fire, or used in the window embrasures to make comfortable seats.

An attempt was made in many houses to improve the appearance and comfort of the rooms by covering the rough walls in
some way. In the Stonor farmer's house there was a hanging
for the wall and a piece of tapestry to throw over the bench
when the family sat by the fire. There was also a growing
demand for fabrics for such purposes, and tapestries at first
and then "painted cloths," which were a cheaper substitute,
were to be found in most houses, except those of the very
poor. Tapestries were mostly imported from Flanders and the
north-east of France, especially from the neighbourhood of
Arras, and are often spoken of as "Arras cloths." The beauty
and richness of effect which a set of these tapestries must
have given to a hall can still be understood when we look at
them even now, after centuries have dimmed their colour and
they are torn from their original surroundings. The beautiful
tapestries designed by Burne Jones to illustrate scenes from
Malory, and executed by William Morris with all the skill and
magic of colour his love and understanding of the crafts of the
Middle Ages gave him, remind us of the brilliance and mass of
colour many English homes must have presented during this
century. When Philip of Castile came to Windsor as a guest
of Henry VII he was given a private suite of rooms, which are
described by an eye-witness as being "the richest hanged that
ever I saw. Seven chambers together [are] hanged with cloth
of arras wrought with gold as thick as could be; and, as for
three beds of state, no King christened can show such three."[3]
The list of tapestries possessed by Sir John Fastolf alone gives
us an indication of the enormous wealth and variety of this

[1] *S.L.* No. 140.   [2] *P.L.* Nos. 336, 988.   [3] *Id.* No. 953.

kind of work existing in England in 1460. Tapestries were woven to illustrate all kinds of subjects,—religious, mythological, classical; and Sir John had a wide assortment. Among religious pieces, he could admire his cloth of Arras, "called the Shepherd's Cloth," probably reproducing the Adoration of the Shepherds, while another showed the Assumption of Our Lady. A tapestry which hung in the Winter hall pictured a Morris dance, and another on the east side of the hall showed the Siege of Falaise. In one of the chambers there was a tapestry depicting scenes of hunting and hawking, while over the dais of the middle hall hung another with the figures of a savage bearing off a child, and in the same hall a third depicting a giant in the midst of it, carrying off the leg of a bear in his hand!"[1]

Besides these beautifully made tapestries, many people used woven hangings, which were not so lasting, but much less expensive than cloth of Arras. Usually these hangings were of bright colours, sometimes one colour being used for the hangings of a whole room, while often gaily striped hangings would cover the walls. In the Stonor house the bed-chambers were hung with striped green and purple, and striped green and red material, while the hall had a black hanging, though perhaps this was only a temporary measure after the death of Thomas Stonor.[2] A fine cloth called "say," very like serge, was much used for hangings. Dame Elizabeth Browne hung one of her chambers with a set of eleven pieces of this material which was of a green colour and had a bordering of acorns.[3]

There was little else in the chief living room, or the hall, besides tables, benches, stools, tapestries and the fireplace accessories. These last are often mentioned in inventories. At Stonor we have record of a pair of andirons, a fire-fork and spit-irons. A fifteenth century vocabulary detailing the contents of a hall, gives the following articles in connection with the fire, and its utensils. "A fire, a hearth-brand, logs, andirons, tongs, and bellows."[4] When we remember the draughts which were always blowing in medieval houses, we can understand how much the inhabitants appreciated a good fire. "A room

[1] *P.L.* No. 336.   [2] *S.L.* No. 140.   [3] *P.L.* No. 988.
[4] *Volume of Vocabularies*, T. Wright, 1857, p. 197.

with a chimney," was one of the signs of a decadent age noted by Langland. Instead of sitting in the hall after meals, or even for meals, some people found it more comfortable to withdraw to the solar or the bedroom, and to sit by the fire there.[1] The fireplace in the hall at this time was usually built into one of the walls, and was not in the centre of the hall where it had sometimes stood in earlier days. Chimneys were becoming more common, although it was another century before many small houses had them. When the fire burnt on an open hearth in the middle of the hall, there was often no possibility of getting rid of smoke and fumes, except by letting them escape through the unglazed windows, and through an opening in the roof called the louvre. The wall fireplace was gradually introduced into houses when repairs or alterations were made to meet the changing needs of the time. Thus, when John Paston was having alterations made to his house at Mauteby, chimneys were built into several rooms, and we have his instructions to the builder that instead of two chimneys as he had ordered at first, he now wanted three.[2] Harrison does not seem to have welcomed the change, and grumbles:

Now haue we manie chimnies, and yet our tenderlings complaine of rheumes, catarhs, and poses. Then had we none but reredosses, and our heads did never ake. For as the smoke in those daies was supposed to be a sufficient hardning for the timber of the houses, so it was reputed to be a far better medicine to keepe the goodman and his familie from the quacke or pose, wherewith as then verie few were oft acquainted.[3]

After the hall, or main living room, the chief bedroom was the next most important room in the house. Judging by inventories of the furniture in this room, as well as from the evidence of manuscript illustrations, poems and romances, we find that the bedroom was used for many purposes other than merely as a sleeping chamber. As we have already seen, it was often the retiring room of the women of the house, where they would sit at their spinning or embroidery. The chief article of

---

[1] *P.P.* xi. B text, ll. 94–100.
[2] *P.L.* No. 186. For fig. of central fireplace, see Wright, p. 450; for wall fireplace, *Dom. Arch.* iii. p. 171.
[3] *Eliz. Engl.* p. 119. Reredose: Parker in his *Dom. Arch.* describes this as a "brazier for the fire of logs, in the centre of the hall," iii. p. 57.

furniture was the bed. Often this took up a great part of the
room, for beds had large wooden frames, with a high back from
which projected a canopy frame. Great pride was taken in the
possession of one of these beds. This pride is indicated by the
manner in which they were bequeathed by will to relatives, as
well as by Harrison's remarks.[1] Our farmer in 1425 left in his
chief bed-chamber, one bed of black and white woods with a
head piece and a canopy. Then there was a mattress, probably
of wool or straw, which rested on cross-ropes slung to the frame
work. A pair of sheets and two blankets, besides a headsheet.
were provided as a covering, and on top of all was a coverlet.
There were side curtains hanging down from the seler which
could be drawn at night to keep out the draughts. Most inventories of a later date include feather-beds, as well as the
ordinary mattresses. When the Duke of Suffolk's men rifled
Paston's house at Hellesdon, among the spoil they bore off were
two feather beds as well as four mattresses.[2] Dame Elizabeth
Browne left to her heirs no less than seven feather beds, most
of them being described as "overworn."[3] The canopy and the
side curtains were often of tapestry or some other rich material.
The Pastons used blue buckram and worsted for this purpose,
while at Caister Castle there were sets of tapestry for a bed
showing "a lady crowned, and a great roll about her head, the
first letter N." Another canopy there was made of tapestry,
with a fringe of red, green and white silk, and a tester of the
same colours. The coverlets to the beds were often very gorgeous.
Sir John Fastolf had a silk coverlet lined with buckram, another
made of green and blue silk, and a third of pale green and white,
with leaves of gold. A green coverlet for the Stonor's bed-
chamber was bright with spots and ostrich feathers glowing on
it, while Sir John Fastolf's cook dreamt at night under the
pleasing combination of roses and blood-hounds' heads![4]

Besides these large well furnished beds, there were often
smaller beds which could be pushed out of the way in the day-
time. These were known as truckle beds, from the truckles

---

[1] See above, p. 88.
[2] *P.L.* No. 978, and cf. No. 533. Cf. also *Bury Wills*, pp. 3, 4, 22, 44, etc.
[3] *Id.* No. 988.
[4] *Id.* No. 388 and *S.L.* No. 140. For figs. of beds, see Wright, pp. 413,
416, 417, 419.

or small castors on which they stood, which enabled them to be run underneath the big bed at will. The personal servants of the rich lay on these, generally at the foot of the big bed. One such bed stood in the big bedroom at Stonor in 1474, and was furnished with "a pair of sheets, a pair of blankets and a mattress."[1] Sometimes not even beds of this description were provided, and people lay on mattresses on the floor. Harrison describes this as common even in his early days.[2] Sir John Fastolf had a little pallet in his chamber, and no doubt his personal attendant slept on this so as to be at his master's call.

Apart from the bed, there was sometimes a chair or two, or some stools in the room. Many contemporary illustrations, however, show both men and women sitting on the bed as if no other seat were available. One chamber at Caister had in it a chair, a joint-stool, and four cushions of red say; but probably few rooms were so well furnished as this. Most of them had a large chest or hutch standing at the foot of the bed, which served as a seat. Often these chests were of considerable beauty, for they were carved, or sometimes painted in bright colours. In them were kept clothes, documents and a miscellany of belongings; for these chests were almost the only place in the house where things could be stored out of harm's way. There are many references to such chests in the *Paston Letters* which confirm this. At one time young John Paston writes home to his mother asking her to "undo the coffer that stands at my bed's feet, and there in a little square box you shall find two deeds."[3] Other letters ask for money, or plate, or clothes, or books, which have been left stored in such coffers.[4]

The walls of these bed-chambers were also covered with tapestries, or hangings of some kind, similar to those used in the living room. Often sweet-smelling boughs and plants were hung about the room to sweeten the air. From occasional references, it would appear that a few people used carpets or matting on the floor of their rooms, but usually rushes were still used. The stone floor of the hall, or the uncovered floor of

[1] *S.L.* No. 140.   [2] See above, p. 88.
[3] *P.L.* No. 678.
[4] The chests or coffers of the Pastons contained (*inter alia*) legal documents (352, 365, 408, 678); money (515, 566); account books (975); clothes (670 and 739) and books (954).

the bedroom made some kind of covering a necessity; and the cheapness of rushes, combined with their warmth, made them very acceptable. Often these rushes were allowed to remain so long without being changed that they became offensive. Erasmus when writing to Wolsey's physician says the rushes in houses are "only occasionally removed, and then so imperfectly that the bottom layer [is] left sometimes for 20 years, harbouring ...abominations, not fit to be mentioned."[1]

The other furniture of a well-equipped bedroom may be soon described. No such things as chests-of-drawers, or wash-stands, or dressing-tables seem to have been at all common. An ewer and a basin of pewter, or laten, was kept in the bedroom, or near by; and the top of a chest, or a table, if there happened to be one in the room, no doubt served as wash-stand and dressing-table in one. Soap was not very expensive, for a pound of black soap could be purchased for a penny, while only five farthings were asked for the best Castell [*i.e.* Castile] soap of Bristol.[2] Occasionally we find a cupboard provided in the bedroom, but these were still rare, and the chest at the bed's foot had to serve. The fireplace has already been alluded to. Here there burnt a log fire in the open fireplace, the logs being piled up on large andirons, such as may still be seen in some old country houses.

The following inventory of the things in Sir J. Fastolf's bedchamber will give a summary view of the furniture and fittings which surrounded the rich.

In primis, a featherbed. Item, a mattress of fine blue.
Item, a bolster. Item, two blankets of fustian.
Item, a pair of sheets. Item, one stitched [coverlet?].
Item, one set of Arras hangings for the bed. Item, one canopy.
   Item, one supporting framework.
Item, one covering.
Item, three curtains of green worsted.
Item, one piece of tapestry to throw over a seat, etc.
Item, three pieces of green worsted for "hanging" [round the wall].
Item, one cupboard cloth.
Item, two standing andirons. Item, one pair of tongs.
Item, one pair of bellows. Item, one staff [to beat the featherbed?]
Item, one little pallet. Item, two blankets.

[1] *Hist. Bicester*, Blomefield, i. u. p. 19, and cf. *Dom. Arch.* pp. 101 and 111.
[2] Redstone, p. 181.

Item, one pair of sheets. Item, one coverlet.
Item, six white cushions. Item, one folding [*i.e.* trestle] table.
Item, one long chair. Item, one green chair.
Item, one hanging candlestick of laten. Item, two little bells.[1]

Candles were the most common means of lighting at this time. When we remember how comparatively costly they were, it is difficult to believe that most houses were ever well lighted. We have already seen Fitzherbert's advice to the master of the house that he should not allow his family to sit up late at night, burning candles and fuel unnecessarily. The difficulty of fattening medieval cattle made the price of tallow sometimes amount to four times that of lean meat.[2] Most families, however, provided themselves with a cheap substitute in the form of the home-made rush-light. This was manufactured by using a strip of rush for the wick, which was dipped into the melted waste fats of the kitchen. Naturally these home-made articles were only a partial success, and gave a poor uncertain light. Better articles were produced by the chandlers, which were made of wax or tallow, and had a cotton wick. Dame Elizabeth Stonor bought such candles from a London wax-chandler.[3]

These candles hung in wooden or metal candelabra suspended from the ceilings, or else stood in candlesticks made of the same materials. In Sir John Fastolf's bed-chamber there was "an hanging candlestick of laten,"[4] while three candlesticks of laten were taken from John Paston's chamber at Hellesdon.[5] In these large houses, it was clearly necessary to have a plentiful supply of such candlesticks. Margaret wrote to her husband on one occasion, and asked him to bring home a dozen new ones when he came; and at Stonor in 1472 there were sixteen little candlesticks, besides twenty-seven others, in good and bad conditions, lying in the buttery.[6]

. By the fifteenth century glass was being used more frequently for windows. The Pastons' ancestors had been accustomed to live in rooms either having unglazed windows, through which the wind could blow, or else stopped with some kind of semi-

---

[1] *P.L.* No. 336. Cf. *Cymbeline*, Act II, scene IV, for a poet's summary of a similar chamber.
[2] See Rogers, *Prices*, IV. pp. 332, 356, 367
[3] *S.L.* No. 227, and see Rogers, *Prices*, IV pp. 367 ff.
[4] *P.L.* No. 336. See fig. in Wright, p. 386.   [5] *Id.* No. 978.
[6] *Id.* No. 429, and *S.L.* No. 308.

transparent material, such as thin horn or oiled linen, which allowed a certain amount of light to enter. Glass windows implied a much higher standard of comfort than had hitherto been common, and such windows were therefore much prized. The care that was taken of glass windows at this time is shown by the fact that window frames were often so constructed that they could be taken out bodily, and stored away in a place of safety when they were not wanted. The Earl of Northumberland's Household Book gives detailed instructions concerning this; and, as late as 1556, a surveyor of Alnwick Castle reports:

And because throwe extreame wind the glase of the windowes of this and other my Lord's Castells and houses here in this countrie doothe decaye and waste yᵗ were goode the whole height of everie windowe, at the departure of his Lordship from lyinge at any of his said Castells and houses, and deuringe the time of his Lordship's absence or others lying in them, were taken down and lade appart in safetie; and at such time as either his Lordship or any other shoulde lie at any of the saide places, the same might then be set up anewe, with small charge to his Lordship; when now the decaye thereof shalle be very costlie and chargeable to be repayred.[1]

The Pastons experienced considerable trouble over this new-fashioned practice of glazing. It was so novel, and comparatively expensive a thing, that very often the windows were regarded as the personal property of the tenant, and as such, removeable at will. When the Parson of Oxnede quarrelled with his diocesan superior, he left the Rectory, taking care to carry off with him both the doors and the windows of the house.[2] One of the Pastons' tenants left the window frames of his house boarded up, and it was reported that the windows were "broken and gone."[3] Another tenant refused to "stop the lyts," as he only held the house on a lease, and evidently was afraid that after he had been to the expense of glazing his windows, Paston would claim them for his own when the tenant left.[4] The law was uncertain in the matter, and it was not until the time of Henry VIII that the judges decided that glass casements were fixtures and not moveables.[5]

We have seen the most important of the fittings and arrange-

[1] *Dom. Arch.* III. p. 122.   [2] *P.L.* No. 819.   [3] *Id.* No. XXXIII.
[4] *Id.* No. 149, and cf. *English Life and Manners in the Later Middle Ages*, Abram, A., p. 178.
[5] *Dom. Arch.* III. p. 123.

ments for the comfort of a medieval household. It now remains to examine the arrangements which were made for the preparation and storage of provisions. The importance attached to food and drink in medieval times, and the necessity for preserving and making at home many more things than is customary now, necessitated a large kitchen. Consequently, the kitchen was a very important part of every house. Often, in the case of large houses, the kitchen stood apart from the main building, possibly as a protection against fire. Many of these large kitchens were handsome lofty structures, having a louvre in the roof which enabled the fumes and steam of the cooking to escape.[1] Generally there were two or more huge open fireplaces. Here the great cauldrons would hang over large fires, and stews and broths would be concocted; while, before the open fire on slowly turning spits, joints and poultry would be roasted. Then there were the ovens for baking. These were heated by thrusting a mass of wood into them; and then, by the time this was burnt to ashes, the oven would have absorbed enough heat to bake the bread or cakes. Even the ashes of the open fires could be used for cooking purposes. A rough kind of oven was constructed by raking a hole in the hot embers, into which the joint was placed, protected by metal covers. Then the hot ashes were raked back over the cover, and the whole left to cook slowly.

The Pastons' kitchen at Hellesdon contained the following utensils:

2 dozen pewter vessels.	4 great brass pans.
3 pots of brass.	1 gridiron.
2 broaches (i.e. spits).	1 dressing knife.
1 marble mortar and 1 pestle.	1 little brass pan holding $\frac{1}{2}$ gallon.
2 pot hooks.	2 iron rakes.
2 brendlets.	An almary to keep meat in.
1 wood axe.[2]	

Sir John Fastolf's kitchen goods illustrate fully what was the normal equipment of a very large kitchen. In it there were:

1 great brass pot.	3 cupboards.
6 coarse brass pots.	1 frying pan.
4 little brass pots.	1 slice.
4 great brass pots.	2 great square spits.

[1] See illustration in *Dom. Arch.* III. p. 151, of magnificent kitchen at Stanton Harcourt.

[2] *P.L.* No. 978.

3 brass pike pans.	2 square spits.
2 ladles and 2 skimmers of brass.	2 little round broaches.
1 cauldron.	1 brass sieve.
1 "dytyn" pan of brass.	1 brass mortar and 1 pestle.
1 dropping pan.	1 grate.
1 gridiron.	1 wooden sieve or cullender.
4 rakes.	1 flesh hook.
3 trivets.	2 pot hooks.
1 dressing knife.	1 pair tongs.
1 fire shovel.	1 strainer.
2 trays.	1 vinegar bottle.[1]

A careful comparison and study of these two lists will enable us to understand fairly accurately what were the contents of a kitchen of the fifteenth century; and will show that these kitchens were very well furnished for the work they had to do.[2]

The kitchen, however, was only one department of several given over to the preparation and storage of "mete and drinke," in houses such as the Pastons inhabited. The buttery, the pantry, and the larder were all separated in really large houses. In smaller houses they were naturally often found in one room, sometimes to economise space, and sometimes because so much space was unnecessary for the few materials to be stored. The lack of storage we have noticed in the hall made it imperative to have some room where the napery, cutlery and glass could be kept. Although the buttery originally was used for the distribution of liquids, and the pantry for the distribution of bread and such things, this distinction was fast vanishing, especially in small houses, and one office was made to serve both functions. In the Pastons' buttery at Hellesdon they kept among other things:

6 table cloths.	2 pewter basins with 2 ewers.
6 towels.	1 barrel vinegar.
12 napkins.	1 barrel verjuice.
6 laten candlesticks.	12 ale stands.
2 silver salts.	2 pantry knives.
2 pewter salts.	A piece of silver [plate].
An ale stool.	12 silver spoons.[3]

At Caister, as we have already seen in other directions, the

---

[1] *P.L.* No. 336. Cf. numerous inventories and figs. in *Dom. Arch.* III. pp. 151 ff.

[2] See also *S.L.* Nos. 50 and 140.   [3] *P.L.* No. 978.

contents of the buttery were much more sumptuous. First of all there were:

2 carving knives.	4 leather gallon pots.
3 knives in sheaths with ivory handles.	3 leather pottlers.
	1 great tankard.
1 trencher knife.	2 great bottles.
1 pair of gallon bottles.	14 laten candlesticks.
1 pair of pottle bottles.[1]	Certain pieces of napery [unspecified].
Another pottle bottle.	1 quartlet for wine.
1 pair of quartlets.	

Besides this, the buttery at Caister housed a fair collection of plate. This is described as comprising dishes, plates, saucers, pottles, salts and basins of silver, some of them richly decorated, such as "a basin of silver, parcel gilt, with a double rose; his arms enamelled at the bottom, beneath his helm and his crest."[2]

The larder also had an important place in medieval life, because in it were stored the preserved meats and salted provisions for the winter. We have already seen how the Pastons laid in stocks of beef to be salted down, so that they could live through the winter until the following Lent.[3] Every housewife was accustomed to preserve meats in this way, and the necessary operations were continuously in progress. Not only meat, but fish of various kinds were bought, salted down in the larder, and stored for winter and Lenten use. In Sir John Fastolf's larder he had:

3 great standing tubs.	1 barrel.
2 salting tubs.	1 butcher's axe.[4]

Sometimes this same place was also used as a brewhouse. Although ale was bought from outside sources and from professional brewers, a certain amount was made at home; and the inventories of the Paston and the Stonor houses show that the brewhouse and pantry were under one roof. At Stonor there were:

1 mashing vat.	1 trivet.
1 great cauldron.	2 boiling vessels for meal.
9 barrels.	7 carvers.
1 eel tub.	1 axe.[5]

It will be seen from the above that the fifteenth century house possessed most of the features we find in our modern

---

[1] A pottle contained 2 quarts. [3] *P.L.* No. 336.
[2] See p. 56. [4] *P.L.* No. 336. [5] *S.L.* No. 140.

dwellings. The hall of those days has been made smaller, and has become the dining-room of to-day. The bower of the lady still exists in the modern boudoir; and, although the buttery has long since passed away (except in Colleges at Oxford and Cambridge, and possibly in a few great houses), the title of butler is still retained by the domestic responsible for the care of the plate and the service of meals. Other rooms and offices have been adapted to meet the needs of modern times; and some refinements, then entirely unknown, have since been introduced.[1] But, by the close of the fifteenth century, the standard of comfort was already rapidly rising; although we must not close our eyes to the fact that this standard was still far from meeting with modern requirements. A glance at any contemporary book of manners indicates that the habits of even well-to-do people were very primitive. Hence it was considered necessary to warn men that, when invited to a meal, they should not cram their cheeks with food like an ape, pick their teeth with their knives, or spit on the table, or in the bowl brought round after the meal, in which the hands were cleansed.[2]

[1] See *Dom. Arch.* III. pp. 171–2, where this is fully worked out.
[2] *Meals and Manners*, pp. 301–3. Cf. p. 344, and for contemporary French manners Part II. pp. 1–20.

CHAPTER VIII

EDUCATION AND BOOKS

It will be remembered that the "unfriendly hand," who drew up the description of the origins of the Paston family, did not fail to remark that Clement Paston himself was merely a hard-working husbandman.[1] In order to emphasise his case, the writer pointed out that, when Clement wished to send his son William to school, he could only do so by borrowing money. Whatever may be the truth as to the origins of the family, it is remarkable to find that Clement cared enough about education to go to the lengths of borrowing money for that purpose. Certainly there were material advantages possible as a result of such an action; for education was the only channel by which a youth such as William Paston might rise to something better than husbandry. Even so, however, it required courage and foresight for an humble countryman to adopt such a course. We know, from William Paston's subsequent career, that his father's action was fully justified;[2] and it is of great interest to see how William himself, and then his sons, dealt with the problem, each in turn.

As one might expect, William (or the Justice, as he had then become), knew the value of education too well from his own experience to think of allowing his sons to grow up without sending them to school. By the fifteenth century grammar schools were to be found throughout the land. In Norwich itself there was a Grammar School, and there were also several other such schools scattered about the county at Thetford, Shipden, Saham Toney and other places.[3] Unfortunately, we do not know whether John Paston or any of his brothers went to any such school. We know that the Pastons had a domestic chaplain, and it is most probable that the sons of the family, while

---

[1] *P.L.* Intro. p. xxv, and see p. 1.   [2] See pp. 2–3.
[3] *Schools*, pp. 168 and 224.

still young, were taught by him.[1] We certainly know that this was so many years later when these sons had children of their own, for a letter to Margaret Paston, from her younger son John, asks her to see that Sir John Still (the family chaplain) was "a good master to little Jack, and learns him well."[2] Except for this one reference, there is no mention of education until the children had begun to arrive at the adolescent stage.

When once they were old enough to leave home, the usual plan seems to have been to send them off to Cambridge. We know that John Paston was at Trinity Hall when he was fifteen or sixteen, and he appears to have been in Cambridge until he was about twenty or twenty-one.[3] Besides this, it is certain that two of his brothers were at Cambridge for a time. Neither of them was there very long, and we find them in London when one is aged fourteen and the other sixteen; so, it is probable, they were about thirteen and fifteen respectively while they were at Cambridge.[4] The remaining son, Edmund, is never mentioned in the *Letters* until we read of him as a student of Clifford's Inn, when he was probably twenty years of age or more. As we shall see later, his brother John did not enter one of the Inns of Court until he had been to Cambridge, and probably Edmund had also been there, or elsewhere, before beginning his study of the law. Obviously, he had received some education before going to London. Hence we have good reason for supposing the four sons of the Justice were all fairly well educated.

Although the modern reader may be surprised to find boys at the University as young as fourteen or fifteen, this was a common custom in the fifteenth century. The young student was usually placed under the care of a Master of Arts; otherwise, he became a scholar of one of the existing Colleges or Halls. The Pastons, no doubt, found themselves crowded together in some hostel with many other youths of their own age and up-bringing. By this time, the Universities were beginning to admit students who were sons of the nobility or of the landed classes. Hitherto, all members of the University had been clerics; indeed there seems to be no evidence for the abandon-

---

[1] See *The Booke of the Governour*, Sir Thos. Elyot, ed. Croft, H. H. S., 1880, I. p. 113.
[2] *P.L.* No. 585.   [3] *Id.* Nos. v and 29.   [4] *Id.* Nos. 66, 69, 311, XIII.

ment of this theory even in the case of the young Pastons, for the "first tonsure" was very liberally given, and committed the recipient to very little. On the other hand it may be argued that in the absence of any specific reference to clericality, the presence of such boys as the sons of Justice Paston supports the view that a new type of undergraduate—the "literate layman"—was making use of the opportunities afforded by the University.[1] We may perhaps say that the majority of men, when they went down from the University, took major orders, or obtained positions in great households as secretaries or clerks. University life in these days was a wild and careless affair. Complaints are numerous concerning the bands of "night-walkers," and "chamber-deacons," and other lawless persons who roamed about as they would, and made themselves a nuisance to all peaceful inhabitants. Altogether, the impression one gets from a study of contemporary evidence is that discipline was more difficult to enforce, and more sporadic than in modern times. As there was so little opportunity for most students to live in Colleges, or even in those semi-collegiate lodgings called halls or hostels, they generally lived in private rooms, nominally under the care of a Master of Arts, in whose books they were inscribed, and who was theoretically responsible for their discipline. Hence their undergraduate life depended largely on the character of this man. If he was easy-going, students were able to enjoy the greatest liberty; and very many Masters were easy-going, because experience had shown them that such an attitude gained most pupils. We find them even touting for students. Once the Master had enrolled his pupils, he was supposed to see they attended certain lectures daily. The Pastons went through some of this routine, and perhaps found themselves in charge of a careless master, for we find William complaining that his master had ignored his complaints of being unwell, so that he was determined to suffer in silence in future.[2] Perhaps the worthy master considered illness an unwarrantable luxury for a young undergraduate. We have no definite evidence of the studies pursued by the Pastons, except that John Paston

---

[1] See *The Lollard Bible*, Deanesly, M., 1920, p. 209, for discussion of the problem of the "literate layman."
[2] *P.L.* No. xiii.

was asked to send two books to his brother at Cambridge—
a "nominale" and a "book of sophistry."[1] The methods of
teaching adopted by many masters are described by Agnes at
a later date, when she speaks with approval of the boys' master
at Cambridge. She writes:

> Pray Greenfield [the new Master in London] to send me faithfully
> word by writing, how Clement Paston has done his duty in learning.
> And if he hath not done well, nor will not amend, pray him that he
> will truly belash him till he will amend. So did the last master, and
> the best that ever he had, at Cambridge.[2]

But this teaching and "belashing" would doubtless be a matter
of private contract; the master in question would be under-
taking work as a "private coach."

John Paston himself seems to have been at Trinity Hall,
and later at Peterhouse. Since we find him at the Inner Temple
a few years after this, it is not unreasonable to suspect that
the Justice had sent him to Trinity Hall to commence his study
of the law. By its original foundation statutes, this college was
designed for the study of civil and canon law. To some fathers,
a study of the law was chiefly a means whereby their sons
might "form their manners, and be preserved from the con-
tagion of vice"; but, to the far-seeing practical eye of Justice
Paston, such a study was a necessity for his heirs. The Paston
fortunes would need much careful guarding, and a sound knowledge of the law, if they were to be preserved intact from outward
aggression. So Agnes advised her son to remember his father's
shrewd advice: "I advise you to think once [every] day of your
father's counsel to learn the law, for he said many times that
whosoever should dwell at Paston, should need to know [how
to] defend himself."[3]

It is from these scanty references that we have to reconstruct
our picture of the education of the sons of Justice Paston.[4] The
next generation is more enlightening; and from the career of
Walter, the son of John Paston, we get fuller information on
University life in the fifteenth century. Walter was born after
1455; and in January 1473 we find his mother making arrange-

---

[1] *P.L.* No. 66. "Book of sophistry," the *Sophistici Elenchi* of Aristotle.
Students often hired from stationers or their tutors, as books were very
expensive.
[2] *Id.* No. 311.   [3] *Id.* No. 46.   [4] *Id.* Nos. 29 and 36.

ments to send him up to Oxford. Walter was to go there in
the charge of Sir J. Gloys, the domestic chaplain of the family.
Margaret explicitly ordered Gloys to see that the boy was "put
where he should be," and that he should be "set in good and
sad rule." Since he was "going up" in January, and not at
the end of the Long Vacation, as most students did in those
days, there was little hope of his meeting a "fetcher" or
"bringer" at Cambridge, who would take him on the rest of
his way. Gloys was therefore bidden to arrange for a horse to
carry his goods, unless by a happy chance they met a carrier
going from Cambridge to Oxford. Margaret's injunctions to
her son are interesting and throw some light on contemporary
conditions. She desires him to "do well, learn well, and be of
good rule and disposition," and also warns him not "to be too
hasty in taking Orders that should bind him[1] till that he be
24 years of age or more, though he be counselled to the contrary,
for often haste rueth." She concludes, "I will love him better
to be a good secular man than to be an unworthy priest."[2]

From the time he thus set out for Oxford, until the 19th May
five years later, we have no information of Walter's life at the
University. When he breaks silence at last, it is to ask for
money. He is evidently living under the Mastership of a certain
Edmund Alyard, who had lent him about eight shillings, since
he was penniless. If we assume that Walter had been home in
the previous Long Vacation, the financial statement he furnishes
gives us the cost of his half-year's expenses from (say) October
to the following Easter. He found that his expenses were
£6. 5s. 5¾d., while his total receipts were only £5. 17s. 6d., and
therefore he had been forced to borrow.[3] He might have got
money in other ways, for the University had "chests" set up
by rich men so as to relieve the necessitous, who had to deposit a book, or a garment of value, as a pledge for repayment.

Although Margaret had originally so strongly advised his
waiting before he took Orders, by this time she began to make
preparations for his future. She enquired of a friend at the
Bishop's Court whether she could present her son at once to

---

[1] I.e. Major, or Holy Orders (Subdeacon, Deacon or Priest) which would
commit him to a life of celibacy.

[2] P.L. No. 716.   [3] Id. No. 816.

a family living. She was met with a decided negative,[1] and
seems to have abandoned the idea; for, a few months later,
Master Alyard wrote to say that his pupil was almost ready
to take his Bachelor's degree, and could go on to Law after the
Vacation. Walter had now been at Oxford over six years, and
should nominally have taken his B.A. at least two years earlier.[2]
From time to time he had had to make his appearance at the
schools, both to hear disputations and to take part in them.
Finally he was called upon to sum up, or determine one of these
disputations, after which he could proceed to his degree. So,
towards the end of May, we find Walter making preparations
for his "determining feast." This feast marked the successful
ending of the Arts course, and was given by the newly-made
Bachelor. At first Walter hoped to graduate at the same time
as Lionel Woodville, the Queen's brother, and he expected the
noble Lord would materially aid the newly-made Bachelors in
settling the bill for the feast. Plans were changed, however,
with the result that Walter wrote home saying "it will be some
cost to me, but not much."[3] His brother, Sir John, was to come
to Oxford for the ceremony; but, owing to a delay in the delivery of letters, he was not warned in time. Nevertheless one
June day Walter took his degree, and held his feast despite dis-
appointments. His Oxford career closed happily; for he tells us:

And if you will know what day I was made Bachelor, I was made
on Friday the seventh [of June], and I made my feast the Monday
after. I was promised venison for my feast by my Lady Harcourt,
and of another man too, but I was deceived by both; but my guests
held them[selves] pleased of such meat as they had, blessed be God.[4]

At the time when Walter was finishing his studies at Oxford,
his brother William was making his acquaintance with the most
famous of schools, Eton College. So far as we know, no other
members of the Paston family had received any education there,

---

[1] *P.L.* No. 826.

[2] *Id.* No. 829. It is probable that the original Arts course, of which the
B.A. concluded the first stage, was a good deal changed by now from the
ideal method of study set forth in Rashdall, II. pp. 455, 456.

[3] *Id.* No. 830. See Rashdall, II. p. 444.

[4] *Id.* No. 831. It may be noticed that Walter was destined never to
"go to law," as was proposed; for, about a month after he left Oxford, he
died at Paston Place, Norwich, and was buried before the image of S. John
the Baptist in the family church of S. Peter, Hungate. Blomefield, IV. p. 333,
and *P.L.* Nos. 834–6.

and we are without any information which will help us to decide why the Pastons should have sent William thither. Eton had been founded by Henry VI in 1440; but, during the Wars of the Roses, its income had greatly diminished:

"This," says Mr Leach, "perhaps hastened rather than retarded the development of the school into a great public school for the upper classes and the aristocracy, who, while paying nothing for their education, paid large sums for boarding in the houses of the fellows, and in the town of Eton, whence they came to be called Oppidans."[1]

Whatever may have been the reasons, William was certainly at Eton in November 1478, and in all probability he had then been there about a year. While he was at Eton we find that he resided in a dame's house in the town, under the tuition of a ellow of the College. Much as we know the Pastons to have appreciated the value of education, they seem to have been loath to pay for it. Consequently we find several references in the *Letters* to William's debts at Eton. At one time, his school-fees and boarding expenses were nine months in arrears; then, a year later, his tutor had advanced him twenty shillings for board and lodging; and again the next year his account was 13s. 4d. in arrears.[2]

"The Eton curriculum," writes Mr Leach, "was summed up in the one word grammar, taught in a way to fit the scholars for the University....We know that grammar meant Latin grammar and the Latin classics, with composition in Latin verse and Latin prose, and conversation carried on in the Latin tongue, both in and out of school."[3]

Despite these opportunities, young William Paston does not seem to have become an accomplished Latinist. Perhaps he managed to evade, or to placate, the "lupus" or spy to be found in schools at this time.[4] This spy was definitely appointed by the authorities to inform upon anyone he heard talking in English. However this may be, William was well satisfied on the whole with his own progress, and wrote to his brother shortly before he left Eton, "And as for my coming from Eton, I lack

[1] *Schools*, p. 259.   [2] *P.L.* Nos. 824, 827.
[3] *V. C. H. Buckingham*, II. p. 161.
[4] See *Schools*, p. 306; *Eng. Gram. Schools to* 1660, Foster-Watson, pp. 314–5, 317; and cf. *Hist. Eton*, Maxwell-Lyte, 4th edn, p. 140, referring to Malim's *Consuetudines*, 1560.

nothing but versifying, which I trust to have with a little continuance." He then quotes:

> Quare, Quomodo non valet hora, valet mora,
> Unde di' [dictum, vel deductum?]
> Arbore jam videas exemplum. Non die possunt
> Omnia suppleri; sed tamen illa mora;

and adds with complacency, "And these two verses aforesaid be of my own making."[1]

Despite frequent debts and uncertain Latin he was not depressed. Like his brother John, he loved amusement and excitement, and once proposed that he should vary the monotony of College life by coming to London for a day or two "to sport with his brother."[2] There is a curious modernity about this suggestion which reminds us how little the character of youth is changed by the passing of the centuries. But, when he could not go to London, he was not entirely without amusements, for once we find him at a wedding. His friend the bridegroom had invited him, and he soon found the sister of the bride worthy of his attentions. The girl was urged on by her mother "and made him good cheer." William was much impressed, and his report to his brother of the maiden's beauty and her fortunes is strictly in accordance with medieval thought. He writes:

> She is not abiding where she is now, her dwelling is in London, but her mother and she came to a place of hers five miles from Eton, where the wedding was, in order to be near to the gentleman which wedded her daughter....If it please you to enquire of her, her mother's name is Mistress Alborow; the name of the daughter is Margaret Alborow, the age of her is by all likelihood eighteen or nineteen years at the farthest. And as for the money and plate, it is ready whensoever she were wedded....And as for her beauty, judge you that when you see her, if so be that you take the labour, and especially behold her hands, for if it be as it is told me, she is disposed to be thick.[3]

The girls of the Paston family, like the girls of most families of their position, probably received little education except that imparted by their family chaplain. The way in which both Agnes and Margaret Paston were able to deal with practical affairs, as well as the confidence their men folk had in them,

---

[1] *P.L.* No. 827.   [2] *Id.* No. 824.
[3] *Id.* No. 827. "She is likely to grow fat."

make it clear that their education was not entirely neglected. There was probably little of book-learning in it, but rather a very thorough training for the responsibilities of domestic life. Both while at home, and when they were "put out," in accordance with prevailing custom, girls learnt to be capable and self-reliant. Thus at an early age they were able to shoulder the burdens and responsibility that inevitably came to the medieval woman with marriage.[1]

It is clear from the above evidence that, for at least two generations, the Pastons cared enough about education to make sure their children did not grow up without it. They could all read and write, and the men at any rate had some knowledge of Latin. There are signs that some members of the family knew French; and, when we remember that both Sir John Paston and his brothers saw some service in France, this is not very surprising. Altogether the whole family must probably be regarded as possessing rather more than the average of education for their times. In no way does this show itself more clearly than in their writing and reading. The evidence with regard to letters and writing will be discussed in detail in a later chapter. Here it will be interesting to see what part books and reading played in the lives of this family.

There can be little doubt that, when the business of the day was done, the Pastons were accustomed to turn to books for relaxation, and that their reading was not confined to utilitarian purposes. Since the art of printing was not introduced into England until 1474, it is not very probable that the Pastons saw anything but manuscripts until after that date. It is, however, significant of their interest in books to find that within ten years of Caxton's starting work in England they possessed a copy of the *Game and Play of Chess*, "in preente." During the fifteenth century certain MSS. were plentiful. Copies of poems by Chaucer and Langland and Sir John Mandeville's travels had a great vogue; while works of a specifically religious and didactic nature appeared side by side with the old romances and tales of daring. As early as 1434 we find that Agnes Paston had a copy of the *Stimulus Conscientiae* in her possession. This was not her own, however, but had been lent to her by Robert

<hr />

[1] For further details, see Chapter V.

Cupper, a burgess of Great Yarmouth, and was to be given to his son Robert when he came to years of discretion.[1] As the years went on, the Pastons began to amass books of their own, and perhaps their friendship with Sir John Fastolf encouraged this. In 1450, the old knight had a collection of books at Caister, which are catalogued thus:

In the Stewe house;
  Of French books.

The Bible.	The Cronycles of France.
A book of Jullius Cæsar.	The Cronicles of Titus Livius.
Lez Propretez dez Choses [by Barth Glanville]. [Astronomie.	
Petrus de Crescentiis.	Liber Geomancie cum iiij aliis
Liber de Roy Artour.	Romaunce la Rose.
Cronicles d'Angleterre.	Veges de l'arte Chevalerie.
Instituts of Justien Emperor.	Brute in ryme.
Liber Etiques.	Liber de Sentence Joseph.
Problemate Aristotelis.	Vice and Vertues.
Liber de Cronykles de Grant Bretayne in ryme.	
Meditacions Saint Bernard.[2]	

Besides these books, Sir John had provided for use in his chapel at Caister:

2 antiphoners.   1 legend of Holy service.
2 Missals, the one noted and closed with silver, and the other not noted.
1 Psalter clasped with silver, with the arms of Fastolf and of Millicent Fastolf upon it.[3]

What happened to most of these books when Sir John died is unknown, for there is no evidence that any of them went to the Pastons.[4]

This collection of Sir J. Fastolf may be regarded as a fair example of the library a rich man might have collected at this period. It was certainly an age of book-buying and collecting. Henry VI himself, the Duke of Bedford and others of the Court set the fashion. Bedford's brother, the famous Duke Humphrey, had given the wonderful collection of books to Oxford, which were afterwards housed in the library which bears his name. Others were fired with a like zeal, and Dick Whittington and his friends had founded the public library in the City of London. Not only England, but France and Italy were diligently searched

[1] *N.A.* iv. p. 326.   [2] 8 *Hist. MSS.* p. 268a.
[3] *P.L.* No. 336.   [4] *Id.* Nos. 690, 696–7, 739, 869, etc.

by a few enthusiasts for their precious manuscripts; while, at Oxford and Cambridge, Colleges began to make provision for housing their growing stores of books.[1]

As we have said, the Pastons evidently loved reading, and more than one member of the family is mentioned as the possessor of a book or books. Anne Paston, for example, had a copy of Lydgate's *Siege of Thebes* of her own; Walter Paston had *The Book of the Seven Sages*, and Sir John's other brother, John, was the owner of a book containing "The Meeting of the Duke and Emperor."[2] But it is Sir John Paston who seems to have been the most enthusiastic bibliophile. This is well illustrated by the efforts he made to obtain the books of Sir J. Gloys, who had been the family chaplain. When Gloys died, Sir John lost no time in asking his mother to pack up the chaplain's books, and to send them to London. Books were still too valuable to be disposed of so easily, and indeed were often left by will, so that one particular book would go to one friend, and another book or books to another friend. Sir John had therefore to add that, if it were afterwards discovered that Sir James had thus disposed of any of the books, it should be returned. A few days later he again asked about the books, and in yet another letter emphasised his desire for them. Apparently there was some delay, and he writes three weeks later, "I hear no word of my books. I marvel." It was not until nearly two months later that he had any news. His mother then told him that the best of the books had been claimed, although she was doing all she could to get it for him. The rest, she said, would cost twenty shillings and sixpence, if he cared to have them. The long wait, and the knowledge that the cream of the collection had been skimmed, evidently lessened his original enthusiasm, for his only reply was that the books could wait; "My mind is now not most upon books."[3]

Not only was Sir John Paston a buyer and collector of manuscripts in their completed form, but he was accustomed to hire professional scribes and illuminators to work for him, and to produce new copies of famous or useful works. We have an interesting record from a certain William Ebesham, who sets

[1] *Libraries*, pp. 186–7.   [2] *P.L.* Nos. 696, 697, 739.
[3] *Id.* Nos. 745–7, 749, 752, 754.

out in full the details of his labours. He also takes occasion to bemoan the high price of living, "among right unreasonable askers," which makes it necessary for him to request his patron to pay his long overdue bill. Among the books he had copied for the Pastons he mentions a little book of physic, which he completed at a cost of twenty pence. Then he had written what he rightly called a Great Book. This contained 26 pages of writing concerning the Coronation and the duties of Knighthood. Then followed a 120 page treatise on War in four books, then an 86 page treatise on Wisdom, and then the rules of chivalry were set out in 28 pages. Finally he had copied the *de Regimine Principum* of Lydgate on 90 pages, and had rubricated the whole book. For all this labour he only charged 31s. 1d., which was estimated at the rate of 2d. a leaf [*i.e.* two pages] for all the work, except the Lydgate manuscript, which he reproduced for 1d. a leaf. He did not find scrivening very profitable, for he asked Paston to send on any old gowns which were of no further use to the family. His pathetic conclusion runs, "I have great need...God knows, whom I beseech preserve you from all adversity. I am somewhat acquainted with it."[1]

It will be seen, from the various items that went to the making of the Great Book, that MSS. concerning the most diverse matters were bound within the same covers. Thus among his books Sir John Paston had one volume in which were *La Belle Dame sans merci*, *The disputation between Hope and Despair*, *The Parliament of Birds* and *The Life of S. Christopher*. Another volume contained Chaucer's *Parliament of Birds*, *The Legend of Ladies*, *La Belle Dame sans merci*, *The Temple of Glass* and *The Green Knight*. Manuscripts which had not thus been bound up into volumes are referred to in the inventory of Sir John's books as existing in quires—that is, just as they were received from the scrivener, or merely stitched in paper covers. His Latin manuscripts seem to have been left in this condition, and we find in quires copies of Ovid's *de Arte Amandi*, and Cicero's *de Senectute, de Amicitia, de Sapientia* and others.[2]

[1] P.L. No. 596. The Great Book is now Lansdowne MS. 285, Brit. Mus.
[2] Id. No. 869. See Appendix I for full list of books owned by the Pastons.

CHAPTER IX

LETTERS AND LETTER-WRITING

A STUDY of the originals of the *Paston Letters* throws considerable light on epistolary methods and difficulties in the fifteenth century. The complex and obscure constructions often used by the writers indicate the difficulty many people felt in expressing their thoughts clearly. Also the letters are the best possible evidence that a fairly large variety of people were able to write with some degree of skill. Thorold Rogers long ago pointed out that there are still extant accounts of bailiffs, and bills written by artizans, which afford evidence that these classes of men were not entirely illiterate.[1] The originals of the *Paston Letters* support these statements. Very many are written by servants, or friends, or business acquaintances of the Pastons, some in a beautiful hand, others barely legible. Besides the Pastons and their friends, we see that men like Richard Calle, the Paston bailiff, were in the habit of writing about business affairs, and there are also many letters written by stewards, upper servants and domestic chaplains.

Mr Kingsford, in his edition of the contemporary *Stonor Letters*, quotes with approval Dr Gairdner's statement:

"No person of any rank or station above mere labouring men seems to have been wholly illiterate. All could write letters: most persons could express themselves in writing with ease and fluency."[2] He adds, "This judgment is fully confirmed by the Stonor Letters. Sir William Stonor, his father, and brothers...wrote their own letters, and spelt passably well. Jane Stonor wrote tolerably but spelt atrociously. Her daughter-in-law Elizabeth generally employed an amanuensis, but could write well enough if she pleased. Generally the country squires of Oxfordshire and their women folk, and the better class merchants of London could write with ease. The worst writers and spellers are the inferior clergy...or humble mercantile people."[3]

---

[1] Rogers, *Work*, p. 165. [2] *P.L.* Intro. p. ccclxii.
[3] *S.L.* Intro. p. xlvi.

Further, in his *Prejudice and Promise in XVth Century England* Mr Kingsford reiterates his approval and adds:

I agree also that there has been too much readiness to undervalue the culture and civilization of the age. Certainly capacity to read and write was no longer an accomplishment confined to the clerical class. ...The wives and sisters of country gentlemen could often write as well as their husbands and brothers, and both they and their servants could and commonly did keep regular household accounts. The shop-keeper made out his bill in writing and sent it to his customer with an explanatory letter. The physician wrote out his prescription in a fashion similar to that still in use and sent it to the apothecary to make up. In the merchant's office a capacity to read and write must have long been required; of its universality we can obtain proof from a single instance. In 1442 Robert Chirche, when taking an apprentice, bound himself to find him to school for a year and a half to learn grammar and for half a year to learn to write. After some years the boy's friends complained that this had never been done, to his great harm and loss. Chirche replied, denying some of the statements, and alleging that the apprentice had been sufficiently instructed both in reading and writing as unto such apprentices reasonably may suffice.[1]

Yet, however many people could write, there can be little doubt that this collection of letters represents an infinitude of labour, oftentimes unwillingly expended. Letter-writing had not yet come to be an easy accomplishment; and no doubt many of these writers sat down to their task with little relish. Naturally this is reflected now and again in their work. As we read letter after letter, we cannot fail to notice their absorbed and solemn tone. In a very few cases only does any conscious humour lighten the pages.[2] Letter-writing was too difficult and lengthy an operation for most people to indulge in playful paragraphs. Usually the writers plod on, anxious to say what is necessary, without any tarrying over superfluous subjects. Many of the documents in this collection are not actual letters, but only rough drafts. This is in itself a proof that the writers did not find expression easy. They needed to collect their thoughts, and arrange them, before they could give them a final form. When the originals of these rough drafts are studied, one can see how much labour often went to the making of a letter. There is, for instance, the rough copy of a letter written

[1] See also the important paper by Prof. J. W. Adamson, "The Extent of Literacy in England in the Fifteenth and Sixteenth Centuries." *The Library*, New Series, Vol x. p. 162.
[2] But note *P.L.* Nos. 528, 686, 794 and 919.

by John Paston to the Duke of Norfolk, complaining of the way
he had been attacked outside Norwich Cathedral.[1] In this may
be seen all the interlineations and alterations which he had to
make before it was fit to be copied. Other members of the
family followed this plan, and we have nothing but the drafts
of many of their letters.[2] The fair copies were sent off and so are
lost.

These drafts show that the pen was still an unfamiliar instru-
ment. Many could use it; but, if an amanuensis could be obtained, so much the better. Now and again this is acknowledged
by the writers themselves. Young John Paston, in the midst
of his labours to win Margery Brews, wrote to his mother:

> All the circumstances of the matter, which I trust to tell you at
> your coming to Norwich, could not be written in three leaves of
> paper, and you know my lewd head well enough, I may not write
> long. Wherefore I defer all things till I may await on you myself.[3]

Margaret Paston often made use of a scribe, especially when
she was growing old. Hence we find Pamping, Lomnor, Gresham
and Sir J. Gloys, among others, serving her purpose from time
to time.[4] This was well known to members of her family, and
Sir John wrote on one occasion, "I am acquainted with your
state of old, that you care not who writes more letters than
you."[5] Agnes Paston usually wrote so little herself that she
thought it necessary to apologise for her handwriting, when
her haste would not let her wait for "a good secretary."[6] The
old lady could write quite well, however,[7] but probably found
it easier to make use of an amanuensis.[8]

Since people like the Pastons used scribes whenever possible,
it is not surprising to find that the nobility seldom wrote letters
at all themselves. Many great lords, like Sir John Fastolf,
seem to have been able to do little more than sign their own
names. Their letters were written for them by their private
chaplains, or by a secretary. William Worcester, who was
Sir John Fastolf's faithful secretary, wrote most of his master's

---

[1] *P.L.* Nos. 174–6. See Add. MS. 27,444, ff. 13–16.
[2] *E.g. Id.* Nos. 623–4, 842, 848, 850, 885, 919, etc.
[3] *Id.* No. 787, "lewd," ignorant.   [4] *Id.* Nos. 93 n., 647, 812.
[5] *Id.* No. 812.   [6] *Id.* No. 25.
[7] *Id.* Nos. 59, 160. See Add. MS. 39,848, f. 2, and Add. MS. 27,444, f. 9.
[8] For letters written by secretaries cf. also *S.L.* Nos. 185, 200, 244.

letters; and, towards the end of Sir John's life, even signed them for him.[1] The old man was always impatient of letter-writing, and there is an interesting example of his impetuosity in a postscript to one of his letters: "And because I might [not] abide till the writing of the matters that I commanded Worcester to write, I signed this letter so near the beginning."[2] His signature comes after the first few words of the letter. Letters received by the Pastons from great ecclesiastics, like the Archbishop of Canterbury, or from such people as the Duke of Norfolk, or the Earl of Warwick, were all written by secretaries.[3] Only the signature is autograph. Lord Hastings appended a postscript in his own hand; but usually a signature, with sometimes "your trusty frend," or "your faythefull cosyene," had to suffice.

The student of manners will find much to interest him in little occasional touches, which help to reveal men and women as they really were. Then, as now, excuses for bad letter-writing were not unknown. Agnes Paston was apologetic, as we have seen, because she wrote in haste without waiting for the services of a good secretary. William Paston, while still at Cambridge, thus admitted his fault, "I am sorry I may write no better at this time, but I trust you will [have] patience."[4] Another writer found the time had passed so quickly that he had to allow his letter to go as it was. "I had thought," he wrote in a postscript, "to have written the above letter anew, because of the foul writing and interlining, but now I lack leisure."[5] A particularly human note was struck by William Lomnor, when he wrote to tell the Pastons of the murder of the Duke of Suffolk. The tragic nature of the whole affair evidently so strongly affected him that the tears fell while he wrote and blurred his writing. He interlined near the beginning his pathetic excuse: "I...have so washed this little letter with sorrowful tears that you shall read it uneasily."[6] Touches such as these relieve the business details of this correspondence, and remind us that these people are not shadowy personages, but real men and women with emotions as keen as our own.

[1] P.L. Nos. 308, 324, 328. See Add. MS. 39,848, ff. 44, 48, and 49.
[2] Id. No. 128. See Add. MS. 39,848, f. 10.
[3] Id. Nos. 43, 213.
[4] Id. No. 69.   [5] Id. No. 575.   [6] Id. No. 93.

Lack of leisure was a frequent excuse for bad writing. Some
of the letters give us glimpses of further conditions which made
letter-writing difficult; while others simply explain the circumstances which influenced the writers while they were at work.
The writer's words sometimes conjure up a vision for us, so that
we see the messenger outside eager to set off, while within the
letter is hurriedly written, then dried by shaking ashes over it,
and quickly sealed.[1] As a contrast to such hasty and urgent
composition, we may notice the amusing candour of a man who
wrote to John Paston, and ended his letter by saying "I had
little to do, when I scribbled this letter."[2] Details are added
at times giving us information as to the time of day the letter
was written. More than one letter was finished by candle light.[3]
Henry Windsor took advantage of a quiet afternoon on Whit
Sunday to compose his letter, and concluded by remarking that
it was written "in his sleeping time."[4] Elizabeth Stonor was
similarly deprived of sleep in order that she might write to her
husband. "No more unto you at this time," she says, and
naïvely continues, "Written at Stonor, when I would fain have
slept, the morrow after Ladyday, in the morning."[5] Sir John
Paston, on the other hand, sat up late into the night writing
to his brother, but consoles himself by the reflection that he
"will sleep an hour longer tomorrow, because I wrote so long
and late tonight."[6] But few end more delightfully than Thomas
Betson's letter to his child-sweetheart, which he tells her was
written:

At great Calais, on this side of the sea, the first day of June, [1476]
when every man was gone to his dinner, and the clock smote noon.
And all our household cried after me, and bade me "Come down;
Come down to dinner at once!," and what answer I gave them, ye
know it of old.[7]

The medieval writer did not begin his letter in modern fashion,
with an address at the head of the page followed by the day of
the month or year. He started to write at the top of the sheet,
and got to work at once with his preliminary salutation. This
has a certain formality and deference about it, which reflects
the manners of the day. "Right worshipful sir, I recommend

[1] P.L. Nos. 315, 525.   [2] Id. No. 269.   [3] Id. Nos. 71, 369.
[4] Id. No. 283. Cf. Hamlet, Act I, scene v.   [5] S.L. No. 237.
[6] P.L. No. 704.   [7] S.L. No. 166.

me to you," is a common opening phrase used by many of John Paston's correspondents. Inferiors were more deferential, and began "Right worshipful and my especial good master, I recommend me unto your good mastership." Then came the body of the letter, which set forth all the writer wished to say. There was no trouble taken to break it up into paragraphs. From start to finish, the letter usually goes straight on. Only at the end was there any indication of the place or date of composition.

A brief examination of the methods then used for dating letters shows that few people knew the exact year according to the Christian chronology. Only ecclesiastics were in the habit of dating their letters by reference to this method. Ordinary folk were inclined to reckon by other means. Most of these letters, however, bear upon them no indication of the exact year in which they were written.[1] If any reckoning in years is made at all, it is usually in terms of the King's reign. Sir John Fastolf's letters are for the most part very carefully dated by this means, and conclude for example with "Written at London, 27 day of May in the 28th year of King Henry VI."[2] Few people troubled to be so exact as this, and many letters are dated by reference to the day and month only, just as people often do now. We find many letters conclude "Written at Hellesdon the 20th day of May" or "Written the 5th day of March." We have still to notice that the majority of letters were dated by reference to Sundays, Festivals, and Saints' Days. The Church had brought these into such prominence that everyone knew what day was meant if it was described as Pulver Wednesday,[3] or Crouchmas Day[4] or the Utas day of Peter and Paul.[5] Letters written on days that did not happen to coincide with an important day in the Church Calendar, were easily identified by reference to a past, or a coming feast. When Margaret Paston wrote a letter six days before S. Catherine's day, she dated it " the Thursday next before S. Catherine's day."[6]

---

[1] E.g. P.L. Nos. 400–500 only give four cases.
[2] P.L. No. 98. Cf. Nos. 115, 152, 154.
[3] Id. No. 197. Pulver Wednesday or Ash Wednesday.
[4] Id. No. 472. Crouchmas Day, or the Invention of the Cross, 3rd May.
[5] Id. No. 189. The utas or octave day is the eighth day of the Feast, i.e. 6th July.
[6] Id. No. 705.

Hence we get such dates as "the Tuesday next after the Conversion [of] S. Paul," "the Monday after Twelfth Day," or "Written the Saturday, late at night, next after Candlemas Day."[1]

We have now seen something of the conditions under which the medieval letter was written; how it was often prepared in a rough draft, or written from dictation by a secretary; how the uncertainty of messengers, or lack of time, or want of skill accounted for bad writing, and how the letter began with a ceremonial flourish and concluded with, or without, one of several methods of indicating the date. We have now to examine the evidence offered by the *Paston Letters* as to how the letter reached its destination, what dangers and delays it met with on the road, and how these were guarded against. Finally, it will be interesting to see what happened to letters after their mission was accomplished.

The absence of any official postal service gave letters an importance, and an air of romance, which more modern methods have destroyed. At the same time, such conditions made it difficult to keep up a very regular correspondence. People apparently had to be prepared to send off one of their retainers as post-boy, or to rely on the good offices of a friend, or to entrust their letters to the common carrier, or to a passing traveller. All these methods had obvious drawbacks, and only too often people must have found it impossible to get a messenger to go to the required place at the desired moment. When John Paston's younger son was travelling in the train of the Duke of Norfolk, he wrote to his brother from Newcastle, but was forced to admit, "I sent no letter to my father, ever since I departed from you, for I could get no man to London."[2] He found himself in similar difficulties the next year, when he was in Wales.[3] Even at a time when Margaret Paston was in great anxiety about her husband's return to Norfolk, she was unable to get a suitable messenger for three weeks. She writes "I could get no messenger to London, unless I would have sent by the Sheriff's men; but I knew neither their master nor them, nor whether they were well-willing to you or not."[4]

[1] *P.L.* Nos. 185, 567, 569.   [2] *Id.* No. 464.
[3] *Id.* No. 486.   [4] *Id.* No. 134.

Messengers must usually have been more plentiful than this, although the sender had to be prepared to take certain risks. The letters were entrusted to a bewildering variety of men: clerks, servants, carriers, "a man of S. Michael's parish," "T. Holler's son"; in short, anyone who would take them. Most of the bearers of letters are complete strangers to us. They are mentioned once, perhaps by name, or merely as the bearer or messenger, and we hear no more of them. Probably many of them were retainers, or servants, of the Pastons and their friends, and so were known to be trustworthy.[1] The ordinary farm servant and the mass of people had few opportunities of sending letters, even had they been able to read and write. The great world beyond their little village could have meant little to them, and we may notice how this lack of ability to communicate with others was one of the strongest factors in their isolation. The only part played by the poor was to carry the letters of their masters. At certain times of the year there were always messengers in plenty. England was still a land of great fairs, to which people came from far and near. After, and during these fairs, the roads were busy with men going to and fro, and many of these acted as messengers, and would leave letters at places as they passed. Sir John Paston complained of lack of news about the time of the great Bartholomew Fair at Smithfield, for, as he said, "I marvel that you sent never writing to me since you departed. I heard never since that time any word out of Norfolk. You might at Bartholomew Fair have had messengers enough to London."[2]

Comments in the letters themselves help us to appreciate the risk involved in thus employing messengers promiscuously. In some cases, the writer vouches for the messenger, as Margaret Paston does in a postscript, "If it please you to send anything by the bearer hereof, he is trusty enough."[3] The Earl of Oxford, in writing to a lady, adds, "You shall give credence to the bringer of this letter."[4] This was very necessary if the bearer was a stranger, for oftentimes he was given verbal messages to

---

[1] An analysis of 74 cases in which any mention is made of the messenger gives the following results: 44 messengers are mentioned by name; 16 as the retainers of known folk, and 14 by vague references such as "the bearer," "the next messenger," etc.

[2] *P.L.* No. 675. [3] *Id.* No. 530. [4] *Id.* No. 669.

deliver, as well as his letter. He was thus able to supplement
any news the letter contained. "Pecock shall tell you by mouth
of more things than I may write to you at this time,"[1] says
Margaret Paston at the end of a letter. Sir John Paston concludes a letter hastily by adding, "Other things Bachelor Walter,
bearer hereof, shall inform you."[2] His brother goes farther
and says, "The bearer hereof can tell you tidings such as be
true for very certain."[3]

These bearers of letters were very welcome, for in those days
London must have seemed very far from Norfolk, and a letter
from the absent husband, or son, a very reassuring thing. "Send
an answer soon," or "by the next messenger," is a frequent
cry in these letters. The writers often lost no time, but wrote
while the bearer was still in the town, so that the letter might
be delivered on his return home. Sir John Paston warns his
father that if he will send an answer, "the messenger will tarry
at London a day or two, and not more."[4] We have already
seen how one letter had to be sent off in all its crudity because
an unexpected messenger was leaving; and how another was
written while the messenger was waiting on horseback outside.[5]
It was often essential not to let slip a chance of getting a letter
taken, so that some letters were answered within an hour of
their receipt,[6] or the messenger waited overnight for an answer
to be penned before he returned.[7]

Unfortunately there are few records of the actual payment
made to any messenger for his trouble.[8] From the scanty
references scattered about the *Paston Letters*, it seems as if
messengers were often paid before setting out. This is confirmed
by various payments noted down in Lord Howard's Account
Books, wherein the sum paid and the service to be performed
are both stated. We read of 12d. being paid "to Henbury is
man to bere lettres to London."[9] The price of a messenger from
Stoke [Essex] to London is given as 4d. in one entry, although
a letter sent the same distance by the common carrier is taken
for 2d.[10] A King's Messenger obviously expected to be rewarded

[1] *P.L.* No. 499.   [2] *Id.* No. 648.   [3] *Id.* No. 670. Cf. Nos. 442, 567.
[4] *Id.* No. LXII.   [5] *Id.* Nos. 315, 575.   [6] *Id.* Nos. 100, 772.
[7] *Id.* No. 367   [8] Cf. Rogers, *Prices*, IV. p. 712.
[9] *Howard*, II. p. 62, but cf. *P.L.* No. 398.   [10] *Id.* pp. 165, 180.

handsomely for his pains, and one of these men received 6s. 8d. for bearing a message to Lord Howard from the King.[1]

It is probable that some letters went astray. Sometimes, the casual messenger must have felt considerable temptation not to deliver a letter, especially if it meant going out of his way. Besides this, in many cases, letters were not actually delivered to the individuals themselves, but only left for them at a friend's house, or at an inn they frequented, and were given to them when occasion served.[2] Sometimes a letter would arrive too late to catch the recipient before he left for another town, and then it had to wait until he returned, unless a lucky chance produced a messenger who would take it on.[3]

Despite this, there are few references to missing letters in this correspondence. Now and again there is some question as to whether a letter has been received or not, or else a definite statement that an expected letter has not come. Even such complaints are not frequent, though one or two interesting examples may be quoted. John Paston apologises to his father for leaving him so long without news, because he says, "God help me, I sent you a letter to London anon after Candlemas, by a man of my Lord's; and he forgot to deliver it to you, and so he brought to me the letter again."[4] On another occasion, the Pastons were expecting to hear from Walter at Oxford, so that they might know on what day he would be made a B.A. No news came, and, when they complained, Walter was able to explain the long silence. The original letter asking Walter to send word of the exact day was sent by the hand of a certain Master Brown. Unfortunately:

Master Brown had that same time much money in a bag, so that he durst not bring it with him, and that same letter was in that same bag. He forgot to take out the letter, and he sent all [the contents] together by London, so that it was the next day after I was made Bachelor before the letter came, and so the fault was not in me.[5]

Not all cases of missing letters were so easily cleared up. Margaret Paston had to complain once, "As for the letters that Tom Holler's son should have brought me, I see neither him

[1] *Howard*, II. p. 70. [2] *P.L.* Nos. 703, 753, 772, 790, 817.
[3] *Id.* No. 392, and see No. LXII. [4] *Id.* No. 486. [5] *Id.* No. 831.

nor the letters"[1]; while, on another occasion, an apprentice returning to his master's shop in London failed to deliver the letters entrusted to him.[2]

Writers also took pains to make sure their letters were not opened and read en route. In those days when any unguarded reference to royalty or to the King's ministers might have meant the gravest penalties, men had to be as sure as possible that their letters were not tampered with. Letters were carefully folded, and sealed, before being despatched. One letter from Margaret Paston to her husband was folded and marked in such a way that any attempt to open it before John Paston received it would have been noticeable.[3] Sir John Paston writes to his brother on another occasion, "I would not that [the] letter were seen [by] some folks. Wherefore I pray you take good heed how that letter comes to your hands, whole, or broken."[4] His suspicions are obvious when he concludes another letter with the words "Item, look that you take heed that the letter was not broken before it came to your hands etc."[5]

The same fear of espionage and incrimination is shown by numerous pleas made to the recipients of letters to destroy or burn them, once they were read. An interesting device was adopted by one of John Paston's correspondents. The whole of the confidential part of his letter was written in a postscript, and was unsigned, concluding, "I write to you thus, that you may cut away this lower part of this letter."[6] "I pray you burn this letter when you have read it," writes one man; and no doubt this was the wish of many. People were still a little uneasy of entrusting their secrets to paper, and felt that only when the letters were burnt, or otherwise destroyed, would they be safe. When Elizabeth Clere told her cousin of the cruel treatment his sister was receiving, she was careful to add "Cousin, I pray you burn this letter, that [neither] your men nor any other man see it, for if my cousin your mother knew that I had sent you this letter, she would never love me."[7] Sir John Paston was equally cautious when he wrote his first love letter

---

[1] *P.L.* No. 716.   [2] *Id.* No. 523.   [3] *Id.* No. 369 note.
[4] *Id.* No. 703.   [5] *Id.* No. 656.
[6] *Id.* No. xxvi, and cf. *S.L.* No. 65, "Moreover Sir I write apart that it may be cut away."   [7] *P.L.* No. 71.

to Anne Haute. "When you have read this letter," he wrote, "I pray you burn it, or keep it secret to yourself, as my faithful trust is in you."[1]

The Pastons, fortunately, had a family tradition which led them to ignore their own advice, and to keep all their letters. When the originals went to people who were not members of the family, they sometimes preserved even the rough drafts, so that they might have a record.[2] Even so careless a man as Sir John Paston had learnt this lesson in his turn, as no doubt his grandmother Agnes had previously learnt it from her husband the Justice. This great collection of letters is evidence enough of the assiduity with which they gathered up and treasured every written scrap of paper.[3] Margaret reminded Sir John of this family tradition, shortly after his father's death:

> Always I advise you to beware that you keep wisely your writings that be of charge, that [they] come not in their hands that may hurt you hereafter. Your father, whom God assoil, in his troubled season set more by his writings and evidences than he did by any of his moveable goods. Remember that if they were had from you, you could never get any more such as they be.[4]

Later on, we see how this tradition was still surviving in a younger son. When Walter wrote to Sir John from Oxford, he told his brother that not only could he produce the last letter he had received from home, but also "all the letters that you sent me since I came to Oxford,"[5]—a period of five or six years!

Finally, a short account must be given of the actual paper on which the letters were written. The large extent of this correspondence gives us ample material for an examination of fifteenth century writing paper. This varied very much. Some of it is of a fine texture, with a fairly smooth surface, while some sheets are coarse and thick. The paper is tough and strong for the most part, and is all hand-made. In the light of present evidence, it seems probable that all the paper used in England until the close of the fifteenth century was of foreign manufacture. The earliest recorded English paper is that used by Wynkyn de Worde in 1495. He printed an edition of Bar-

---

1 *P.L.* No. 588.   2 See above, p. 115.
3 Cf. *S.L.* Intro. p. xl, in which Mr Kingsford notes a similar characteristic of the Stonors.
4 *P.L.* No. 560.   5 *Id.* No. 831.

tholomew's *De Proprietatibus Rerum*, and in the proem we read of:

> John Tate the yonger,...
> Which late hath in Englond doo make this paper thynne,
> That now, in our Englyssh, this boke is prynted inne.[1]

John Tate the younger, son of a Lord Mayor of London, is said to have erected a paper mill at Hertford about 1494. This would agree with the above statement of Wynkyn de Worde. There is no doubt that a mill was erected about this time; for in 1498, when Henry VII was staying at Hertford Castle, he visited the mill; and an entry in his accounts records that he paid 16s. 8d. "for a rewarde geven at the paper Mylne."[2]

The *Paston Letters* are written on paper made in France or in North Italy. South-east France was well known throughout the fourteenth and fifteenth centuries for its paper making; and the watermarks on the sheets of paper used by the Pastons and their correspondents leave no doubt as to its foreign origin. M. Charles Briquet's great work on watermarks reproduces 16,112 actual specimens; and, from references given to the books and documents in which these occur, there is no doubt as to their date.[3] Most of the watermarks to be found in the *Paston Letters* may be traced by this means, and are seen to be the marks of widely used paper. The bull's head, for example, with its many minor variations, is a common papermark in the sheets of this correspondence. This watermark, says M. Briquet, "est le plus abondant de tous les filigranes pour la période 14°–16° siècle." Others are almost equally common. Then, when we examine any contemporary English documents of which the exact date is known, we find the paper bears similar watermarks to those on the *Paston Letters*. "Bishop Alnwick's Visitations of Monasteries, circa 1437–1446" for example, contains such watermarks as an ox's head, a pair of scales, a fleur de lys, or a slung hunting horn, and all of these varieties occur among the Paston papers.[4] No doubt the Pastons, their friends, and the Bishop's secretary

---

[1] Fenn, I. p. xx.
[2] *Excerpta Historica*, ed. Bentley, S., 1831, p. 117.
[3] *Les Filigranes: Dictionnaire historique des marques du papier dès leur apparition vers 1282 jusqu'en 1600*, Briquet, C. M., Paris, 1907, 4 vols.
[4] *Visitations of Religious Houses in the Diocese of Lincoln*, ed. A. Hamilton Thompson, II. pp. xiii–xiv.

bought their paper in the towns, which in turn bought it from overseas.

The sheets of paper on which the letters were written varied a little in size, but most of the sheets are from 10 to 12 inches wide. A whole sheet was from 16 to 18 inches long, so that an uncut sheet presented a very formidable area for an unpractised writer to have to fill. This difficulty was avoided by the simple device of cutting off the sheet at any place they wished, when they had written enough. Thus some letters take up a whole sheet,[1] and contain a great deal of matter; while others are only a few lines long, and the width of the paper makes these look even shorter than they are.[2] Finally, the letters were folded into small oblong packets, about 3 or 4 inches long, and 2 or 3 inches wide, and fastened by passing a thread, or thin strip of paper through the folded thicknesses. Then the ends of the threads or paper were sealed, and the address added. The superscriptions were usually straightforward, though the bearer was often adjured to make haste. "To my right worshipful husband, John Paston, be this delivered in haste,"[3] is a common form. Others of more interest are addressed, "To John Paston, and to none other,"[4] "To Thomas Green, good man of the George by Paul's Wharf, or to his wife, to send to Sir John Paston, wheresoever he be, at Calais, London, or other places,"[5] and best of all Margery Brews' inscription, "Unto my right well-beloved Valentine, John Paston, Squire, be this bill delivered, etc."[6] But this, we may suppose, was delivered by a confidential messenger.

[1] E.g. P.L. No. 99 (11¼″ × 16½″), No. 637 (11½″ × 17½″); cf. Rogers, *Prices*, IV. p. 592.
[2] E.g. Id. No. 212 (12″ × 4″), No. 292 (10½″ × 4″). [3] Id. No. 260.
[4] Id. No. 625. [5] Id. No. 790. [6] Id. No. 783.

CHAPTER X

ROADS AND BRIDGES

THERE can be little doubt that the general condition of the roads in the fifteenth century was deplorable. The old Roman roads had been so magnificently constructed that, even as late as this, they were in use, although much decayed. Many new roads had been made, while a vast net-work of smaller roads had grown up, joining hamlets to towns, and serving the needs of an agricultural countryside. But these roads had been built without much of the care the Romans had lavished on their work, and must always have been inferior to those triumphs of engineering. Indeed, we shall not be far wrong if we imagine many of the so-called roads of the Middle Ages as little better than tracks or bridle-paths linking up the various manors and villages one with another, and also providing a means of passage to the larger roads which went from town to town. Many of these new roads most probably had their origin in the tracks made by men moving across country from one ford to another, or driving their pack-horses across open spaces. It is necessary to forget all modern conceptions of roads which run for the most part fenced in on either side by hedges; for the medieval highway was in fact little more than the legal right of way from one place to another.

Between market towns it was recognised that a clear safe road was necessary, and in 1285 the Statute of Winchester ordered:

That highways leading from one market town to another shall be enlarged, whereas bushes, woods, or dykes be, so that there be neither dyke nor bush whereby a man may lurk to do hurt, within 200 feet of the one side, and 200 feet on the other side of the way.[1]

If this statute had been obeyed, the traveller on such roads would have had no fear of losing his way, but there were many miles of road in England which never benefited from this act.

[1] 13 Ed. I, § ii, c. 5.

In fact, there is abundant evidence to show this law was never well kept at all,[1] and that it affords only another instance of the "almost incredible gulfs which are frequently to be found between fourteenth century theory and practice." Too often the road must have been much the same as is described in Trevisa's translation of Bartholomew, where

strange men ofte erre and go out of the waye: and take uncerten waye, and the waye that is unknowe, tofore the waye that is knowen. ...Therfore ben ofte knottes made on trees and in bushes, in bowes and in braunches of trees: in token and marke of the highe waye, to showe the certen and sure waye to wayfaring men.[2]

Yet, if the care of Parliament and the constant passage of travellers had ensured the way being "certen and sure," it by no means follows that the journey was simple and comfortable. John Paston must often have ridden out from Norwich on his way to London; and, on such journeys, once he had passed the city gates, he must soon have found himself riding along lanes, and crossing meadows, following a road which varied with the season, but which never could have been much better than a present-day country lane. It so happens that as late as 1599, after several Acts for the reparation of the roads had been passed, John Kemp passed along the same way John Paston often used. Kemp describes the road he danced along as "this foule way [in which] I could find no ease, the lane being full of holes, sometimes I skipt up to the waist."[3] Faulty initial construction, and very uncertain and ineffectual repair, made travelling very difficult in the winter. The roads were much like an up-country trail at the present time in Alberta, or in the Great North West, where the traveller "breaks trail" as he goes along, avoiding the worst places by the simple expedient of taking a wide sweep round them.

Unfortunately none of the contemporary records of travel in England seem to concern themselves with the condition of the roads. Various men have recorded with scrupulous care their expenses at every stage of their journey, and where they baited, dined, or slept; but no one has left any note for us concerning the ease or difficulty of travel.[4] Indeed, it seems clear from the

---

[1] E.g. 4 Hist. MSS. p. 431b. [2] Trevisa, lib. VII. c. 20.
[3] Wilde, p. 362.
[4] E.g. Arch. xxv. pp. 411 ff. The Lestrange Household Accounts.

silence of the *Paston Letters*, that the state of affairs revealed
by contemporary records was so widespread that it was regarded
as inevitable and unworthy of comment. Throughout the
Paston Letters, only one reference to the state of the roads has
been noticed.[1] The Pastons come and go about their business
in Norfolk, or further afield to London or up to Yorkshire,
seemingly oblivious of the roads. If we had only these *Letters*
to go by, we might be inclined to agree with a great authority
that "the means of communication were fairly good, and the
principal roads, even in winter, were kept in decent repair."[2]

But there is, in fact, a mass of evidence to contradict this
optimistic view. John Wyclif wrote in one of his tracts late in
the fourteenth century, "We speken over litel for to visite and
offre to pore men, and making briges and causeis where men and
bestis and catel perischen ofte."[3] If we turn from this plain
statement as mere rhetoric to actual contemporary legal documents, the result is the same. A recent volume, published by
the Selden Society, entitled *Public Works in Medieval Law*, gives
us an interesting picture of the roads at the end of the fourteenth
century. An examination of the entries for the single county
of Berkshire shows that in many cases the roads had been allowed
to fall into disrepair, and were dangerous. A typical entry runs:

Juratores [of Wantynge] presentant quod est quedam regia via
ducens de villa de Faryndon usque Ratkotebrigge que est confracta
profunda et lutosa pro defectu reparationis sic quod homines cum
equis et carectis suis ibidem absque magno periculo transire ne-
quiunt.[4]

In other cases it is represented that the roads are out of repair,
covered with water and miry, to the danger of passengers, both
in winter and summer.[5] The jurors of Ock declare that "the
king's highway is broken, hollow and ruinous,...and is dangerous in winter,"[6] while other roads are declared to be ruinous
and flooded.[7] Such was the state of the roads in one county
during a single year, and we can easily imagine the weary

---

[1] *P.L.* No. 787. "The causey ere ye can come to Bokenham Ferry is so
overflown that there is no man that may scarcely pass it, though he be
right well horsed; which is no meet way for you to pass over, God defend
it."

[2] Rogers, *Work*, p. 135.   [3] Arnold, III. p. 283.   [4] *Public Works*, p. 4.
[5] *Id.* p. 9.   [6] *Id.* p. 13.   [7] *Id.* p. 19.

traveller hoping to reach Abingdon by nightfall. He hastens on as the dusk is falling, only to find himself on the causey leading from Marcham scarcely able to move forward without grave risk, because of the "broken, hollow, and ruinous condition" of the ground beneath his feet.[1] In the same way the road from Abingdon to Dorchester

over the water of the Thames by the places of Burford and Culhamford ...was lately by the Increase of Water so much surrounded, that no one could have passed there, nor make any such Carriage there without Danger of losing their Lives, Goods, Chattels, and Merchandises.[2]

It is characteristic of the way in which repairs were done, and then no further care taken, to observe that, although this road was mended in 1408, by the year 1421 it had been allowed to get into a thoroughly bad state again, and needed a new statute to arrange for its further repair. The difficulty of moving from one place to another was greatly increased by this carelessness, even if the unavoidable difficulties in themselves were not sufficient. Dr Wylie's untiring industry has enabled us to get a bird's-eye view of the state of the roads in 1406.[3]

"The year," he says, "had been remarkable for floods and rains of exceptional severity." The result was that in 1406 along the Thames, "the dykes and causeways were broken between London and Greenwich; the bridges were in danger at Wallingford, Staines, Windsor, Weybridge, Kingston, and Maidenhead; the Lea marshes were under water; the king's road was broken up between Stratford and Bow; 800 ac. of corn land were flooded, and £2000 worth of enclosures belonging to the Abbess of Barking were swept away. The swollen Severn had well nigh wrecked the bridges of Montford and Bridgenorth, and the lands about Torkington, Littleton and Rockhampton, were all under flood. At York, the Fossbridge was in ruins and the Ouse bridge weakened. The bridge over the Wharfe at Tadcaster was damaged and the causeway thence to Boroughbridge destroyed. So also were the bridges over the Eamont and the Lowther on the north western roads passing by Penrith to Carlisle. The Wye was in flood between Bradwardine and Whitney, and the cartway between Whitney Bridge and Hereford was nearly swept away. Arundel, Pulborough, Lewes and the Kentish marshes from Rye to Blackwose (or Blackooze) above Hythe, all suffered again. There were floods in the Waveney at Beccles; the bridge over the Nene at Thrapston was broken, and that over the Wensum at Attlebridge could no longer bear the great traffic passing to and from the worsted

[1] *Public Works*, p. 13.   [2] 9 Hy V, § 2, c. 11.
[3] 3 Hy IV, Wylie, II. pp. 470-1.

seld at Norwich, and miles of country were drowned in the flats of Holderness. The banks of the Humber were swamped from Hessel to the Derwent; and, in the Isle of Ely around Cambridge in the Marshland between Lynn and Wisbeach, and in the Fen country from Holland-bridge to Donnington, roads, bridges, and causeways were wrecked and washed away. The sheriffs posted their outriders requesting immediate contributions from abbots, priors, and landowners, and indulgences were freely offered by the Bishops to all who helped in making good the damage.

Nor was the condition of affairs in towns much better. The roads leading to the City of London were so bad in the middle of the fourteenth century that

all the folks who bring victuals and wares by carts and horses to the City do make grievous complaint that they incur great damage, and are oftentimes in peril of losing what they bring, and sometimes do lose it, because the roads without the City gates are so torn up, and the pavement so broken, as may be seen by all persons on view thereof.[1]

Between the City and Westminster roads were equally bad, although efforts had been made from time to time to repair them.[2] Even as late as 1482 there is an indictment against the Bishop of Norwich

for not repairing the highway in the parish of S. Martin in the Fields lying between his inn and the inn of the Bishop of Durham, which way is so overflowed with water that the lords both spiritual and temporal, the King's justices...and all persons journeying by that way to Westminster to administer and observe the laws...are often hindered.[3]

In the second half of the fifteenth century many towns in England tried to get their streets into a better state by repairing them,[4] and Gloucester, Canterbury, Taunton, Winchester and Bristol all obtained permission from Parliament to compel every occupier of a house abutting on a main street to "make as ofte as it shal be nede hereafter, sufficient pavement at their owne costes and charges from their said Burgagiez, Meses, and Tenementes, and as farre as it extendith to the myddes of the Strete."[5] Incidentally the preambles to these acts reveal the

[1] *Memorials*, p. 291.
[2] *Syllabus of Fœdera*, Hardy, T. D., I. pp. 350, 377, II. p. 597.
[3] *Hist. Shrewsbury*, Owen, H. and Blakeway, J., I. p. 279.
[4] *Rot. Par.* VI. pp. 49, 177, 179, 180, 333, 390–1.
[5] *Id.* VI. p. 49 a.

condition of the streets. At Winchester the petition confesses
that

of late, and in dyverse tymes past, dyverse and many of the Kinges
Subgetts, as well by day as by nyght there rydyng, goyng, and
travelyng, hath taken and susteyned greate hurtes and harmes
within the seid Citee...for lakke of due, convenient and convenable
Pavyng of the high Streetes of the same Citee, and boundes of the
same; which said Streetes, by water fallyng out of Gutters, raveyn
of water there being many tymes, be holed and founded, to the grete
unease of all the Kinges Subgetts.[1]

But the traveller had not only the "broken, pitted and hol-
lowed" streets themselves to trouble him, but had also to
make his way as best he could through garbage and filth of all
kinds that was thrown out upon the highway. The Hundred
and Leet Rolls for this century are full of examples of fines for
this offence. The Norwich Leet Rolls for 1390–1 furnish us
with the following cases:

Isabella Lucas has and maintains a foul gutter running from her
messuage into the King's highway, to the nuisance etc.... Fined 6d.
Wm Gerard has had a horse lying for a long time in the King's
highway, near the church of S. Michael de Colegate to the abominable
offence and poisoning [of the air].   Fined 12d.
The Churchwardens of S. Martyns at the Bale, for noyeing the
King's highway with muck and compost.   Fined 3d.[2]

The Hundred Court of Hythe, in the same way, had to deal
year by year with men who brought the town into "a state of
utter filth and squalor." One such man caused the highway to
be "almost stinking and a nusiance"; another obstructed "the
King's highway opposite his kitchen with the dung of his cows";
while a third had "ploughs in the King's highway, to the
nusiance of the people."[3] At Lynn in 1424–5 a bye-law was
made forbidding butchers to slaughter their animals in the
street. Such a law adds a vivid trait to our conception of a
medieval street. One can imagine the overhanging houses,
partially shutting out light and air, and there in a dark corner,
by his open shop, the butcher at his slaughtering. The paved
way must have become slippery with blood and offal, some of

[1] R.P. VI. p. 333 b.
[2] Leet Jurisdiction in Norwich [S.S.], Hudson, W., pp. 72, 75, 87, and cf.
pp. 69, 76; Norwich Records, II. p. 88 for sixteenth century.
[3] 4 Hist. MSS. pp. 431 b, 432 a, 433 b.

which might run away into the kennels, but much of which soaked into the cracks of the broken pavement, and there stagnated.[1]

The Coventry Leet Book gives us a detailed account of how this state of things was combated by the municipal authorities. First they ordered "that every man repaire his pament afore his tenementes betwyxt this and the next leet upon the payne of 3/4."[2] Evidently this was not very successful; the amateur efforts of the citizens would not stand the wear and tear of the traffic. Consequently after a few years it was agreed that the Mayor was "to provide paviors to pave streets, and wages to be raised by distraint."[3] Even when this was done, it was difficult to keep the new paving clean and decent. Again and again ordinances were made against leaving refuse in the streets, and it was ordered "that euery person euery Seturday fro hensfurth for euer let swepe the stretes before their groundes. And if any person fayle any Seturday in that partie, he to lose 2d. furthwith to be paide and gadered be the comien serjant."[4] Contemporary records disclose a similar state of affairs in many other towns.[5]

The traveller's troubles arising from the state of the roads were increased by the irresponsible fashion in which men dug up the highway to suit their own convenience, without any regard to possible dangers arising from their action. For example the jurors of Nottingham present "Robert Melors for gettyng clay, holyng the hye wey at the Wodgate, thoro the which the hye wey shall be parles [dangerous] both for man and beste,"[6] and other cases might be quoted from Manchester and Coventry. At Aylesbury a pit was dug in the highway, of such a size that an unfortunate itinerant glove seller fell into it and was drowned. The local miller who dug the pit was acquitted by the jury, who said there was nowhere else he could get the clay he needed.[7]

[1] Hillen, I. p. 169.	[2] Cov. Leet, p. 58.	[3] Id. p. 199.
[4] Id. pp. 23, 43, 170, 217, 425, 587, etc.; cf. Sandwich, Boys, II. p. 674.
[5] E.g. Chester, Morris, R. H., pp. 260–273; Nottingham, III. p. 357, IV. pp. 161–2.
[6] Nottingham, III. p. 340.
[7] Town Life, II. p. 31. See also The Manor and Manorial Records, Hone, N. J., p. 142. Court Rolls of Hales, Intro. pp. lxxxix, cxi, cxviii, and II. 564.

A brief consideration of the system of road maintenance reveals its essential weakness. The feudal idea of delegating power and responsibility had thrown the care of the King's highway principally upon the lords of the manor, or upon the township. Supervision was exercised by the Justices of the Peace, the Sheriff at his turn, or the Judges of the King's Bench, who had laid before them presentments concerning roads and bridges which had been allowed to fall into disrepair.[1] The documents printed in *Public Works in Medieval Law* show how frequently a higher authority was necessary; but they also reveal a very interesting example of how the law was evaded by the local agents of great lords. For many years, a certain stretch of road near Colchester had been in a bad state of repair. It was found on enquiry that this was partially due to the fact that the ditch alongside the road was not cleaned out, and consequently overflowed and flooded the road. This ditch was within a manor of the Abbot of Westminster; and, whenever any attempt was made to get an order against him to clean the ditch, his agents and steward refused to let the matter be discussed in the leet courts. This had gone on for 30 years, and all that time the Abbot was neglecting his duty, to the ruin of the neighbouring highway.[2]

With the gradual decline of the manorial system during the fifteenth century, there was a corresponding decline in the care of roads and bridges. The shortage of labour after 1381, and the new system of stock and land leases played their part so thoroughly that there can be little doubt that the serious lack of labour at the disposal of the Lord of the Manor compelled him to do as little as possible to the roads. This lack of labour was emphasised by a lack of money. Every penny that could be got was needed for the wars in France. In addition, the declining power of the monasteries contributed to the tendency to neglect the roads. In their palmy days, the monks viewed the state of the roads with keen interest; because, as they grew richer by the gifts of the faithful, it is clear that their lands became more and more widely dispersed. Consequently they were forced to take a very active part in the upkeep of the roads, if they wished to make full use of their properties. But

[1] *Public Works*, p. xxvii.   [2] *Id.* p. 67.

the fifteenth century saw the condition of the regular clergy steadily deteriorating, so that their care and administration of their properties became weaker and weaker. It is clear that this combination of circumstances required continuous supervision, and a definite central policy to check gradual disintegration. Unfortunately, the bitter faction quarrels which led up to and accompanied the Wars of the Roses gave little time for adequate central control. Hence the lawless and unquiet state of the whole countryside must have told heavily against any effort to ensure adequate attention being paid to the roads. As a result of all this, by the time of Henry VIII it was reported:

Many common...ways in Kent be so deep and noyous, by wearing and course of water, and other occasions, that people cannot have their carriages, or passages by horses upon, or by the same, but to their great pains, peril and jeopardy.[1]

A few years later in 1530 a statute was enacted empowering Justices of the Peace to enquire into "all manner of annoyances of bridges broken in the highways, and to make such process... for the reparation of the same against such as owen to be charged."[2] This, however, was not sufficient, and in 1555 the first General Highways Act was passed, "for amending highways ...now both very noisome and tedious to travel in, and dangerous to all passengers and carriages."[3]

Throughout the middle ages the evil of bad roads was so widespread that it was a recognised charitable deed to leave money for their repair.[4] Many fifteenth century wills leave money for the "repair of bridges and highways, and other pious and charitable uses." The frequency and terms of these bequests show very clearly how well-known and urgent was the need; for it was surely bitter experience which prompted these folk to describe roads as "perilous highways," or as "noyous and jeoperdes weyes"; and there seems to be more than a touch of reminiscent feeling in one testator's description of a road as "foule and feeble."[5] Citizens of London were constantly leaving money for this purpose. Sometimes their directions are merely general, but very often their knowledge of the condition of some

[1] Stat. Realm, 14–15 Hy VIII, c. vi.   [2] Id. 23 Hy VIII, c. v.
[3] Id. 2 & 3 Phil. and Mary, c. viii.
[4] See passim, North Country Wills, Early Wills, Test. Ebor. i–iv. etc.
[5] London Wills, ii. pp. 422, 548, 626, etc.

particular highway causes them to be specific. John Plot, for example, left £5 "to be yspendyth betwene London and Ware, of fowle ways...there most nede ys."[1] In Norfolk too, Margaret Paston did not forget to leave five shillings for "the reparation of the highway in Woollerton."[2]

Besides such difficulties as arose from the state of the roads, the traveller was also sometimes in very real danger of being met or waylaid by his private enemies, by bands of armed men who scoured the countryside, or by thieves and cut-throats who took full advantage of the wild and unsettled days in which they lived. Contemporary records depict the greater part of England as suffering under almost incredible lawlessness and terrorism. This state of affairs will be illustrated at length in another chapter, but a few extracts from the *Paston Letters* will mirror what was happening. In 1424, so important and influential a man as William Paston, a sergeant at law and well known throughout Norfolk, was in so "great and intolerable dread and fear of an enemy of his that he durst not...go nor ride about such occupation as he is used [to do]."[3] In 1452 information was laid against

a great multitude of misruled people...sometime six, sometime twelve, sometime thirty or more, armed with cuirasses and helmets, with bows, arrows, spears, and bills, and override the country and oppress the people, and do many horrible and abominable deeds like to be the destruction of the shire of Norfolk.[4]

And again in 1461 John Paston the youngest writes, "There is...made [a] great gathering of people, and hiring of harness, and it is well understood that they go not towards the King, but rather the contrary, and in order to rob."[5]

Amid such wild and troublous happenings the ordinary peasants and townsfolk had to live and carry on their varied occupations, for the most part bearing the most unjust treatment with patience, and only under great provocation were they roused to passion and to "waxing wild." Murderers, robbers and lawless gangs rode to and fro, terrorising wherever they went, and ever adding fuel to the smouldering unrest, which the King and his advisers seemed powerless to check. More

[1] *London Wills*, II. pp. 433, 467, 487, 499, 514, 534, etc.
[2] *P.L.* III. p. 470.   [3] *Id.* No. 4, and see p. 186.
[4] *Id.* No. 179.   [5] *Id.* No. 384.

remarkable than this, the *Paston Letters* show us the Pastons, their friends and servants, messengers, merchants and many others riding about on their business in the midst of all this unrest, and facing all with apparent calm. Dangers they evidently regarded as inevitable. The Statute of Winchester had tried to safeguard the roads to some extent, by clearing them on either side for 200 feet, so that robbers could not lurk among the bushes and trees bordering the edges of roads between neighbouring towns. By the fifteenth century this statute was very imperfectly observed, and neighbouring hedges and heaths were full of danger for the traveller. Parliament complained bitterly of the lawless bands of men in the time of Richard II, who "rode in great routs in divers parts of the country...and in some places lying in await with such routs, do beat and maim, murder and slay the people...and do many other riots and horrible offences."[1] The Rolls of Parliament for 1450 give us a vivid account of the dangers of the road, and of the whole course of events at one of these encounters, which may serve as an illustration of what was happening throughout the land. William Tresham had to ride to meet the Duke of York, and by a ruse his enemies learnt the hour of his departure. Thereupon, they

gathered and assembled with them divers misdoers and murderers of men to the number of 160 persons and more, arrayed in form of war with cuirasses, light helmets, long swords,...and all other unmerciful [and] forbidden weapons. In the night next following...[these men came] to a place called Thorplandclose, [in Multon, Northants.] and there lodged them under a large hedge adjoining to the highway,... and thence lay in wait for the said William Tresham in order to execute their malicious purpose, from the hour of midnight...till the hour of six before noon;...at which hour the said William Tresham, riding in the highway to the said long hedge towards the said Duke saying the Matins of Our Lady, the said William King, who was sent by the said misdoers to await and give them perfect knowledge of his coming, made to them a sign accorded between them, whereby they knew the person of the said William Tresham, the day being then dark. Whereupon, the said misdoers feloniously ...issued out upon the said William Tresham, and smote him through the body a foot and more, whereof he died,...and gave him many and great deadly wounds, and cut his throat.[2]

---

[1] Stat. 2 Ric. II, § 1 c. VI.   [2] *R.P.* v. pp. 211–12.

Nothing could be more vivid. One can almost see this great ambushing party gather overnight, and hide in the long hedge for their midnight vigil. Their victim starts from home just as the light begins to show up the road before them. He is rehearsing his morning office, and the words are still on his lips when he meets his swift and terrible end.

Besides the more open stretches of road, much of the way must have run through woods and over heaths and moors, for England was still rich in woods and forests. Even close to the gates of London was the "Great Forest" of Epping, with the heaths of Highgate and of Hampstead nearer at hand: while the Bishop's Wood, where year by year the Mayday revels were held, was only a mile from Aldgate. Such places, and the far wilder nooks in many a forest, were frequently the haunts of the outcast and fugitive, where "He must needes walk in wood that may not walk in town," and where, as an old writer says, "Oft in woods thieves are hid, and oft in their awaits and deceits passing men come, and are spoiled and robbed, and oft slain."[1] The contemporary evidence as to the frequency of robbery and assault on the highway is so voluminous and widespread that it cannot be questioned. What the *Paston Letters* reveal to us in Norfolk, is only a condition of affairs which the *Coroners' Rolls*, or the *Early Chancery Proceedings* show to have existed all over the country. Sir John Fortescue, the Lord Chief Justice, actually boasted of the number of robbers England harboured, and regarded them as a sign of the great spirit of the country.

It hath often ben seen in England, that three or four thefes, for Povertie hath sett upon seven or eight true Men, and robbed them al. There be more Men hangyd in England in a Yere, for Robberye and Manslaughter, than ther be hangyd in France for such Cause of Crime in seven years.[2]

The Italian Envoy's words are equally emphatic, even allowing for his customary exaggeration:

There is no country in the world, where there are so many thieves and robbers as in England; insomuch that few venture to go alone into the country, excepting in the middle of the day, and fewer still in the towns at night, and least of all in London.[3]

---

[1] *Bart. Ang.* trans. Trevisa, lib. VII. c. 20.
[2] *Works*, Fortescue, J., 1869, I. p. 466.   [3] *Ital. Rel.* p. 34.

The *Paston Letters* from time to time reflect the results of such a condition of affairs. John Paston's aunt, who owes a London merchant 20 marks, "dare not adventure her money to be brought up to London for fear of robbing, which causeth her to beseech [John Paston] to pay the said money in discharging of the matter."[1] The fears of Margaret Paston for her husband's safety when he was away were only too well founded, and now and again her anxiety rises above her usual business-like news, and her relation of minor affairs. At the end of a letter of 1461, she writes, "At the reverence of God, beware how you ride or go, for naughty and evil-disposed fellowships.... God for his mercy send us a good world."[2] Ten years later, the fear of robbers still troubled men wishing to send money to London. "I should send you money... but I dare not put it in jeopardy, there be so many thieves stirring. John Loveday's man was robbed unto his shirt as he came homeward."[3] Yet no doubt John Loveday's man, relating his adventure to his cronies, and thinking it over, considered he had escaped lightly, with no bones broken and only the loss of his clothes to lament. Perhaps nothing throws a more sinister light on the methods and barbarities of the robbers of those days than the story in Capgrave's *English Chronicles* which relates that in 1416 three beggars stole three children at Lynn. They put out the eyes of one, broke the back of a second, and cut off the hands and feet of the third, in the hope that these infirmities would draw forth abundant alms from all who beheld them.[4]

The frequency of ambushes is so marked at this time that it serves to prove very conclusively the neglect of the Statute of Winchester. Almost every mile of the road in the fifteenth century must have had its convenient lurking places, either at some awkward turn, or else where the road had become so bad that tracks round the "perilous and broken" parts led the traveller to pass by a knoll, behind which men could watch and listen for their victims. In Norfolk, as the *Paston Letters* show quite clearly, these facts were known and appreciated, and we get racy accounts detailing how the Pastons, or their

[1] *P.L.* No. 260.   [2] *Id.* No. 400, and see No. xxi.   [3] *Id.* No. 685.   [4] *Chronicle of England*, Capgrave, J., 1858, [R.S.] p. 316, and cf. *P.P.* c. x. ll. 169-70 and Wright, p. 338.

enemies, or the professional robber made use of holes, or woods, or of the heath when lying in wait.[1] A quiet roadside gave a man all he asked for in those days: he was prepared to supply the accessories himself. So, when Thomas Daniel wished to revenge himself upon a certain Walter Ingham, he sent him a forged letter ordering him to meet his Lord at a certain place and time. This done, Daniel arranged his plans, even going so far as to lay two ambushes, as his victim plaintively remarked, "knowing well that your said beseecher must come by one of these two ways for there were no more." When Walter Ingham came to one of these ambushes, they

him then and there grievously beat and wounded, as well upon his head as upon his legs, and other full grievous strokes and many gave him upon his back, so that he is maimed upon his right leg, and fain to go on crutches, and so must do all days of his life, to his utter undoing, notwithstanding the said misdoers and riotous people in this conceit left your said beseecher for dead.[2]

Such occurrences made travel dangerous, if not actually fatal, and sometimes the shock and ill-usage consequent on a meeting such as that related above proved fatal. An uncle of Margaret Paston's met with an ambush coming back from the Sessions where

ten persons of the said rioters lay in await in the highway under Thorpe wood upon Philip Berney esquire and his man,...and shot at him, and smote the horse of the said Philip with arrows, and then over-rode him, and took him and beat him and spoiled him.[3]

After this, he never recovered:

For a time he lay so sick...that I thought he should never escape it, nor is he like to do unless he has ready help; and therefore he shall to Suffolk this next week to my aunt, for there is a good physician, and he shall look to him,[4]

writes Margaret Paston. But his injuries and the attendant shock were too deep seated even for the good physician to overcome, and on Monday the 2nd July, 1453, after fifteen months' lingering illness, he "passed to God with the greatest pain that ever I saw."[5]

Naturally the very frequency of such ambushes made men

[1] *P.L.* Nos. 146, 179, 201. [2] *Id.* No. 198. [3] *Id.* No. 201.
[4] *Id.* No. 182. [5] *Id.* No. 188.

cautious. Sir James Gloys, household chaplain and confidant of the Pastons, writes to Sir John and relates his failure thus:

And if he had kept his way that night I should have kept him true covenant, for I lay in wait upon him on the heath as he should have come homeward....But he had laid such watch that he had espied us ere he came fully at us; and he remembered...that four swift feet were better than two hands, and he took his horse with his spurs and rode...as fast as he might ride.[1]

The *Early Chancery Proceedings* frequently record cases which show that Norfolk was not alone among counties, but that this state of affairs prevailed throughout the kingdom. We may read how a chaplain and a tailor lay in wait for a man so that they might murder him, and pursued his step-son into a churchyard where they cut off three of his toes;[2] or how Robert Dane, a citizen and mercer of London, while riding into Kent to survey his lands, was ambushed by one Thomas Holbein who had twenty archers waiting in concealment.[3] Another case tells us how a parson of Cumberland, while riding along the highway on the eve of Palm Sunday, met his enemies lying in wait, "with their bows strung and swords drawn, who would have killed or maimed him had it not been that the swiftness of foot of his horse delivered him out of their hand and power";[4] and a fourth relates the sad story of how the right arm of Ralph Fryday was broken by certain evil-doers who lay in wait to kill him, and how the arm mortified through the malpractice of a physician.[5] Let us look at one case more fully, and observe the light it throws on the disregard of law and authority. John Stenby had issued a writ against a certain John Hellewell's tenants. On learning this, Hellewell "did lie in wait on the highroad near the town of Bytham, in the County of Lincoln, armed with a hauberk and an iron cap and a sword, and having other evil-doers in his company arrayed in warlike manner, in order to have killed the said suppliant." When Stenby came along, they all set upon him,

whereupon...knowing the great power of the evil-doers and for fear of death, and to save his life, [he] fell on the earth on his knees before the said John Hellewell, offering him all that he had to dispose of at his will, and crying him mercy, so that he would spare his life.[6]

[1] *P.L.* No. 146.   [2] *E.C.P.* Bundle 3, No. 120g.   [3] *Chanc. Pro.* p. 8.
[4] *Id.* p. 56.   [5] *Id.* p. 123.   [6] *Id.* p. 36.

The *Coroners' Rolls* also present the outlines of many a highway tragedy, and record, briefly and without any comment,
facts which doubtless set the ale houses in neighbouring hamlets
buzzing with eager talk on the morrow of their happening.
They record how John Waltham, a saddler, came to the village
of Brill one Saturday evening at the hour of vespers, and killed
the village tailor Elias Smith with a blow from a knife;[1] or how
Walter Walker slew Thomas Weston in the King's highway by
striking him on the head with a pole-axe.[2] The dangers which
beset merchants and travellers are strikingly shown by the
report of a Coroner's Inquest at Marston, Staffs.,

on view of the body of John Swale, by the oath of [twelve] jurors
of four neighbouring townships. They say on their oaths, that on
Monday next [after the feast of the Holy Trinity], Nicholas of
Cheddleton was going along the King's highway with linen and
woollen cloths and other goods, when he was met by certain thieves
who tried to kill and rob him. And the said Nicholas, in self defence,
struck one of the robbers named John Swale, right over the head
with a staff worth a penny, of which blow he died forthwith.[3]

Along such roads as those described above, and constantly
attended by the possibilities of ambush, robbers or other
enemies, the medieval traveller had to make his way. Before
we try to follow him from stage to stage on such a journey, we
must notice one or two other important features of medieval
wayfaring.

A brief survey of the routes followed by the medieval traveller
shows that his course was determined to a large extent by the
position of fords and bridges. He was constantly making detours
to reach convenient crossings; the very absence of hedges made
it possible for him to strike out into the adjacent lands. Little
by little, through continuous usage, a succession of travellers
would beat out a new track leading to a more convenient ford,
or to a newly built bridge. Throughout the centuries after the
Conquest, the wooden bridges, which were a legacy of Saxon
times, were replaced in many parts of the country. These
wooden structures had served their turn; but, as they fell into
decay, the growing desire for something more permanent, and
more beautiful, found expression in the numerous stone bridges
which were built. The most notable of these was London Bridge.

[1] *Cor. Rolls*, p. 41.   [2] *Id.* p. 48.   [3] *Id.* p. 101.

M. Jusserand writes of it, "This was a famous bridge. No Englishman of the Middle Ages, and even of the Renaissance, ever spoke but with pride of London Bridge; it was the great national wonder."[1]

The whole story of the bridges of these days resembles the story of the roads. The same lack of system allowed both to be built without any effective central control: the same jumble of religious and secular interests was displayed in their upkeep; and the same tale of neglect and troubles ensued. The upkeep of all bridges, however, was undoubtedly a part of the "tri-noda necessitas," and therefore by rights, the bridges should have fared rather better than the roads did. But from very early days this obligation was found to be so difficult to enforce, that accessory means were invented from time to time. The reasons which actuated the clergy in their concern for the upkeep of roads held good in the case of the bridges. Hence, the bishops frequently tried to stimulate the giving of money for repairs, by offering "indulgences" to all the faithful who contributed to this end. Almost any Bishop's Register might be quoted to show the efforts they made. For example, the Archbishop of York granted a hundred days' pardon to all those who contributed to the repair and to the building of new bridges at Oxnede,—one of the Pastons' homes.[2] In the same way, the *Papal Registers* abound with the details of indulgences granted for the repair, or upkeep, of bridges and bridge chapels.[3] Then again, there were religious gilds of laymen, which to some extent took the place of the "Frères pontifes" of the Continent.[4] Such gilds made themselves responsible in part for the repair of roads and bridges in, or near by, their township or city. The Gild of the Holy Cross at Birmingham was one of these, and the Commissioners of Edward VI said in their report that the Gild "maintained...and kept in good reparation two great stone bridges, and divers foul and dangerous highways, the charge whereof the town of itself is not able to maintain."[5] There can

---

[1] Jusserand, p. 48.
[2] Blomefield, VI. p. 493, and cf. *Ely Epis. Records*, ed. Gibbons, A, 1891, pp. 397, 398, 400, 403, etc.
[3] *C.P.L.* IV. pp. 48, 249, 351, 399, 406, V. pp. 242, 272, 274, 313, 317, 318, 339, 379, 408.
[4] Jusserand, pp. 38–9, 42.   [5] *Gilds*, p. 249, cf. p. 256.

be no doubt that these gilds did a very fine work, and preserved many structures which otherwise would have had the same disastrous record as characterises the majority of English medieval bridges. Hence Leland was able to say of one such bridge:

> The bridge at Bideford [co. Devon] is a very notable work, and has 24 arches of stone and is fairly walled on each side....There is a fraternity in the town for the preservation of this bridge, and one waits continually to keep the bridge clean from all ordure.[1]

Actuated by this religious spirit, it became quite customary for people to leave bequests for the repairs of bridges, as unquestionably charitable and pious acts. Naturally they usually left money to be spent on bridges near their own neighbourhood, and contemporary wills abound in such phrases as, "I leave to the fabric of the bridge of Hebethe £10, to be expended on reparacion of the said bridge,"[2] or "the remainder...to the repair of bridges and highways."[3]

The uncertainty of this form of income led many men, who had a real concern for the upkeep of bridges, to endow them with lands.[4] By this means, the bridge had a certain income and funds available whenever repairs were necessary. The upkeep of Rochester Bridge affords an interesting example of how people tried to make sure bridges should not be neglected. In the first place, the bridge had funds which were provided by the income from certain manors, which were called "contributory lands." Besides this, the whole fabric of the bridge was theoretically under the especial care of some great lord, or city, or group of towns. For example, the Archbishop of Canterbury was made responsible for the maintenance of one pier, and of a certain number of beams; the Bishop of the Diocese was charged with very similar duties, while the "contributory lands" provided the money, and were held responsible for the rest of the structure.[5] "The Biidge at Bedeforde," mentioned by Leland, was also aided in like fashion by funds from lands, and his account is worth quoting, because it indicates the simple faith and religious fervour with which many bridges must have been

---

[1] *Itinerary of J. Leland*, ed. Smith, L. T., London, 1907, I. p. 171.
[2] *Nottingham*, II. p. 89, cf. II. pp. 82, 220, 244, III. pp. 2, 4, 8, 12, etc.
[3] *London Wills*, II. p. 548, cf. II. p. 626.
[4] *North Country Wills*, No. CXLVII.   [5] *9 Hist. MSS.* p. 285.

built. Leland writes, "A poor priest began this bridge; and, as it is said, he was animated so to do by a vision. Then all the country about set their hands unto the performing of it, and since, lands have been given to the maintenance of it."[1]

The story of Hethbeth Bridge, in the town of Nottingham, illustrates so many aspects of the troubles and varying fortunes of medieval bridges, that it is here set forth at some length. Hethbeth Bridge has long since been replaced by newer structures, the latest being the well-known Trent Bridge which is one of the glories of municipal Nottingham. The ancient bridge over the Trent had fallen into disrepair early in the thirteenth century, and the Archbishop of York granted an indulgence of 12 days to those who contributed to its repair.[2] Whatever may have been the result of this, the next century saw the bridge so ruined that a ferry service over the Trent had to be established. In the conditions laid down by the King, it was stated that he had granted

to the Mayors of Nottingham, our passage over the water of Trent near Nottingham, to have together with our barge pertaining to that passage, and all profits arising...on condition that all the profits aforesaid shall be employed on the repairing and making of the bridge called Hethbethbridge, which is now broken down, under the supervision and testimony of our Sheriff of Nottingham, and of the Constable of our Castle of Nottingham.[3]

This measure does not seem to have been very successful, and a few years later, in 1376, a petition was presented to the Good Parliament, in which were related the troubles and dangerous condition of the bridge at some length. The petitioners said it was "ruinous and oftentimes have several persons been drowned, as well horsemen as carts, man, and harness," and that since nobody "to the making and repair is bound," and since "alms only are collected," they prayed that two bridge-wardens might be appointed to care for the bridge, and also to administer the funds and properties given to it. The King refused to grant their request.[4] Time, however, brought them their desire, and we have for the year 1457-8 the first extant Bridgewardens' Accounts. Unfortunately these only disclose the unhappy fact that the bridge was in little better order than

[1] Leland, I. p. 171.   [2] *Nottingham*, II. p. 440.
[3] *Id.* I. p. 183 [Nov. 9th, 1363].   [4] *R.P.* II. p. 350a.

it had been eighty years earlier, when the people thought that the appointment of two wardens would solve all their troubles. The Bridgewardens sorrowfully report at the head of their accounts that, during the past year and a quarter, "the Bridges ...fell down for want of repair."[1] Hence they have to present a heavy account of their costs in repairing the damage, "to wit, two arches of timber with standard timber," and a great deal of other material.[2] All the crowds of people passing over the bridge, both before and after its repair, only gave eight shillings and sixpence in alms for the fabric. The cost of the repairs unfortunately amounted to £20. 2s. 11½d. It was clear that some energetic measures had to be taken to secure money for the upkeep of the bridge, and collectors of alms were appointed. One such appointment, issued to William Thomas and William Chase, authorises them "jointly and severally to seek and receive alms and charitable gifts for the reparation, sustentation, and mending of the bridge aforesaid," because the bridge "has nothing whereby it can be sustained, except by gifts of charity."[3] Nine pounds ten shillings was secured by one collection of this nature, and thirteen pounds by a second.[4] The collectors do not seem to have handed over the whole sum, or else it was a well-paid office and much sought after; for in 1491–2 one collector had to sue the other for selling their letter of appointment.[5] The Bridgewardens' accounts also show that the needs of the bridge were not forgotten by dying men, and they record many sums received from bequests, although most of them were small. Thus, for the year 1485–6, they have to report thirteen such bequests; the largest only amounted to thirty-three shillings and fourpence, while one testator could only leave one penny. During the same period, five money gifts were received, ranging from eightpence to twenty shillings.[6] Gifts in kind were often made, especially when repairs were in progress, and the Wardens received great beams, loads of stone, loads of poles, etc., to be used in the work of rebuilding.[7] Besides leaving money, or sending gifts, some people made grants of land to the bridge. In 1480 Ellen Gull gave one garden and one messuage

[1] *Nottingham*, II. p. 221. [2] *Id.* II. p. 364. [3] *Id.* II. p. 267.
[4] *Id.* II. p. 245. [5] *Id.* III. p. 22.
[6] *Id.* II. pp. 82, 89, 220, 244, 306, III. pp. 2, 4, 8, 12, 96, 196, etc.
[7] *Id.* II. pp. 221–3.

to the Mayor and Bridgewardens, so that "the issues and profits of the said messuage and garden yearly as they grow [might] be applied and expended to and for the sustentation of the works and reparations of the said bridges."[1] Even the little chapel,—a common feature of medieval bridges—contributed its mite, for in 1457–58 it gave two shillings "for half the offering in the chapel of S. James there, for this year."[2] The bridge chapel was frequently visited by passing travellers, for there was to be found "a fit priest in the chapel built upon the said bridge, daily celebrating divine service in honour of Our Saviour...for all helpers and benefactors of the bridge."[3]

Legally, as in the case of roads, the obligation for the repair of bridges fell upon the Lord of the Manor and his tenants, or upon townships and municipal authorities. Pollock and Maitland say definitely enough, "It is planted in the soil, and to the soil it has ceded: it is apportioned according to hideage or acreage."[4] Yet, despite this legal obligation, the varied accessory aids we have mentioned, and the common interest of landlords to keep the bridges in repair, they were frequently as badly kept as the roads. Indeed, at times they were so shamefully neglected as to become dangerous, and even to collapse for want of repair.[5] The same authorities who were ordered to supervise the care of roads, had also the upkeep of bridges under their survey. Wilkinson, in his famous treatise, tells the Justices that,

[they] shall enquire if any common Bridges over Common Streams bee broken, that by reason thereof the King's subjects cannot passe about their affaires and businesses, and [they] must present those which ought to make them.[6]

It is only on looking over a collection of the presentments of such Courts, that the condition of medieval bridges can be realised.[7] This evidence is overwhelming: bridge after bridge is spoken of as being "broken and dangerous in winter," or it is "flooded and impassable in winter."[8] The brief wording of the originals only hints at the hardships and added difficulties

[1] *Nottingham*, II. p. 311. [2] *Id*. II. p. 221.
[3] *Id*. II. p. 267. [4] *Hist. Eng. Law*, I. p. 602.
[5] *Nottingham*, II. p. 221; *R.P.* II. p. 111; *Pub. Works, passim.*
[6] *A Treatise...concerning the office...of Coroners and Sheriffs, etc.*, Wilkinson, J., London, 1638.
[7] *Pub. Works, passim.* [8] *Id.* Nos. LXX, LXXIV, LXXVIII.

created by such conditions. We can only guess the feelings of the people of Tortworth and Stone in Gloucester, who for a year were unable to use the bridge at Syndleforth between their villages, because the Lords of the Manor did not trouble to repair it. The villagers said the Lords of the Manor were responsible, and that the bridge was completely broken down. The defaulting knights came before the Sheriff in due course, acknowledged their liability, were ordered to repair the bridge, and were only fined ten shillings.[1] There are many similar cases recorded, and the verdicts returned leave us wondering what comfort the unfortunate traveller, and the still more unfortunate local rustics derived from them. For, although the law was possibly satisfied when it was established that no one was responsible for the upkeep of a bridge, the neglected bridge still remained a danger to every passer-by. The township of Scampton, and the Abbot of Kirkstead came before the King at Westminster in the Easter Term of 1369, and both denied that they ought to repair the Till bridge (Lincoln) on the east side, or that they had ever done so. The case was enquired into at Lincoln in 1374; and, after several postponements, it was not until the Michaelmas Term of 1381 that it was decided that neither the township nor the Bishop was responsible.[2] A further attempt was made to fasten the responsibility upon the neighbouring townships of Thorp, Carlton, and Broxholme. This fresh suit lasted even longer, but finally a verdict was given "that neither the said townships, nor any holder of land there, ever made or ought to repair the aforesaid bridge."[3] Nothing at all is said of what had been done during the dispute, or what steps were now to be taken, to prevent the bridge from becoming dangerous and useless.

Such accounts as these illustrate the continued attempts which were being made to fix the liability for the repairs on some individual, or some corporate body. The lack of any organised system, in earlier days, had allowed bridges to grow up, for the most part, as a result of local or private enterprise. After the lapse of years, or even centuries, it was often almost impossible to fix the liability. As we have seen, at Bideford

[1] *Pub. Works*, No. LXIX.   [2] *Id.* No. XCVIII, § 6.
[3] *Id.* No. XCVIII, §§ 7 and 8.

a "poor priest" began the bridge: another bridge is reported
to the jury as being begun "by an hermit, after the first pesti-
lence, who set a plank across a certain ford." Among our early
bridge-builders and tenders, the hermits must always deserve
an honourable place. They were well-known figures by many
a bridge, and often received a pension, or small sums of money
from time to time. At Lynn, for example, an hermit received
an annuity of thirteen shillings, to keep the town bridge in
order; while William Warde, a hermit of Beccles, kept the great
bridge there, and also its chapel, in a state of repair.[1]

All the above evidence leaves us little reason to doubt the
truth of M. Jusserand's conclusion, "The chronicle of even the
most important of English bridges, when it is possible to trace
it out, is a long tale of falls into the river, rebuildings, and ever-
recurring catastrophes."[2]

It is clear, from what has already been said of the state of
roads and bridges, that travel was not always easy. In the
winter, and during the bad weather, when the roads were reduced to deep miry tracks, and the swollen fords were dangerous,
guides were often necessary. The controller of the Duke of
Rutland's household at Belvoir made use of a guide sometimes,
both for his master and for himself. He enters in his accounts,
"Payd to Roger Meddylton, off Beywer, for beyng gyde v dayes
to my Lord Rosse from Beywer to Grimsthorpe, and from
Grimsthorpe to Lynhollene at viij[d] the day." Another entry
throws a little more light on this man's local knowledge, and
runs "Payd the xxviij day January to Roger Myddylton off
Beywer, for gyddyng off the controller from Beywer to the
Eeygle in a fowll mysty day."[3]

Similarly, the accounts of the Howards, in the latter part of
the fifteenth century, show that when they were riding in unknown country guides were frequently employed. There is a
wealth of romantic possibility in an entry which coldly states
that money was given "to a mayde that tawte the wey over
Tyddgsbery forthe" [Didsbury Ford].[4] It would be interesting
if we could withdraw the veil, and know whether the party

[1] Redstone, p. 192.   [2] Jusserand, p. 67.
[3] *Hist. MSS.* Rutland MSS. IV. p. 321 ["Beywer," Belvoir Castle] and
p. 354.   [4] *Howard,* I. p. xciii.

was lost, and what their adventures had been, before they met
this timely country maiden. On a previous occasion, soon after
leaving home, Sir Thomas Howard had paid twopence "ffor a
gyde ovyr the Wayssche."[1] This well-known crossing seems
still to have been as dangerous as King John had found it
several centuries earlier, and a local guide was very necessary.
In spite of its dangers, it was much used, being the only short
route into Lincolnshire from Norwich, or North Norfolk, on
account of the Great Fen. While riding into "the northe
kontery," Sir Thomas hired another guide after passing the
Wash; and, having completed his business at York, went across
to Chester aided by several guides.[2]

The Privy Purse Expenses of Elizabeth of York, wife of
Henry VII, also show that guides were employed when the
Queen was travelling. Eightpence was "payed to a guyde that
went from Monmouthe four myles bakeward towardes Flexley
Abbey, to gyde a wagne laden with stuf of the Warderobe."[3]
If there were any doubt at all concerning the condition of the
roads, such entries as these would help to dispel it. Undoubtedly
the wisest and quickest course very often was for the traveller
to hire one of the boys or men standing about the village ale-
house where he baited, to act as his guide. Such men knew the
whole face of the countryside well enough to be able to take
their patrons by the least broken roads and tracks, and over
the safest bridges or fords. It is necessary to remember that,
while the main routes up and down the country received a
certain modicum of attention—though inadequate it certainly
was—the very numerous secondary roads and connecting lanes
were almost entirely neglected. It was therefore reassuring
to have a native at one's stirrup who could find his way over
difficult untracked country, where the way might be over
dangerous and well nigh impassable roads and bridges. Riding
out from Rye in 1458, the Mayor and Town Clerk went across
country to Sittingbourne, where they hoped to fall in with the
Earls of March and Warwick. Unfortunately, the Earls had
left, and were rumoured to be at Leene, a few miles distant.

[1] *Howard*, I. p. 227.
[2] *Id.* pp. 227, 230, xciii, and see *Howard*, II. pp. 115, 154, 307.
[3] *The Privy Purse Expenses of Elizabeth of York*, ed. Sir N. H. Nicolas,
London, 1830, p. 46, and see pp. 32, 46.

The Mayor and Town Clerk at once hired a guide, giving him a penny "to lead us on the way between Sedyngbourne and Leene." Not finding the Earls here, they had to hire another guide, this time on horseback, who cost them twopence. Their reason for doing this is made clear in their return of expenses. "Paid to one of Leene with his horse to lead us to Forde Mylle, for the way between...was a nuisance [nociva] to us, who had never gone by it."[1]

[1] 5 *Hist. MSS.* p. 493.

CHAPTER XI

WAYFARING

THE great main routes throughout England followed fairly closely such old Roman roads as the Watling Street and the Icknield Way. Highways had certainly multiplied enormously, but the conditions of English life had not altered sufficiently to make the work of the Romans useless. Indeed, in many cases, the reasons which had led the Romans to site their roads as they did still held good. Hence travellers still used the same, or parts of the same ways, as were used originally more than ten or twelve centuries earlier. The old surfaces had been much broken by the wear and neglect of centuries, yet it was still possible in many places to see the lay-out of the Roman work where the newer medieval road had swerved from it to gain some advantage of ground. A man coming to London from East Anglia, for example, would find that much of his journey led him along bridle tracks and roads which were the remnants of an earlier civilisation. This partial continuity of highways throughout the centuries may be well illustrated by studying some journeys from Hunstanton to London in the late middle ages. Fortunately we possess the records of a considerable number of such journeys undertaken by members of the Lestrange family in the early years of the sixteenth century, by means of which we can follow their progress from start to finish.[1]

About 20 miles S.S.E. of Hunstanton is the Roman station of Castleacre, and the two places are joined by a Roman road, still known as Peddar's Way. This is a characteristically straight stretch, and the Lestranges came along it on the first part of their journey, sometimes halting awhile at Castleacre to drink.[2] Then the same road led them on over open heath country through Pickenham, as far as Thetford. They often avoided this detour by riding south from Castleacre, and making for

[1] *Arch.* xxv. pp. 411–569.   [2] *Id.* p. 464.

Brandon Ferry.[1] This was probably a comparative innovation, as there is no known Roman road through Brandon. Once at Thetford, our travellers were on the Icknield Way, and rode across open downs over the chalk, and then through wild heath country to Newmarket, and so on to Barkway. Here they turned south along a post-Roman road, and went across the Cam valley as far as Braughing. Here again they met an ancient road, believed to be Roman, which took them through Ware and Waltham into London. Thus, by far the greater part of their journey had been on routes, either definitely Roman, or dating from very early times. Travellers from King's Lynn followed a medieval route across Stoke Ferry, and thence to Brandon Ferry, just south of which they met the Icknield Way, and continued as described above. Similarly, the traveller from Norwich came west to Thetford, and so on the Icknield Way through Newmarket, Barkway and Ware, to London.

Along these roads, which had been used by generations of travellers, villages and hostelries had gradually multiplied. Halts were chiefly determined by the position of fords and bridges, and by the need for food and shelter at reasonably equal distances. On their frequent journeys to London, the Lestranges usually halted at Castleacre, Brandon, Newmarket, Babraham, Barkway, Ware and Waltham. Most of these are situated on, or near, a river crossing, and are spaced out at intervals of twelve to eighteen miles. Accounts of journeys in 1411,[2] in 1452[3] and in 1520,[4] all show that travellers called for refreshment or beds at one or another of these places, and there can be little doubt that these were the recognised medieval stages. Such stages had an additional use for men whose business caused them to ride fast and to tire their horses quickly on the bad roads, for here they could hire fresh horses, and speed on again. Sir Thomas Howard, riding hastily to join the King at Dover, went from London to Gravesend by barge, and there hired horses for himself and thirteen retainers and rode to Canterbury. The next morning he obtained a fresh set to post on to Dover.[5]

[1] *Arch.* xxv. pp. 439, 463–4.   [3] Hillen, I. p. 156.
[2] Grace Book A, p. 36   [4] *Arch.* xxv. pp. 411 ff.
[5] *Howard*, II. pp. 217–9, and cf. *Meals and Manners*, p. 310, for price of hire, and 20 Richard II, c. 5.

The extant records of journeys at this time show that it was occasionally possible for men to cover large distances very quickly, despite all the difficulties. In the majority of cases, however, it must be remembered that these records only tell us how the rich fared. Their journeys were likely to have taken place under the best of conditions. The travellers would be well mounted, able to get fresh horses when necessary, and often were riding on affairs that required urgent attention. Therefore we cannot regard their daily stages as being at all normal. The most generally accepted view of the average rate of travel seems to put it at between 20 and 30 miles a day. The detailed evidence given below suggests that it was more probably between 30 and 40 miles a day. Travellers were so early astir, and so many hours on the road, that one would expect them to have covered even more ground than this in a day. The fact that the normal rate was no higher must be accounted for by the state of the roads. One or two examples of what the fifteenth century traveller could do may be quoted. John Shillingford, Mayor of Exeter, seems to have been able to ride from that city to London in four or five days—a distance of 170 miles. In 1447, he writes to his City Council, "Worthy sirs, I greet you well all; giving you to understand that I rode from Exeter on Friday and came to London on Tuesday by time, at 7 at clock." Riding in the bright May weather the next year, he does even better, "On Wednesday next after Corpus Christi day, at seven at clock in the morning I rode out of Exeter to Londonward. The next Saturday thereafter at seven at clock by the morning, I came to London."[1] Another important traveller, Bishop Redman, Visitor of the Præmonstratensians in England, during his visitation journeys, rode between 40 and 50 miles a day on several occasions. On the morning of July 27th, 1494, he left Salisbury, and was in Exeter, which is 90 miles distant, by the next evening. A few days after this he left Torre Abbey, and started on his 175 mile ride to London, and was only four days on the road.[1] Men on important business could evidently travel quickly, and we find a deputation leaving Shrewsbury on Wednesday, and arriving in London in time for dinner on Saturday. They had covered

[1] *Coll. Ang. Pre.* III. pp. vi–vii.

153 miles in 3½ days. On the Thursday they left Wolverhampton and slept at Daventry; the next day reached S. Albans, and so rode into London the next morning. Both on Thursday and Friday they must have ridden at least 50 miles.[1]

Such long journeys were beyond the capabilities of the ordinary traveller, and must have entailed great fatigue. The usual practice followed in the fifteenth century by people riding from Norfolk was to try to reach Newmarket on the first evening, and to have supper there, and put up for the night. Once after supper, however, the Lestranges rode on to Babraham, probably quite two hours' riding. As they completed the journey to London the next day, they rode over 50 miles each of these two days they were on the road. This is the only time they made such an effort; usually they took three days on the journey.[2] The ordinary course was to leave Newmarket in the morning, and to ride as far as Ware, a distance of 41 miles, by nightfall. This enabled the traveller to reach London the next day in time for dinner, so that the journey was completed in 2½ days on the road.[3] The road between Ware and London was greatly used, and seems to have been often in want of repair. Wills of the fifteenth century leave money for the repair of highways, "especially between...London and Ware," while one testator left " 100/- to be yspendyth between London and Ware, of fowle ways, of my goods, there most nede ys."[4][5]

The journey from Norwich to London could also be made in under three days, but only when there was urgent need. A letter of 1450 among the Paston Correspondence says, "Thomas Skipping rode to Londonward on Friday last past in great haste, and purposed him for to be at London on Sunday by noon."[6] More usually, the traveller rode a little slower and, if fortunate, could reach London by nightfall of the third day. Often, however, it was not until the next morning he could get there. Margaret Paston, for example, got a letter on Wednesday, written by her husband in London the Monday previously; and Sir John Paston, writing to his mother on Good Friday, 1473, says,[7] "I let you know that on Wednesday last past, I wrote

[1] *Hist. Shrewsbury*, I. p. 279.   [2] *Arch.* xxv. p. 463.
[3] *Id.* pp. 439, 464; Hillen, I. p. 156.   [4] *Early Wills*, p. 15.
[5] *London Wills*, II. p. 685.   [6] *P.L.* No. xxi.   [7] *Id.* No. 506.

you a letter, whereof John Carbold had the bearing, promising
me that you should have it at Norwich this day, or else tomorrow in the morning."[1] His letter of 26th November, 1473,
substantiates the fact that it was possible to cover the distance
in about three days, for he entreats his brother to act quickly,
"so that I hear from you again this day seven nights."[2]

But not all travellers were so expeditious, or perhaps so
fortunate. A letter from Norwich, written on Tuesday, 23rd
January, 1476, must have arrived in London on Friday, or
Saturday morning at the latest, as it was answered then. The
answer, however, only reached Norwich on February 3rd, so that
the luckless traveller had been six or seven days on the road.[3]
It is not too fanciful, perhaps, to imagine him unable to get
along over "highways foundered and flooded," and trying to
cross "fordes deep worne" with the heavy rains, or moving
with trembling care over perilous bridges. During the winter
months, and after heavy storms, it must have been almost
impossible on some days to use the roads, and the vagaries of
the weather were a continuous source of anxiety and uncertainty
to the traveller.

The daily log book of a carter of this century shows that he
was unable to work at times during the winter because of the
bad weather, as his business consisted of transporting loads of
clay, wood, stone, etc. from place to place in the vicinity of
Norwich. He enters, concerning the 16th December, 1428, "On
Thursday nothing at all before noon because of the rain,"[4] and
again for the week ending 13th February, 1429, "In Fastgoing
week no more because of weather than 12d."[5] There can be
little doubt that such enforced abstention from work was the
common lot of all whose business made them frequent the roads
of medieval England.

The journey to Canterbury from the time of Becket appears
to have been reckoned as one of two days and one night on the
road, for all except folk like Chaucer's pilgrims, who took their
pilgrimage very leisurely indeed. An early MS. dating from the
middle of the thirteenth century contains a map showing the
Stations of a pilgrimage to the Holy Land. London, Rochester,

---

[1] *P.L* No. 723.   [2] *Id.* No. 733.   [3] *Id.* No. 770.
[4] *N.A.* xv. p. 144.   [5] *Id.* p. 146.

Canterbury and Dover are the English stations. Between the first two is written "jurnee," and also between Rochester and Canterbury, but between Canterbury and Dover is written "pres de jurnee."[1] Now, an examination of extant records of fifteenth century journeys on this road shows this was still the prevalent rate. The Envoys to Henry V from Ferdinand of Aragon left London 31st July, 1415, and reached Rochester the same night. The next day they reached Canterbury, and the return journey was also performed in two days and a night.[2] Towards the end of the century, Sir T. Howard left Dover after noon on the 18th August, and slept that night at Canterbury. The next day he rode as far as Rochester; and, after resting on the 20th, he finished the journey by arriving in London on the 21st August.[3]

All this evidence tends to show that, besides passing over routes which had in very many cases been used for centuries previously, the fifteenth century traveller rested at nights, or halted to bait his horse, or to have dinner, at places which had many generations of hospitality behind them. A very early map, of the late fourteenth century, affords interesting evidence on this point.[4] Besides marking a certain number of towns and villages, it indicates some main roads, and even gives the mileage between them. A careful examination of the places marked on this map, in the case of the Norwich route for example, shows that they are the very villages and stages at which we happen to know that travellers halted; hence, it is almost certain that, if a place is indicated on this map, a medieval road ran through it.

The general conclusion would seem to be, that men whose affairs necessitated their riding fast could travel between 35 and 40 miles a day, at almost any time of the year. The Lestranges, and the Cambridge University authorities, are known to have ridden over the 41 miles between Ware and Newmarket, or the 35 miles between Barkway and Cambridge frequently, and there can be little doubt that these represent a normal

[1] *British Topography*, ed. R. G[ough], London, 1780.
[2] *Henry V*, Wylie, i. p. 95.   [3] *Howard*, ii. pp. 217–19.
[4] *British Topography*, Plate VI. See illustration to face p. 158.* Since the above was in print the authorities of the Bodleian Library have kindly drawn my attention to a modern facsimile reproduced in the *Ordnance Survey's Facsimiles of National MSS. of Scotland*, iii. (1871), No. 2; and the map is fully described in the *Reports of the Deputy Keeper of Public Records*, xxxii. p. v. and xxxiv. p. 288.
* Omitted from paperback edition.

day's travel. Undoubtedly, given good weather and good going, 50 miles a day was not at all impossible; but this must be regarded as an extraordinary effort.[1] The figures given here for separate days' journeys, representing travel at different years during the fifteenth century, show that the average distance travelled was over 34 miles a day.[2] In several of these cases, the journey was terminated by the exigences of the traveller's business, or by his arrival at his destination. Therefore, if we take any account of this, the correct figure would be even higher than 34 miles a day. This result is supported by the figures quoted below of five journeys made by people of widely differing circumstances, and many years apart. Each of these journeys was of over 100 miles, and the average daily mileage is 39.[3] Carriers could also travel at this rate, and the *Paston Letters* show that they were able to get to Norwich from London in little more than three days, if necessary.[4] This was the ordinary traveller's rate, and represents about 30 to 35 miles a day. This speed, however, was high for carriers, and only possible when packhorses were used—a common practice at this time. When carts were used, the speed was considerably reduced. A carter from Norwich to Ipswich took four days on the out and home journey, which represents a daily pull of 22 miles.[5]

We have now considered the state of the roads and bridges, the dangers that beset travellers, and the methods and speed by which the individual horseman could get from one place to another. Besides this, we must remember that trade, and the needs of the community, necessitated some provision being made for the carriage of goods. To meet this need there sprang up the public servant known as the common carrier. He was not universally needed, for it is probable that the rich often provided

---

[1] Even greater distances could be covered. "The almost incredible speed with which express journeys could be made is illustrated by the case of Thomas de la Croix, who was in London, March 19th, 1406, and 6 days afterwards presented himself at Milan, having travelled a distance of 600 miles as the crow flies." *Henry IV*, Wylie, III. p. 172, and see other refs. there.
[2] See Appendix II for details. [3] *Id.* [4] *Id.*
[5] *N.A.* xv. pt ii. p. 119. When we remember that the medieval traveller was early astir, and often on the road by six or seven at the latest, it is difficult to explain why he had usually only travelled between 30–40 miles if we assume, as some writers do, that the roads were good. If we bear in mind the real state of the roads, as implied by the above evidence, we have little difficulty in understanding why progress was so slow.

their own means of transport. This we can see from entries in the Northumberland Household Book, or by the proviso in the Order of the City of London for the imposition of "a tax on all carts entering the City with victuals or wares for sale," except "for carts and horses of great people and other folks, that bring their own victuals and other goods."[1] Most people, however, had to employ the services of a carrier if they wanted to send or fetch goods from one place to another; and consequently the carrier was one of the most well-known figures on the roads. Year after year, the same man would ply between two towns, and interchange their products, while he naturally did whatever business came his way in the towns and villages he passed by en route.

Besides being familiar as a class, these carriers were also well known individually, and their constant passage to and fro made them a link between villages and the larger world beyond. When William Naynow, an Exeter carrier, was giving evidence before the Court of Star Chamber, he said he had been travelling between London and Exeter for over 35 years, and he was at that time [1484] 61 years of age.[2] It is impossible to think he had passed up and down through the towns and villages between London and Exeter for all those years without becoming a well-known figure. The Pastons evidently knew the Norwich carriers well, for they frequently refer to them by name. John Paston tells his brother Sir John, "I have this day delivered your mantle...to Kirby to bring with him to London."[3] Although John Paston does not say so, his brother would know quite well that he might expect his mantle to be delivered by a carrier, and not by a special messenger, for later letters show the modern reader that Kirby was a well-known carrier between Norwich and London.[4] Another carrier, well-known to the Pastons, was Harry Barker. In 1451, Agnes Paston sent a letter, "To Harry Barker, of S. Clements Parish in Norwich, to deliver to my master John Paston, in haste."[5] Twenty-five years later, this same Harry Barker was still working at his carrier's business, and was employed by the Pastons.[6] In the same way, the accounts of Sir T. Howard speak of "Peryn,

---

[1] *Memorials*, p. 291.
[2] *Select Cases in Court Star Chamber*, ed. Leadam, J. S., [S.S.], p. 80, and cf. *S.L.* No. 268.
[3] *P.L.* No. 688.   [4] *Id.* No. 745.   [5] *Id.* No. 160.   [6] *Id.* No. 771.

the caryer of Neylond,"[1] evidently thinking his name would be
well known to anyone whose business it was to overlook the
accounts; whilst the Lestrange accounts also mention individual
carriers by name.[2]

Besides these men, whose names by happy chance we know,
there were many other carriers. A great city like Norwich could
employ the services of several such men to carry its London
traffic alone. Throughout the *Paston Letters*, the knowledge
that there was such a service at frequent intervals was ever
present in the writers' minds. Hence, when something was forgotten, and the carrier arrived in London without it, the cer-
tainty that there would be another messenger in a few days,
smoothed over any difficulty that might have arisen, had their
journeys been very infrequent. John Paston writes, "Item, the
carrier forgot your bill (a weapon) behind him, but it shall be
brought you...by the next carrier."[3] We know that there
could not have been any very long interval between carriers;
for Sir John, writing to his brother on Sunday, 20th November,
1474, asks him to send "the pewter vessel hither by the next
carrier, by the latter end of this week."[4] It is quite clear from
this that there must have been a good service between the two
cities, if Sir John could write his letter on Sunday, and expect
the goods to arrive by carrier within a week.

It would be interesting to know how successful the carriers
were in keeping to any sort of scheduled time on their journeys.
Unfortunately there seems to be little definite evidence on this
point. A remark of Sir John Paston's, complaining that he had
not heard from home, and ascribing the fault to the servants
not enquiring diligently "after the coming of carriers," suggests
that the carrier relied on rumour to spread the news of his
arrival, or else on people keeping a look-out for his coming. The
townsfolk, however, had some data to assist them. The average
time taken on the journey was well known to everyone, so that
no doubt they were able to guess fairly accurately, in the light
of long experience, when the carrier would arrive, within a few
hours. They could appreciate and allow for the weather con-

---

[1] *Howard*, II. p. 197, and cf. pp. 187, 284, 286, 292, 358.
[2] *Arch.* XXV. pp. 421, 470.   [3] *P.L.* No. LXXXII.
[4] *Id.* No. 747, and cf. *Plum. Corr.* p. 36.

ditions, and the consequent difficulties of the road. We have only two records giving any information as to how long it took the Norwich carrier to reach London; one an August journey, the other in November, nine years later. In the first case, the carrier "was at Norwich on Saturday, and brought...letters" to John Paston in London.[1] Now, as he is writing on the Wednesday following, it is clear the journey must have taken less than five days, and probably was not more than four. In the other case, the carrier left London on Saturday, and promised to be at Norwich by Monday night or "else on Tuesday timely,"[2] a little more than three days. It seems probable that in fine weather the carrier hoped to reach London some time before nightfall on the fourth day after leaving Norwich. Evidently this must have been the case of the "loder from Norwich which comes each week to Rossamez Inn, in S. Laurence's Lane."[3]

When it became necessary to fix the rate of wages after the ravages of the Black Death, the Statute expressly included carriers among those who were to receive the accustomed wage for their work, which fact in itself is evidence enough that they were both numerous and important. It is difficult to determine within what radius the carrier pursued his business, and what proportion of carriers undertook long journeys. There seem to have been two very distinct classes; the first of these seldom carried goods so far that they could not return the same night, whilst the second class undertook very long journeys, in some cases entailing several nights at wayside hostelries. The case of the regular carrier between Exeter and London has already been mentioned; and the Shillingford letters also vouch for the existence of a London carrier at that time.[4] Even longer journeys were made, for there are records of money being brought by carrier from Newcastle-on-Tyne to Oxford. The Lestranges had liveries brought for them to Wells in Norfolk by the London carrier, and there was a large and frequent carriers' service between London and both the Universities.[5] Oxford and Cambridge themselves were evidently linked by a carriers'

[1] P.L. No. 519.   [2] Id. No. 745.   [3] Id. No. 967.
[4] Shillingford, pp. 23, 148, 150.
[5] Rogers, Prices, IV. pp. 692–5.

service. When Walter Paston was first going up to the University at Oxford, his mother, like the careful woman she was, arranged he should go via Cambridge, where he might "best purvey an horse to lead his gear." If, however, she says, "you can get any carriers from thence to Oxford more hastily"— and more cheaply she might have added,—he was to send his gear by the carriers.

The University carrier was an important personage in medieval University life. At the end of each Long Vacation, when the University reassembled, the "carrier, or fetcher, or bringer," guarded the young undergraduate on his journey back to his studies.[1] The troubled state of those times, combined with the comparative cheapness of the carrier's cart, no doubt recommended this method to the minds and the purses of careful parents. An indenture of the fifteenth century between the University and City of Oxford includes among those enjoying the privileges of the University,

> Alle common caryers, bryngers of Scolers to the Universite, or their money, letters, or eny especiall message to eny Scoler or clerk, or fetcher of any Scoler or clerk fro the Universite for the tyme of fetchyng, or bryngyng or abydyng in the Universite for that entent.[2]

The most famous of such men is the well-known Hobson, the supposed originator of the dilemma known as "Hobson's choice."

The numerous references to carriers in the *Paston Letters*, and the variety of the goods entrusted to them, indicate how dependent people were upon such men.[3] Whatever was wanted, either in Norfolk or in London, there seldom seems to have been any hesitation about sending it by carrier. Usually the Pastons only employed private messengers, when no carrier was available. This in itself, supports the belief that these men, as a class, were to be trusted. Occasionally, when something of special value was wanted, there was a direction that it must be brought by "some trusty carrier"; but usually the request was only for things to be sent by "the next carrier," or by "a common carrier."[4] There are, however, individual examples of

---

[1] *Mun. Acad.* I. p. lix, and cf. *The University of Cambridge*, Mullinger, I. pp. 345–6.
[2] *Id.* I. pp. 346–7, and cf. *P.L.* No. 716.
[3] *P.L.* Nos. 637, 683, 688, 716, 771, LXXXV, etc.   [4] *Id.* No. 519.

carriers who did not deserve this trust. Here and there, phrases
in the *Letters* show the doubts of the Pastons fairly clearly.
When Margaret Paston wanted a runlet of Malmsey to be sent
to her at Norwich, she directed her son to arrange "that it
should be wound in a canvas, for [fear of] broaching by the
carriers, for she hath known men served so before."[1] Evidently
the constant temptation to slake his thirst, after the labour
necessary to traverse some bad stretch of the road, had been
too much for some former carrier. The fear of the law, and the
knowledge that frequent "losses" would in the end ruin their
trade, must have been strong motives to honesty. The carrier
was liable in common law for the safe delivery of the goods
entrusted to him, and therefore a certain proportion of his
charge represented insurance. When carrying valuables, or
money in bulk, the rate was naturally high. Once John Paston
writes:

> And peradventure, some trusty carrier [comes]...at this time; and
> with him might some money come trussed in some fardel, not knowing
> to the carrier that it is no money, but some other cloth or vestment of
> silk, or thing of charge.[2]

This may have been done simply because the Pastons doubted
the carrier's honesty, but what we know of the parsimonious
nature of John Paston certainly suggests that he also wished
to avoid paying a high rate for the carriage of money.

[1] *P.L.* No. LXXXV.   [2] *Id.* No. LIII, and see No. XVII.

CHAPTER XII

THE LAW

It has already been pointed out how, in the midst of all the lawlessness and confusion which characterise the greater part of the fifteenth century in England, the law still attempted to deal with the ever-growing torrent of business which came under its purview. Indeed, Denton in his well-known *England in the Fifteenth Century* wrote:

> Few things are more striking than to follow the calm dignity of the law and its official administration as the judges passed from county to county, and to note the observance of most of the legal forms of the courts of justice, even in the midst of strife and the noise of angry partisans. The judges from Westminster went their circuits at the proper legal terms; juries were empanelled by the sheriffs to hear all plaints, and to give their verdicts though war was raging around them.[1]

This may be superficially true, but we have only to examine the records of the time to see how very necessary it is to qualify such a statement. Denton points out that it was often very difficult to enforce a judgment gained in the Courts, but he is silent concerning the whole intrigue and finesse which went on before the judgment was given. The truth is rather, that most men of position, and consequently their hordes of followers, laughed at the law, because they knew they could generally overcome it. The *Paston Letters* show a variety of ways in which this was done. Whether the matter in question were simple enough to be dealt with by the local Justices, or required the jurisdiction of a judge at the Sessions, or at Westminster, the methods adopted were much the same. They sprang from a common cynical view of justice, which only saw the Law as a useless and interfering body. Many men preferred to rely on strength and cunning rather than on legal proceedings. The

---

[1] Denton, p. 276, but see *E.H.R.* 1917, pp. 176–7, where Miss C. B. Firth makes clear the total breakdown of administrative government during reign of Edward IV.

only laws they recognised were might and possession. Men whose views were framed on better principles than these found themselves at a great disadvantage, even in the Law Courts. The idea of absolute justice, and the impartial weighing of a case honestly presented, did not interest most men. To them the Law was another pawn in the game, whose pieces were oppression, trickery and force. The unfortunate man who went to law, trusting only in the strength of his own case, must very often have had a rude awakening. A contemporary chronicler puts the condition of England very clearly before us when he writes:

> In every shire with Jacks and salets clean
> Misrule doth rise, and maketh neighbours war;
> The weaker goeth beneath, as oft is seen,
> The mightiest his quarrel will prefer.

> They kill your men always by one and one,
> And who says ought, he shall be beaten doubtless;
> For in your realm Justices of Peace are none
> That dare ought now the quarrellers oppress.

> The law is like unto a Welshman's hose,
> To each man's leg that shapen is and mete;
> So maintainers subvert it and transpose,
> Through might it is full low laid under feet.[1]

Men took care to shape the law to their needs by various means. A writer in the *Paston Letters* indicates what was perhaps the commonest method when he quotes, "Omnia pro pecunia facta sunt."[2] The recognition of this fact is the keynote of much fifteenth century litigation. But there were, as we shall see, many other methods of evading the law. The bribery of justices, of sheriffs, of juries, etc. was scarcely more common than was the subverting, or overawing, or perjury of witnesses. The *Paston Letters* show how justice was meted out according to favour, or to meet the King's wishes, or even to satisfy a personal enmity.

First of all, the unfortunate litigant had to beware, lest for some reason or other, he or his relatives had excited the displeasure of the presiding justice. In 1451, Paston and his friends

---

[1] Hardyng's *Chronicle*, 1457 (*E.H.R.* Oct. 1912, p. 749). "Jacks and salets," armed with coat of mail and light helmets.
[2] *P.L.* No. 350.

raised such a clamour against the notorious oppressions by Sir T. Tuddenham and John Heydon of people in the county, that a commission of Oyer and Terminer was sent to Norwich to investigate the trouble.[1] Unfortunately for Paston and his friends, Justice Prisot was one of the commission, although his friendship with Tuddenham and Heydon was notorious. When the court sat, Prisot's partiality was so marked that his colleague Yelverton remonstrated with him, but in vain. The grave complaints made by the city of Norwich, the town of Swaffham, Sir John Fastolf and many others, "the judges by their wilfulness, might not find in their heart to give not so much as a beck nor a twinkling of their eye toward, but took it to derision, God reform such partiality."[2] Nor was this all. Prisot felt Norwich was too antagonistic towards his friends, so he adjourned the Court to Walsingham, where Tuddenham and Heydon's supporters were strongest. There assembled all the knights, squires and gentlemen who espoused the oppressors' cause, and a body of 400 horsemen rode to the court with them. Prisot would allow no advocate to speak for the plaintiffs, except under great difficulty, for he "took them by the nose at every third word," which, adds the narrator, "might well be known for open partiality"![2] After such a travesty of justice, it is not surprising we hear no more of the charges against Tuddenham and Heydon, but find them at large, pursuing their old tactics.

The part played by private enmity is strikingly illustrated by the conduct of the very man who protested against Prisot's partiality in 1451. By 1465, Justice Yelverton had become John Paston's most determined enemy in the fight for Fastolf's possessions. At this time Paston was struggling to keep Hellesdon, which the Duke of Suffolk coveted; and, in the long fight that went on between the rival parties, so much disturbance was caused, that it was rumoured in Norfolk that a commission was to be sent down to enquire into the matter, with Justice Yelverton and the Duke of Suffolk as commissioners. It was quite clear to Paston's friends what would be the result of such

---

[1] Oyer and Terminer: "A commission specially granted to certain persons for the hearing and determining [Oyer and Determiner] of causes, and was formerly only in use upon some sudden outrage or insurrection in any place." Fenn.
[2] P.L. No. 158.

an enquiry. Richard Calle, the Pastons' bailiff, had been attacked by twelve of his enemies and only rescued by the Sheriff's intervention. Besides this, he had been threatened with instant death if he dared to ride abroad unprotected. This, it would seem, was evidence enough of the lawless tactics of his enemies. Yet when Calle knew who were to be the Commissioners, he wrote to John Paston, asking for advice, for, as he said, "as many of us as can be taken, shall be indicted, and hanged forthwith." He besought Paston to take some immediate action to check Yelverton's revengeful spirit, and it is clear that he fully expected Yelverton to take advantage of his position as a justice, to hurt Paston's prestige and to molest his men.[1]

Justices, as well as lesser men, were not above accepting bribes. Loudly as Paston and his friends cried out when Prisot or some other Justice swayed the law against them, they were never averse from adopting any means themselves to get a verdict in their favour. Justice Paston himself was accused of taking "diverse fees and rewards," although we have no evidence beyond the charge itself to help us form any judgment. When Fastolf's agent, Sir T. Howes, was sued in London, Sir John did not hesitate to write to one of the Justices to ask him to favour the agent's cause,[2] and the friends of Tuddenham and Heydon offered the Speaker of the House of Commons more than £1000 to befriend these two men.[3] No man seems to have been too great to be approached in this way. Mayor Shillingford makes no pretence to hide what efforts he made to bribe influential justices and others. Letter after letter goes home to Exeter detailing his exploits in this direction. What could be done with the great men of the law, was more easily done with lesser folk. Sir John Fastolf, as we might expect, thought all law matters were regulated by bribes. The Sheriff was an influential personage in the shire, and it was necessary to be in his favour to prosper well in law. So Fastolf orders his agent to "entreat the Sheriff as well ye can by reasonable rewards, rather than fail."[4] His correspondence reveals the continuous

[1] *P.L.* No. 512.   [2] *Id.* No. 308.
[3] *Id.* No. 113. Cf. how Roper extols Sir T. More for never taking bribes. *Life*, 1842, pp. 49-50.   [4] *Id.* No. 154.

bribing he found necessary to assist his very numerous lawsuits, and the Sheriff must have reaped a rich harvest if many
litigants followed the old knight's example.[1] That the Pastons
did so, we know from several references, and also from the very
interesting details of an effort once made by them to bribe the
Sheriff of Norfolk.[2] The circumstances were as follows.

John Paston had indicted some men of Lord Molynes for
forcibly ejecting Margaret from Gresham in 1450. Before the
case was tried, Osbern, a friend of Paston's, offered the Sheriff
a bribe. This the Sheriff refused at the moment, but left Osbern
under the impression that he would accept later. Osbern pushed
his advantage by every means he could, and the Sheriff said
he would be Paston's friend in everything except the present
case against Lord Molynes' men. He dared not say more, for
both the Duke of Norfolk and Lord Molynes had written to
him, asking him to favour the men. Lord Molynes, he declared,
was too influential a man to offend; and nothing Paston could
offer would compensate him if he incurred his Lordship's anger.
Osbern offered him more than any of Paston's adversaries had
offered, but the Sheriff would not yield. He agreed that if he
were able to favour Paston in any way, he would take his
money "with a good will," and there the negociations ended.
It will be noticed that fear, and not a moral scruple, was the
factor operating in the Sheriff's mind.

The jurors also could be bribed. When the Justices of the
Star Chamber were asked whether a man should be punished
there and then, or the case be sent to a jury, they decided to
deal with him at once; for they said it was probable the jury
would be corrupted by him.[3] An Act of Parliament in the reign
of Henry VI mentions "the great Gifts that such Jurors take
of the Parties in Pleas sued in the Courts."[4] In the sixteenth
century a Bishop of London, writing on behalf of his Chancellor,
asked Cardinal Wolsey to stop an action against the Chancellor
"because London juries are so prejudiced that they would find

---

[1] *E.g. P.L.* Nos. 223, 224.
[2] *Id.* Nos. 155, 159, 183, 281, and 8 *Hist. MSS.* p. 268. "Minute accounts
of Thos Playter of all expenses [meals, *bribes*, presents] while employed
on law business for Fastolf's executors."
[3] *P.P.C.* III. p. 313.	[4] 11 Hy VI, c. 4, and cf. 11 Hy VII, c. 21.

Abel guilty of the murder of Cain." Fuller quotes a proverb
to the effect "that London juries hang half and save half."[1]
Panels of jurymen were got together who could be relied on to
support one side of a case, and bribes were given freely in order
to get such panels formed. "Labour to the Sheriff for the return
of such panels as will speak for me,"[2] writes Sir John Fastolf;
and on one occasion John Paston was informed that certain
men had no other means of livelihood than by taking bribes.[3]

If some men could be bought over in this manner to deliver
false verdicts, it is not surprising to find that others could be
bribed to give false evidence. Perjury was as common as bribery.
Sometimes men perjured themselves through sheer fear of
offending some powerful man. Juries and witnesses felt the
weight of the vengeance men like Tuddenham and Heydon
could exact, if they were crossed. So the jurors at Swaffham,
although they knew otherwise, were forced to perjure themselves by giving a false verdict in favour of Sir T. Tuddenham.
A petition to Parliament states: "The jury of the said assize,
durst not for dread of the horrible menaces of the said Sir
Thomas, do otherwise but be forsworn in giving their verdict."[4]
Sir John Fastolf, ever anxious to uphold the purity of the law
when it suited his own convenience, exclaimed again and again
to the Duke of Norfolk, or to the Justices, concerning the
"perjury...that many years hath been and yet is used in this
shire."[5] The examination of certain witnesses touching Sir
J. Fastolf's will, shows that even the clergy were not always
above perjuring themselves, while a mariner who gave evidence,
on being cross-examined, admitted he had been suborned, and
that he had deposed falsely.[6] The whole of this detailed evidence
in the great will case is full of investigations and cross-examina-
tions, all of which seek to prove that the witnesses are, or are
not, guilty of taking bribes, and of giving false evidence.[7]

The medieval litigant was therefore in a difficult position if
his adversary cared to employ any of the above means of
evading justice. Even if such methods were in abeyance, there

[1] *Shakespeare's England*, II. p. 170.   [2] *P.L.* No. 154.
[3] *Id.* No. LX.   [4] *Id.* No. 151, and cf. No. 341.
[5] *Id.* Nos. 234, 308.   [6] *Id.* Nos. 488, 550.
[7] For other cases of bribery and perjury see Nos. 133, 144, 342, 389, 591,
706, and cf. *Cely*, No. 91, and *London under Eliz.* p. 200.

were frequently other factors which would intervene, and rob
him of his verdict. If his opponent were the dependent or the
friend of some influential personage, the law often made no
pretence to be impartial. All men from the King downwards
used their influence in this way. "Nowadays, ye know well
that the law goeth as it is favoured," writes one of Paston's
correspondents; and, when John Paston dared to indict Lord
Molynes, for attacking and pillaging Gresham, the Sheriff received a letter from the King, ordering him to see that such a
panel was formed as would acquit Molynes. Apparently this
was far from being an unknown or unusual use of the Royal
prerogative, for John Paston remarked that such letters could
easily be bought for six and eightpence each.[1] We have seen
how the Duke of Norfolk and Lord Molynes both threatened
to hold the Sheriff responsible if Molynes' retainers were not
acquitted,[2] and how Tuddenham appeared at Walsingham
sessions with a great force at his back to overawe the Court,
and any opposition.[3] This fear of the great must have caused
thousands of men to let causes of injury go unredressed, rather
than fight an almost hopeless case in the Courts. William
Paston, before he became a justice, knew the law well enough
to tell a client the best thing he could do was to drop his suit,
because his opponent was befriended by the Duke of Norfolk.[4]
All these many means of securing a verdict must have made
litigation even more hazardous and expensive than it necessarily
always is.

Yet, despite all these drawbacks, litigation flourished.[5] No
one can read any collection of contemporary letters, without
noticing the large place occupied by legal affairs. "Litigation
is indeed always a prominent feature in the private correspondence of the time, though it might be rash to assume that it
had an equal part in everyday life," writes Mr Kingsford; and
he goes on to give an account of the legal business that occurs

[1] *P.L.* No. 159.   [2] See above.
[3] See p. 167, and cf. *E.C.P.* 13/85, where rioters are brought to Court
to intimidate witnesses.
[4] *P.L.* No. 28.
[5] A statute was passed in 1455 limiting the number of attorneys for
Norfolk and Suffolk. Many lawsuits were alleged to be fomented by them,
"more of evil will and malice than of the truth of the thing." *R.P.* v. p. 326*b*.

in the *Stonor Letters*.[1] The *Plumpton Correspondence* also shows how very frequently Sir Robert Plumpton was in the Courts,[2] while the pages of the *Paston Letters* are constantly filled by details of law business.[3] No doubt much of this litigation was due to the changing fashion of the times by which men held lands by lease, instead of by feudal service; and also to the "scrambling and unquiet times," which left only the law courts as a last resort to the oppressed.

All this however more concerns civil than criminal actions, and it is time to turn to the part played by Justice in checking the lawlessness which we have seen was so prevalent. Speaking generally, it seems fair to say that most ordinary felons had a very good chance of escaping punishment. Besides the common method of bribing the judge or jury, or of getting witnesses to perjure themselves, there were many other possibilities open to men. England in the fifteenth century was too near the uncontrolled habits and customs of a more primitive civilization for men to have become peaceful or easily amenable to law. A rough word was still too often followed by a blow, and a blow by the drawing of a weapon, and by scenes of bloodshed. Men took the law into their own hands, and avenged their imagined wrongs to the very utmost, apparently trusting to fortune for their escape from the consequences. The fatal mistake was to be caught red-handed. For such bunglers in the art of crime, medieval thought had little toleration, and the culprit suffered summary justice of a rough and severe type. He was brought before a court competent to try him, and sentence forthwith pronounced. If fortune did not favour him, and his crime were discovered, the hue and cry was immediately raised. On hearing the shouts of "Out! out!" all able-bodied men and youths left their work and rushed out pell-mell to follow the chase. To the yawning apprentice the cry must have come like a huntsman's call to hounds. Aided by the confusion and the narrow streets of most medieval towns, the criminal had a good sporting chance of escape. In villages, his prospect was less favourable,

---

[1] *S.L.* p. xli.　　　[2] *Plum. Corr.* pp. 23, 91, 112, 130, 133.
[3] A roll of seven skins was required to account for all the expenses incurred in ten years by Sir J. Fastolf in a single lawsuit. See 8 *Hist. MSS.* p. 268. John Paston had a dozen actions pending in one term for his sister alone. *P.L.* No. 395, and cf. Nos. 267, 354.

and he had to make full use of the few minutes he had before
the hue was raised, and his pursuers set out on his track. Here
is one account from the *City of London Coroners' Rolls*, which
illustrates what was happening throughout the realm:

> The jurors say that on the preceding Friday at the hour of Vespers,
> the said William struck with his hand a certain Johanna de Lille-
> bourne, as she was standing at the said gate, for opprobrious words
> that had arisen between them. That seeing this, a certain John
> Walsham, a tailor, being moved with anger on her account, drew his
> knife...and therewith mortally struck the said William...so that
> he there fell, and immediately died. Being asked who were present
> when this happened, the jurors say, the aforesaid William, John,
> and Johanna, and a certain Adam le Irisshe came up and raised the
> cry....Being asked what became of the said John, the jurors say
> he fled to the church of S. Edmund the King in Langebourne Ward.[1]

England was full of men, such as this John Walsham, who had
been forced to flee from the scene of their crime; though, as we
shall see, many of them did not seek the refuge of the Church
as he did. Indeed, sanctuary was theoretically only a momentary
remedy, although we must here, as so often elsewhere in speaking
of medieval matters, distinguish clearly between theory and
practice. In theory a man was safe in sanctuary for only forty
days. During this time he dared not leave the precincts of the
church, for his enemies waited and watched without, and once
he left sanctuary he could be taken. While he was there, the
coroner would be sent for to come and parley with him in the
church. There were two courses open to the felon. He could
surrender to the King's peace, or else he could abjure the realm.
The coroner's business was to arrange if possible which of these
courses the man would adopt. If they could come to an agreement the question was settled; but, in many cases, neither of
these alternatives seemed very hopeful to the refugee, and he
would decline both. All the while he remained in sanctuary,
it was necessary to keep watch on his movements, lest he
should escape. Besides the voluntary vigils of any relatives of
the murdered man, or others interested, it was the duty of the
civic authorities, or the parish, to keep watch over the fugitive
during the time he was in sanctuary. Often this was so care-
lessly done that the man escaped, and got away outside the

---

[1] *Cal. Cor. Rolls of City Lond.*, Sharpe, R. R., 1913, p. 95.

jurisdiction of the particular authorities. The *Coroner's Rolls for the City of London*, during a period of about 80 years, contain thirty-seven cases of men rushing to sanctuary, but in no less than twelve of these cases the criminal managed to escape, usually under the cover of night. An even larger number were prepared to abjure the realm. Many men no doubt felt it was worth while to run the risks of re-starting life in a new land, rather than to submit to the grave possibility of ending it by surrendering. So only four men out of these thirty-seven gave themselves up to the coroner. The fourteen who abjured the realm from time to time had each to appear at the door of the church, and to acknowledge his guilt, and to swear to leave England for ever. Then each felon was told by the coroner which port he was to go to, and had to set off "un-gert, unshod, bare-headed, in his bare-shirt, as if he were to be hanged on the gallows, having received a cross in his hands." Every stage in his journey was arranged. He could only stay one night in any place, and might not turn off the high road to the right or left. When he got to Dover, or the port he was to embark at, he had to go down to the sea at once, and do his utmost to get a passage overseas. Day by day, until he sailed, he was bound to walk out into the sea up to his knees, to show his willingness to leave the realm.[1]

All this was well enough in its way, and no doubt helped to satisfy the medieval love for dramatic effects. If the criminal refused to surrender, or to abjure the realm, the difficulty was to know how he could be punished. Violation of sanctuary was too greatly opposed to ecclesiastical law and privilege to be at all common. Any such violation was severely punished, and kings found themselves powerless to prevent all kinds of men from taking shelter in sanctuary, and remaining there indefinitely.[2] During the troubled years of the Wars of the Roses, many nobles and others, fleeing from political persecution, took refuge in this way. We find from the *Paston Letters* that Anne, the widow of the great Earl of Warwick, had been in sanctuary at Beverley in 1473,[3] while Falconbridge, although sore hurt, sought refuge there soon after the head of his brother Thomas

---

[1] See *Statutes*, I p 250 for text of the oath of abjuration.
[2] See Jusserand, pp. 152–66.   [3] *P.L.* No. 725.

was displayed on London Bridge.[1] The Earl of Oxford's
brothers and Sir Thomas Fulford were in sanctuary at Westminster during 1471 after the battles at Barnet and Tewkesbury.[2]

Many men, however, only sought refuge in sanctuary until
the watch over them was relaxed, and then they escaped to
join the vast numbers of men always roaming at large in medieval
England. These outlaws were a continuous menace to all peaceful
folk, yet in some ways they caught the popular fancy; and
around them has grown up a wealth of legend and folk story,
such as we find in the Robin Hood romances. The felon who
was taken red-handed, or who surrendered to the King's peace,
found the walls of his prison a sorry substitute for that home
of outlaws, where

> In summer when the shaws be sheen,
> And leaves be large and long,
> It is full merry in fair forest
> To hear the fowlës song.

They had good reason; for, even when we discount much exaggerated writing, the conditions of life in medieval prisons
were vile. One of the Paston's correspondents evidently found
it so, for he writes:

> In good faith, I had never more need for to have help of my goods
> than I have at this time, for God wot, it stands right strange with
> me, for the false jailer that keeps me treats me worse than [if I]
> were a dog. I am fettered worse than ever I was, and manacled in
> the hands by the day and night, for he is afraid of me for breaking
> away.[3]

This fettered confinement, which loaded men with heavy chains
as though they were wild beasts, was particularly galling to
men of spirit. A man in Norwich prison, for example, paid
five marks to be released from his fetters;[4] and one of Paston's
servants wrote to his master asking for help, for he was in prison
"with the jailer, with a clogg upon my heel."[5] The number of
deaths in prison, and the condition of the prisoners, afford the
most terrible evidence of what men had to endure; e.g. of
forty-nine cases recorded on the *Coroners' Rolls for the City of*

---

[1] *P.L.* No. 676.   [2] *Id.* No. 675.   [3] *Id.* No. 363.
[4] *Id.* No. 144. He might well do so: for it is on record that a former
prisoner had to endure such conditions that his foot rotted during his long
imprisonment. *N.A.* VII. p. 267.
[5] *Id.* No. 414.

London for one year, no less than twenty-two are inquests on men dying in Newgate prison. This is an exceptionally high proportion, but year by year the number of deaths in this one prison is startlingly high, and tells its own tale.[1] When the debtors' prison at Ludgate was closed, the debtors were transferred to Newgate. The horrors that criminals endured were now felt also by these civil offenders, and within a few months an order was made for the re-establishment of Ludgate prison. The light it throws on both of these prisons, and on the medieval conception of the function of a debtors' prison, make it worth quoting at some length. It runs:

> Whereas through the abolition and doing away with the Prison of Ludgate, which was formerly ordained for the good and comfort of citizens and other reputable persons, and also, by reason of the fetid and corrupt atmosphere that is in the hateful gaol of Newgate, many persons who were lately in the said Prison of Ludgate...and who for divers great offences which they had there compassed, were committed to the said gaol [of Newgate], are now dead, who might have been living, it is said, if they had remained in Ludgate, abiding in peace there....[2]

Except in the worst cases, most prisoners were able to ameliorate their conditions by money. The jailer looked on his prisoners as a type of paying guest, and the more they could pay the less irksome became their confinement. John Paston himself must have been able to speak with some authority on the matter, as he was thrice confined in the Fleet prison. It is obvious from his letters that, except for his lack of liberty, he found life there quite bearable. Indeed, once while he was there, Margaret went up to Town, and evidently was much at the prison, where Paston and his friends entertained her. She writes on her return:

> Right worshipful husband, I recommend me to you,...thanking you of your great cheer that you made me, and of the cost that you did on me. You did more cost than my will was that you should do, but [since] it pleased you to do so, God give me grace to do that may please you.[3]

The sums paid to jailers naturally varied very much according to the rank of the prisoner. The Earl of Surrey paid the great

---

[1] *Cor. Rolls, City Lond.* Roll B. Out of 394 deaths in Rolls B–G, 158 perished in prison!

[2] *Memorials*, p. 677. [3] *P.L.* No. 529.

sum of 40s. per week for himself, and 2s. 6d. a week for each of his men.[1] Unfortunately, we do not know how much Paston paid, but one of his tenants was in prison at Ipswich for some time, and had to pay 20d. weekly for his board;[2] while another man was imprisoned for over two years, at a weekly tariff of two shillings.[3]

The same spirit that prompted the picturesque exit of men abjuring the realm, still held its own in other methods of punishing offenders. Throughout this century, every town and village had its stocks, where vagabonds and other offenders against the law might frequently be seen. Apart from the discomfort, the shame of being seen in such a position was evidently keenly realised. Everyone will remember King Lear's indignation and deep anger when he finds his messenger in the stocks outside Gloucester's castle, and this feeling was common to all classes of people. In the indictment drawn up against the wild and lawless fellowship that molested Norfolk in 1451, the fact that innocent men were seized by them, and forced to endure the indignity of the stocks, is mentioned in the notes for the prosecution. The Prior of Swaffham's man, they say, was "set openly and shamefully, and [with] great oppression in the stocks," while another unfortunate man was kept in this disgraceful position for more than three days, till he paid 5 marks to be set free.[4] Sometimes the stocks performed a more proper purpose in holding miscreants until they could receive their due punishment. Margaret writes to her husband in great excitement to say that the parson of Snoring and his accomplices, who had killed a man, had been caught, and were in the stocks waiting to be taken to London for their trial.[5]

Margaret, as well as all the members of the Paston family, must have been very familiar with the sight of people in the stocks at Norwich.[6] Other equally interesting sights were the common joy of the medieval mob. In 1496, a woman was ordered to leave Norwich within twelve days. If she was still found within the City after that time, it was ordered that she was to be led outside the City walls to the strains of a bagpipe![7]

[1] Materials, Hist. Hy VII, Campbell (R.S.), I. p. 208.
[2] P.L. No. 505.   [3] Id. No. 931.   [4] Id. No. 144.   [5] Id. No. 403.
[6] E.g. Norwich Records, II. Nos. CCLI, CCLIII, CCCIX.
[7] Id. II. No. CCLIV.

Such processions, heralded by trumpets or other sounds, would make their way to the stocks, or to the pillory, where the wretched man was condemned to stand for a certain time, while his enemies made sport of him. A man condemned for making a false charge of conspiracy against the chief men of the City of London was sent to prison for a year and a day, besides which he was to be put in the pillory on four separate occasions. The official pronouncement runs:

> The said John shall come out of Newgate without hood or girdle, barefoot and unshod, with a whetstone hung by a chain from his neck, and lying on his breast, it being marked with the words,— "A false liar"; and there shall be a pair of trumpets, trumpeting before him on his way to the pillory; and there the cause of his punishment shall be solemnly proclaimed. And the said John shall remain on the pillory for three hours of the day, and from thence shall be taken back to Newgate in the same manner.[1]

Often while there, the victim would have to endure, besides the taunts and missiles of the crowd, the further indignity and discomfort of seeing his false or rotten wares burnt under his nose, or else he would be forced to drink some of his own bad wine, while the remainder was poured over his head![2] Scolding women, in Norwich, as elsewhere throughout England, were set upon the ducking-stool and ducked in the water, possibly to their own amendment, and generally to the amusement of the bystanders.[3]

Severe in many ways as medieval laws were, the prisoner had a better chance then of getting his sentence reduced or cancelled than he has now. The judgment of the court by no means deprived the medieval prisoner of all hope. He knew very well that there were still many ways in which his friends could work —by making representations in the right quarters, by female influence, by bribes—to secure his release. A man who had money in his purse, or rich friends, could oftentimes get his punishment remitted for a money fine. A London swindler was found guilty and condemned to stand an hour a day on the pillory on three market days, but his rich friends managed to get the order to the Sheriffs cancelled, on payment of £20.[4] Another case is recorded in which a parish clerk was tried, and

---

[1] *Memorials*, p. 316, and cf. pp. 405, 466.
[3] *Norwich Records*, II. Nos. CCLXVI, CCCXLV.
[2] *Id.* pp. 318, 446, 449.
[4] *Memorials*, pp. 623–4.

put into Newgate prison, for having slandered John of Gaunt. "And after that," the official document says in its bald way,

at the suit of the wife of the said Clerk, and by other means employed with that Lord, the release of such clerk was by him assented to, seeing that he acknowledged his offence...and threw himself wholly on the grace of that Lord.[1]

In that phrase, "by other means employed with that Lord," lies the whole secret of the force which continuously undermined medieval justice. Sometimes, more spectacular alternatives than fines were demanded. A man who had been condemned to stand in "the pillory with a whetstone hung from his neck, in token of his being a liar," escaped by doing public penance.

In reverence for our said Lord the King, whose servant the said William then was, and at the entreaty of other lords, who interceded for him,...it was determined that, on his leaving prison, he should carry from the Guildhall aforesaid through the Chepe and Fletestrete, a lighted wax candle, weighing three pounds, to the Church of S. Dunstan before mentioned, and there make offering of the same.[2]

Besides such means as these, there was always the possibility of a Royal pardon. As we have already seen, the King did not scruple to send an order to the Sheriff to empanel a jury such as would acquit Lord Molynes of any charges against him. In the same way, the Royal pardon could sometimes be obtained by those about the King, and the ease and frequency with which such pardons were granted undoubtedly encouraged the lawlessness of the times. In 1452 Henry VI, following the example of the Pope, offered a general pardon, and about 3000 persons took advantage of this offer.[3] Twenty years later, both Sir John Paston and his brother were glad to take advantage of a pardon issued to those who fought against King Edward IV in the battles of 1471.[4]

[1] *Memorials*, p. 425, and cf. W. Hudson, *op. cit.* Intro. xl–xli for frequency of such practices at Norwich.
[2] *Id.* p. 493.
[3] *P.L.* Intro. cxxvii. We do not need to rely on medieval figures with their usual exaggeration for these figures, as the names of those pardoned are all entered on the Pardon Roll of 30 and 31 Henry VI.
[4] *P.L.* Nos. 674–5, 678, 687.

CHAPTER XIII

LAWLESSNESS

THE gradual failure and collapse of the old Feudal régime caused very grave troubles. Men began to feel the injustice of any attempt to confine them to the place in which they happened to be born. As the Feudal rural organisation fell to pieces, the serfs began to shake themselves free, and to wander about the land seeking employment and better conditions of life wherever they might be found. The new economic situation which developed during the fifteenth century was largely responsible for two classes scarcely known to Feudalism proper—a middle class and an urban population.[1] The gradual formation and interaction of these new forces, and their consequent reaction upon the old conditions, assisted to bring about the end of the existing system. However good this emancipation proved to be in the end, it made fifteenth century England a very unhappy place to live in. Men conscious of their wrongs, and only partly conscious of their power, are always inclined to be violent; and the risings and local rebellions at this time were inevitable and are understandable. Under the changing conditions men wandered up and down the country seeking employment, and too often finding none. Many of them eventually took to lawless ways as an only solution. With all its faults, the old system had provided a bare living and a dwelling house, however poor, for most men. The serf had his privileges as well as his disabilities. Now he began to find that in casting off his serfdom he was relinquishing these rights of protection and sustenance which custom had gradually created as a counterpoise to his legal disabilities.

A change must have come even without the new ideas of John Ball and his friends, which had filled many men's minds and hastened events. The history of the fifteenth century shows clearly that landowners were fast ceasing to keep a strong hold

[1] *Factors in Modern History*, Pollard, A. F., 1910 edn, p. 41.

on their serfs, who were indeed becoming unnecessary and a burden to them. A study of manorial life has shown that the lord of the manor very often took no steps to regain a serf who had fled. Many landowners were glad when this happened, especially in the later years of the century.[1] The rapid rise and growth of the woollen industry was gradually changing the face of much of England. Men began to realise that sheep-farming was far more profitable than the agricultural work of their ancestors; and, as more and more land was laid down in sheep walks, so men became more and more superfluous.

In the midst of such far-reaching changes as these, came the Wars of the Roses. It is frequently stated that these wars were almost private wars, that they were fought between rival factions assisted by their partizans, and that the great mass of English people was unconcerned. This is only a one-sided view; for, whether the people took part or not, the same conditions which stirred up the nobles to those battles operated in like manner against the whole nation. The lack of firm government, which was the plague of England during many years of the fifteenth century, was felt by Hodge, as well as by the King-maker. That same lack of control, which allowed small gangs and "evil ruled fellowships" to terrorise Hodge and his friends, also allowed great nobles and their followers to fight at S. Albans. The times were out of joint for all; and, unfortunately, as we have seen, just at a moment when other influences had resulted in the crumbling of an old and intricate system.

The interaction of these circumstances proved very terrible for England. At such a time, when thousands of men were dissatisfied and breaking away from their old allegiance, the firmest, wisest, statesmanship was needed. Unfortunately, statesmanship was the last thing thought of at the courts of Henry VI and Edward IV. All classes of society were affected. The vagrant was quick enough to see that under the livery of a great lord he was practically immune from ordinary justice; and he knew that, so long as he fought when ordered, and gave his master no trouble, few questions were likely to be asked as to how he spent his leisure. The great lords themselves relied on the power of arms, rather than the pleas of their lawyers;

[1] *R.H.S.* xiv. p. 131; xvii. p. 248.

and the rest of England took its lead from them. The Wars of the Roses only repeat on a large scale the same type of lawless action which went on throughout the length and breadth of the land. All this anarchy was able to flourish, whatever its cause, because there was no sufficiently strong power at the centre of government to stamp it out. Not until Henry VII came to the throne was there any appreciable improvement and stabilising of control.

The evidence detailing this wild state of affairs is overwhelming. Whether we look at official records, or at private letters, all alike are constantly recording outrages and lawless deeds of the most flagrant nature. It will be well, perhaps, to quote one or two typical examples which are recorded on the Rolls of Parliament. We should be inclined to discount much said there, as being merely rhetorical, if it were not for the fact that every statement made in these rolls can be substantiated many times over by contemporary records. The preamble to a petition set out in the Rolls of Parliament for 1459 gives a graphic account of the general state of affairs. The faithful Commons tell of

Great and lamentable complaints of your true poor subjects, universally throughout every part of this your realm, of robberies, ravishments, extortions, oppressions, riots, unlawful assemblies, wrongful imprisonments done unto them, unto such time as your said true subjects have made, as well for their enlarging as for the sureties of their lives, fine and ransom at the will of such misdoers. And forasmuch as the said misdoers be so favoured and assisted by persons of great might, having towards them of their livery, expressly against your laws, such multitude of robbers, rioters and mischievous persons, which in riotous and forcible manner disturb and hinder as well your Justices of Assize as of Peace in every part of this your realm, that no execution of your law may be had, so as your said true subjects, though divers of them be persons of great worship, dare not for fear and doubt of their lives, neither complain to your Highness, nor sue for remedy after the course of your laws, but rather to suffer such wrongs without remedy.[1]

How little control there was, is clear enough from the succession of complaints and enactments against robbers, murderers, oppressors and the like from time to time;[2] while the following

[1] *R.P.* v. p. 367 [1459].
[2] *Id.* IV. pp. 421, 427, 456, V. pp. 268, 408, 426, 434, 487, VI. p. 188.

petition of 1472 shows how bold these men had become. The petition reminds the King that, although he has obtained victory over his enemies, and a certain amount of peace, yet this

peace in no wise may persevere or continue therein, or in any body politic, without due execution of the laws within the same used and approved.... We your humble subjects coming for the Commons of the same, were put in right good comfort at the beginning of this your high Court of Parliament by the mouth of my Lord of Rochester, declaring your blessed disposition and tender favour that you bear to the same extent and effect of execution of your laws. Yet sovereign Lord, it is so that in divers parts of this realm, great abominable murders, robberies, extortions, oppressions and other manifold main-tainences, misgovernances, forcible entries, as well upon them being in by judgment as otherwise, affrays, assaults, be committed and done by such persons as either be of great might, or else favoured under persons of great power, in such wise that their outrageous demerits as yet remain unpunished, insomuch that of late divers persons have been slain, some in Southwark, and here nigh about the City, and some here at Westminster Gate, no consideration [being] taken.... that your high presence is had here at your Palace of Westminster, nor that your high court of Parliament is here sitting, and is in a manner a contemelious contempt of your Highness, and your Courts here held and kept, to the great discouraging of your well ruled and true begemen, and to the great emboldening of all rioters and misgoverned persons.[1]

If all this sounds rather general and lacking in definition, we can easily fill in the detail by turning over the pages of the *Paston Letters*. Here in this private correspondence we get the most astonishing picture of the state of England at this time. We have no reason, it must be remembered, to regard what was happening in Norfolk as being at all exceptional. The *Early Chancery Proceedings*,[2] the *Proceedings of the Privy Council*,[3] or the *Coroners' Rolls*[4] all tell the same tale; and therefore we may assume that the evidence we are fortunate enough to possess in the case of Norfolk, thanks to the *Paston Letters*, is only characteristic of almost any other county at this time.

Previous chapters will have given the reader many examples of deeds which could only have been accomplished in a wild and unsettled community. It will be remembered that the Pastons themselves suffered three sieges. First Lord Molynes had attacked Gresham with his men and ejected Margaret,

[1] *R.P.* VI. p. 8.   [2] *E.C.P. passim*, and see Abram, p. 219.
[3] *P.P.C.* v. VI. *passim*.   [4] *Cor. Rolls, e.g.* Nos. 60–3.

before proceeding to pull down the house and rifle its contents. Then, the Duke of Suffolk had sent a force of 300 against Hellesdon and had broken and destroyed everything possible; and finally the Duke of Norfolk had seized Caister. To do this he had to send a force of 3000 men to surround the castle; and the fact that a noble had as many men in his pay, and could so ignore the King's peace, affords an illuminating commentary on the times.[1]

Complaints were naturally frequent, but seem to have been very ineffective. As we have seen, government was paralysed at the centre; and, whether men complained to the King in person, or to his local representatives, it made little difference. Whatever promises, or partial attempts to enforce the law were made, the forces of the wild and lawless parties eventually prevailed. So strongly was the evil state of affairs in Norfolk presented to the King, that at last, in 1452, he was forced to send down the Duke of Norfolk to inquire into the "great riots, extortions and horrible wrongs and hurts" which had made the people "so wylde." The Duke caused a proclamation to be made, in which he asked for full and fearless exposure of any misdoings. But this was useless without a promise of adequate protection. Lord Scales, who was one of the greatest men in the county, had caused much unhappiness by his protection of certain well-known oppressors. Yet, before the Duke came into Norfolk, some of Scales's adherents let it be known publicly that any tales told of them or their friends would be fully revenged after the Duke's departure. Some bold spirits like John Paston and several of his friends felt the times justified the risk, and laid information of "divers assaults and riots made by Charles Nowell and others...upon John Paston and other of our kin, friends and neighbours."[2] John Paston's complaint detailed the outrageous attack on him outside Norwich Cathedral,[3] and also the murderous attempt against his wife's uncle, Philip Berney.[4] The documents setting forth the varied crimes and oppressions of this one gang will give the reader ample material for judging the condition of Norfolk at this time. These men were not mere lawless outcasts of society, but mostly enjoyed the

[1] See p. 20.   [2] P.L. Nos. 173–5.
[3] Id. Nos. 174–6.   [4] See p. 141.

protection of some influential personage or other. Sir Thomas Tuddenham, John Heydon, and Thomas Daniel are three men who seem to have been at the back of much of the trouble. They, and their adherents, were continuously in conflict with the more law-abiding men in the county. Were one of their number indicted, Tuddenham, or Heydon, or their friends, would appear at the court with so overwhelming a force at their back that the jury would be overawed, and justice defeated.[1]

Ten years later, conditions do not seem to have improved. The *Patent Rolls* record innumerable instances of the state of confusion and uneasiness that prevailed. The *Paston Letters* are full of hints and fears caused by the "murders and robberies, as well as the great insurrection" that went on around the writers. One of the Pastons' correspondents warned his master that "the world is right wild, and has been since Heydon's safeguard was proclaimed at Walsingham; for in good faith, I trow unless he be punished, the country will rise and do much harm."[2] The King sent a message to the people of Norfolk by Justice Yelverton, who said the King was displeased to learn that "ill-disposed people" had been so troublesome, but that he knew it was only a small portion of the county, and that the mass of men were well disposed. Yelverton stated that he and the Sheriff were there to receive complaints, and that any man so complaining would be protected; but men doubted the value of such a safeguard. The flood of troubles rolled on. Margaret writes:

God in his holy mercy give grace that there may be set a good rule and a wise [one] in the country in haste, for I heard never say of so much robbery and manslaughter in this country as is now within a little time.[3]

Such was the general state of Norfolk throughout many years of this century. Rival factions, and their adherents, were for ever struggling for the mastery, and in their train came all the horrors and misery attendant on such circumstances. Naturally, under the shadow of greater men, many ruffians and outlaws found shelter and carried on their evil occupations. But, having described the prevailing conditions, both throughout England and also in Norfolk, we can now discuss in detail some of the

[1] *P.L.* Nos. 147–8, 155, 158, 190.   [2] *Id.* No. 399.   [3] *Id.* No. 435.

more important cases of lawlessness reported in the *Paston Letters*.

It is, perhaps, little more than accidental that the first important document relating to the Pastons should be a long information setting out the misdeeds of one Walter Aslak; but the document itself is typical of the wild and boisterous times. It relates how, in 1424, a certain John Grys was attacked in his house at Wighton, the doors broken open, and himself, his son, and servant were carried off in open daylight to a place about a mile away, where stood a pair of gallows. The miscreants were unable to get any ropes to hang these unfortunate men, so they thereupon "feloneously slew and murdered [them] in the most horrible wise that was ever heard spoken of in that country." William Paston, about this time, had the misfortune to offend Walter Aslak by acting against him in the Law Courts. Aslak contemplated asking for a new trial, and so wished to eliminate Paston. This he attempted to do by posting bills on the gates of the city, and on the chief churches in Norwich, which set forth a threat to murder Paston, his clerks, and his servants, and to dismember them "as John Grys in the same form was slain." Worse still, the bills contained "these two words in Latin, et cetera, by which words commonly it was understood that...the makers of the said bills imagined to the said William...more malice and harm than was expressed." It seems incredible that this could have been allowed in so great a city as Norwich, but William Paston had no doubt of the sincerity of Aslak's threats, and durst not stir abroad. Paston naturally appealed to the Law, but got little assistance. Aslak had a powerful patron, who enabled him to evade any writs served against him, and also was able to deprive Paston of the protection of the Duke of Norfolk.[1]

This happened in 1424; but, as the century went on, there was little improvement. Rather the world got more unsettled, and people lived in almost daily fear of molestation. A letter written before 1450 shows us what could happen. William Tailboys had quarrelled with a certain Hugh Withom, but they had agreed to abide with one another according to the law. "Notwithstanding," writes Tailboys, "upon Monday last past, he

[1] *P.L.* No. 4.

and three men with him came unto a servant's house of mine in Boston,...and there, as he sat at his work, struck him upon the head and in the body with a dagger, and wounded him sore and pulled him out of his house, and set him in prison without any reasonable cause, or without writ, or any other process showed unto him.

Withom, as was the common custom, was supported in his misdeeds by one of the nobility, who a little later took the unfortunate servant out of Boston prison, and said before all the crowd gathered about him: "False thief, you shall be hanged, and as many of your master's men as may be got." Then he had the man haled off to some unknown place—probably Lincoln Castle prison, the writer thought—and he adds, "Unless he be had out of prison in haste, it will be right grievous to him to heal of his hurt; he is so sore stricken."[1]

Much about the same time, Norfolk was greatly troubled by a lawless band of men under the leadership of Charles Nowell. They kept the country to the east of Norwich in a continuous ferment, and no man, or place, was safe from their attacks. They had their headquarters in the house of one Robert Ledham, and in the words of the information laid against them,

would issue out at their pleasure, sometimes six, sometimes twelve, sometimes thirty or more, armed jacked and salleted, with bows, arrows, spears, and bills, and over-ride the country and oppress the people and do many horrible and abominable deeds.[2]

Churches were no more sacred to them than the wayside hovel. On Mid-lent Sunday they tried to kill two servants of the Bishop of Norwich while they knelt at Mass. A little later they came to the White Friars at Norwich at Evensong and demanded to enter. This was refused them, as they had previously threatened to seize some of the citizens. A great crowd gathered, and overawed the "evil fellowship," and they had to depart; but no one seems to have dared to molest them, though the Mayor and Aldermen were there supported by the loyal citizens. These ruffians rode about the country, and took sheep and cattle where they would; they pulled men out of their houses, and killed or beat them; they waylaid men on the high road; they even entered the chancel of Hasingham Church and there attacked the parson; they molested and beat old women; and so

---

[1] *P.L.* No. 75.   [2] *Id.* No. 179, 201.

terrorised the countryside that people "for fear of murder dare not abide in their houses, nor ride, nor walk about their occupations" without protection.[1] But they were far too clever to rely on violence only. Charles Nowell himself was a friend of a certain Daniel who, as we have seen, was one of the band of influential men who held Norfolk in their grip for many years. Nowell and his friends relied on the protection of such men.[2] Guile and clever manœuvring at law were frequently employed by all these people to bolster up their lawless deeds.

Roger Church, one of Nowell's friends, as soon as he learnt that the Duke of Norfolk was coming to stamp out violence, caused himself to be arrested by some of his own friends and brought before the Duke. He was accused of having been at an unlawful assembly with the view of stirring up a rebellion. Whereupon Church offered to turn King's evidence, and proceeded to indict many well-known gentlemen, farmers and yeomen. In all, about 300 men were implicated; and Church alleged that they were planning a rising against the King. The whole conspiracy was betrayed by one of Church's accomplices a little later. He admitted that several men had met Church in a little wood, and he had proposed the name of John Amend All for their captain. Then they decided on Church's arrest, so that they might cause suspicion to fall on well-known men in the countryside, hoping perhaps thereby to divert attention from their own doings.[3] As we shall see later, these desperadoes had little to fear in being brought before the Sheriff or visiting Justices. Their powerful friends were stronger than the King's judges!

It is obvious that, once the first battle at S. Albans was fought, from then onwards lawlessness had a certain sanction and encouragement, which must have made it stronger than ever. Thus John Paston's youngest son writes, "There is at the Castle of Rising and in two other places,...great gathering of people, and hiring of harness. It is well understood that they be not to the King ward, but rather the contrary, and for to rob."[4] He goes on to say that, under the circumstances, his father thinks it wise to keep his men about him in Norfolk.

---

[1] *P.L.* Nos. 179, 201.   [2] See above, p. 185.
[3] *P.L.* Nos. 177, 178, 179, 180, 181.   [4] *Id.* No. 384.

The *Letters* of the next few months and years show how necessary this was. A friend of the Pastons' was taken from his house by a parson, led away, and later on was murdered. "The world is right wild" wrote a friend, and we hear of a band of men, led by one Will Lynys, who rode about the countryside, accusing men of being Scotsmen and exacting heavy bribes before they would release them. "I am put in fear daily for my abiding here," wrote Margaret Paston, and not without reason. Within a month of this, her husband was attacked in the Shire house by one of the Sheriff's men, who struck him twice with a dagger. Luckily Paston wore a thick doublet and was unhurt;[1] but that such a thing could happen in the Shire house, and in the face of a crowded assembly, illustrates how fierce and contemptuous of all authority men had become. An interesting account exists in a letter to John Paston, which still further illustrates the high-handed manner adopted by great lords at this time. A certain man named Piers of Leigh was in the Bishop's gaol at Lynn. When the Earl of Oxford learnt this, he hastened at once to the gaol.

My Lord pulled him [Piers] out of the said gaol, and made to put him upon a horse, and tied an halter by his arm and so led him forth....And even forthwith, the said Bishop, the Mayor and others of their fellowship met with my said Lord...and also the said Piers tied by an halter, the Bishop having these words unto my Lord with his pillion in his hands, "My Lord, this is a prisoner, [as] you may know by his tipet and staff. What will you do with him?" Thereto my Lord said, "He is my prisoner now." Whereto the Bishop said, "Where is your warrant or commission thereto"? My Lord said, "I have warrant sufficient for me." And thus they departed, the Mayor and all the Commonalty of Lynn keeping their silence.[2]

While such things could and did happen, the whole countryside must have lived in constant fear. Besides this, however, both the ordinary holder of lands upon a yearly rental and other tenants were always at the mercy of these contending factions. While landowners and others disputed about their property-rights among themselves, the tenants felt little inconvenience; but, unfortunately for them, it usually did not stop

---

[1] *P.L.* Nos. 400, 410.
[2] *Id.* No. 437. "Pillion," the hat worn by a Doctor of Divinity.

there. Both claimants would demand rent, and the wretched tenants would be often forced to pay twice over, or else they would have their goods distrained for not paying up, or would be punished for paying the rival claimants anything at all. We can watch one such case in detail. When Sir John Paston died, his brother wrote hurriedly to Margaret and told her to send Edmund Paston to the manors of Marlingford, Oxnead, Paston, Crowmer, and Caister, to warn the tenants of the death of Sir John, and of his brother's rights of succession. Edmund was particularly instructed to tell the tenants of Marlingford and Oxnead to pay no rents to his uncle William. After his mother's death William Paston had claimed these two manors, because they came to the Pastons when Agnes married Justice Paston. The manors, however, were entailed under the Justice's will, and so Sir John, and now his brother John, was the rightful heir. Despite this, William Paston meant to get them if he could, and fought vigorously. As usual, it was the tenants who suffered most, since they never knew to whom their rents were due. The vicar of Paston writes to Margaret:

When my master Sir John's baily was at Paston, he scared your tenants, bidding them pay no rents to Mr William Paston. On which Harry Warns wrote to Mr William, who bade him warn them not to pay money to anyone else; otherwise he would meet them at London "as the law would," or at some market or fair, and make them pay arrears.[1]

Men were afraid to cultivate their land, as they never knew what would happen to the property.[2] It was not until more than five years later that an agreement was reached between uncle and nephew, and that this family quarrel was removed from the burdens the tenants had to bear.[3]

So far the cases we have described have shown wildness and unlawful deeds in plenty, but have generally stopped short of actual murder. It is very evident, however, that turbulent gangs of men in rough and lawless times would not always be so scrupulous, and murder is appallingly common in the records of the time. The Pastons fortunately lost no relative directly in this terrible fashion, although Philip Berney, a cousin of Margaret Paston, was so ill-treated that, after a lingering illness,

[1] *P.L.* No. 741.   [2] *Id.* No. 742.   [3] *Id.* No. 880.

he died.[1] Many instances are recorded in these pages, and some
of them in words so graphic that they must be given in full.
The first case concerns the murder of Sir Humphrey Stafford's
son, and illustrates the murderous hatred that could arise from
quarrels over property.

Touching the sudden adventure that fell lately at Coventry, please
it your Lordship to hear that, on Corpus Christi Even last passed, between eight and nine of the clock at afternoon, Sir Humphrey Stafford
had brought my master, Sir James of Ormond, toward his Inn from
my Lady of Shrewsbury, and returned from him towards his Inn, he
met with Sir Robert Harcourt coming from his mother towards his
Inn, and passed Sir Humphrey; and Richard his son came somewhat
behind, and when they met together, they fell in hands together,
and Sir Robert smote him a great stroke on the head with his sword,
and Richard with his dagger hastily went toward him, and as he
stumbled one of Harcourt's men smote him in the back with a knife;
men know not whom it was readily. His father heard [a] noise, and
rode towards them, and his men ran before him thitherward, and in
the going down off his horse, one, he knew not who, smote him on
the head with an edged tool,—men know not with us, with what
weapon,—that he fell down, and his son fell down before him as
good as dead. And all this was done, as men say, in a Paternoster
while. And forthwith Sir Humphrey Stafford's men followed after,
and slew two men of Harcourt's, one Swynerton and Bradshawe,
and more be hurt. Some be gone and some be in prison in the gaol
at Coventry....And all this mischief fell because of an old debate
that was between them, for taking of a distress, as it is told.[1]

In the west of England, the disputes of contending lords and
their factions led to scenes of similar lawlessness. The Earl of
Devon and Lord Bonville carried on a quarrel of such ferocity,
that the law was unable to stem the torrent of murders, robberies, and devastation that resulted from their disagreements.
The Earl of Devon alone was said to have been followed by
800 horsemen and 4000 footmen.[3] Although the Privy Council
tried to compose the differences between these two lords as
early as 1441,[4] fourteen years later the Rolls of Parliament
stated that, "there be great and grievous riots down in the West
country between the Earl of Devonshire and the Lord Bonville,
by which some men have been murdered, some robbed, and
children and women taken."[3] The Paston Letters record in some

---

[1] P.L. Nos. 175–6, 188–9, 201.   [3] Id. No. 60.   [3] R.P. v. p. 285.
[4] P.P.C. v. p. 165, and pp. xc, xci.

detail one of the many terrible incidents which resulted from this continuous enmity.

A certain man, Radford by name, was one of Lord Bonville's counsel. One night the Earl of Devonshire's son, with a force of 70 men, came to Radford's dwelling and set an house on fire near to his gate. When the house was well alight, they made a great noise and attracted the attention of Radford's men, who opened their gate, and came out to look at the fire. Immediately the Earl's son and his men got inside the gates, and sought out Radford, who was persuaded to come out to talk, on being assured no injury would be done him. John Paston's correspondent continues:

> In the mean time, his followers robbed his [Radford's] chamber, and rifled his chests, and packed up such [stuff] as they could get together, and carried it away on his own horse. Then the earl's son said "Radford, thou must come to my lord, my father." He said he would, and bade one of his men make ready his horse to ride with him, which answered him that all his horses were taken away. Then he said to the Earl's son, "Sir, your men have robbed my chamber, and they have my horses [so] that I may not ride with you to my Lord your father. Wherefore, I pray you, let me ride, for I am old, and may not go."

Despite his plea, no horse was given him, and he was forced to walk out into the night on foot, to stumble on as best he might. His infirmities would not allow him to walk quickly, and he was little more than a bow-shot from his own home, when nine men sprang upon him, and a blow on the head felled him to the ground. One of this band of assassins bent down and swiftly cut the prostrate man's throat.[1]

Civil war; private wars of the above nature; the strife of nobles and gentry contriving for the mastery of counties or districts; all went on side by side. With them, and sometimes under their patronage, went the grim figures of the cut-throats and robbers. Laws were passed in vain. Statutes against the hire of retainers with a distinctive livery, and against the maintenance of quarrels, were of little avail. The times were troubled and confused; and, in the midst of all this internal anarchy, the weak and innocent masses of common people suffered and endured as best they could.

[1] *P.L.* No. 257.

CHAPTER XIV

RELIGION

No account of life in medieval England could be complete which failed to recognise the very important part played by religion in those times. Few things, indeed, were more familiar to every man, woman and child, than were the parish church and the parish priest. The parish church was the scene of many of the great events of their lives. There they were baptised, married, and in due course buried. There, week by week, from childhood, they were expected to attend to hear Mass, and to receive instruction in the Faith and the mysteries of the Church. There from time to time they made their confessions, received absolution, and yearly partook of the Eucharist. The parish priest was equally familiar to them as the voice of the Church and as the minister of her sacraments. Amidst an almost entirely unlettered congregation, the priest's learning (however scanty it sometimes may have been) obviously gave him prestige, and induced respect for himself and his Church. Belief in the Christian faith and obedience to the teaching of the Church were almost universal. To most people the ecclesiastical system was an accepted part of the scheme of things; and, as a result, everyday life and thought were strongly coloured by the doctrines and claims put forth by the priests in the name of the Church. There was already, under the surface, a good deal of the anti-clericalism voiced in Henry VIII's reign by St Germain; but the large majority of the lay folk were undoubtedly loyal, in the main, to the existing state of things. If, therefore, we examine the medieval attitude towards birth, or death, or marriage, we are enabled to understand how immense was the part the Church played in the lives of the people.

Baptism in the fifteenth century seemed to most people to be the natural and necessary consequence of birth. Church teaching made it very clear that every effort must be made not to allow any child to remain unbaptised for any length of time. If a child seemed unlikely to live, the parents or the midwife might baptise it at once. Midwives, especially, were taught to understand the essential words and actions which made the sacrament valid. In the ordinary way there was no need for such drastic methods, and the infant was baptised at the parish church. This took place as soon as possible, often upon the same day as the child was born. The godparents were hastily summoned, and the baby taken to church by the midwife, accompanied by a crowd of friends and neighbours. When they reached the church, preparations were quickly made for the ceremony. We read that the midwife undressed Mary Barantyne's son William, while she sat beside a fire in the belfry, and that the child's godfather, Sir William Stonor, looked on and declared that the child enjoyed the whole business.[1] When all was ready, the priest was summoned from the vestry, and the ceremony then took place at the font. The scene is set out in detail on many stone fonts of the period still existing in country churches. These picture boys holding lighted tapers by the side of the priest, while others carry the ewer and towels for use after the infant has been anointed with the sacred oil. At the priest's side, the acolyte holds the opened service book, and the midwife soothes the baby until the moment comes when she must hand him to the priest.[2]

Once the actual ceremony was over the child was taken home by the midwife and given back to the anxious mother; an account of the whole ceremony, and the names of those present were related in detail by her gossips who called to see her. The godparents and other friends usually gathered together, and spent the rest of the day in feasting and drinking. All such details as these may be found related again and again by contemporary witnesses in the documents known as Proofs of Age.[3]

[1] S.L. No. 294.
[2] Records of Rochester, Fielding, C. H., 1910, p. 139. "At S. Mary Higham the font has places for the salt, the chrism and the taper."
[3] E.g. see Sus. Arch. Soc. XII. pp. 43, 44. But note articles in E.H.R. XXII. pp. 101, 526, which show that the information in these proofs was often "common form" by the fifteenth century. "John Budd...was present at the baptism, and held a lighted torch. John Steer because on his return from Bosham, he met a woman carrying the said Robert to Cherdham Church to be baptised. John Broker because the godfather and godmothers, and many other persons came into his house on that day directly after the baptism,...to eat and to drink. Another man met the midwife, and yet another the priest who baptised."

The *Paston Letters* never report for us such intimate details of the numerous baptisms which various members of the family doubtless attended. The only baptism mentioned is that of the young daughter of the Duke of Norfolk. She was baptised by the Bishop of Winchester (who was also her godfather) and the whole ceremony is thus briefly described. "On Thursday by ten of the clock before noon my young Lady was christened, and named Anne. The Bishop christened it, and was godfather both, and within two hours and less after the christening was over, my Lord departed."[1]

The actual ceremony of marriage was ignored in much the same way. John Paston the youngest makes a passing reference to the publishing of banns, which was as necessary then as now, and writes: "Ye send me word of the marriage of my Lady Jane; one marriage for another one. Norse and Bedford were asked in the church on Sunday last past."[2] A fifteenth century book of instruction for priests gives the formula as follows:

> The seventh sacrament is wedlock, before the which sacrament the banes in holy church shal be thryes asked on thre solempne dayes—a werk day or two between, at the lest: eche day on this maner: N. of V. has spoken with N. of P. to have her to his wife, and to ryght lyve in forme of holy chyrche. If any mon knowe any lettyng qwy they may not come togedyr say now or never on payne of cursyng.[3]

But there is little other information. Once the exciting financial chase was over, the actual solemnities were too commonplace to be worth the labour of description in a letter. What actually happened we know from the same book of instructions. On the marriage day, the priest met the parties at the door of the church, and there married them with these words:

> N. Hast thou wille to have this wommon to thi wedded wif. R. Ye syr. N. My thou wel fynde at thi best to love hur and hold ye to hur and to no other to thi lives end. R. Ye syr. N. Then take her by yor hande and saye after me: I N, take the N, in forme of holy chyrche, to my wedded wyfe, forsakyng alle other, holdyng me hollych to the, in sekenes and in hele, in ryches and in poverte, in well and in wo, tyl deth us departe, and there to I plyght ye my trowthe.[4]

---

[1] *P.L.* No. 714.
[2] *Id.* No. 696, cf. Myrc, ll. 203 ff.
[3] Gasquet, p. 209, quoting Harl. MS. 4172.   [4] *Id.*

The Wife of Bath, it will be remembered, had five times stood "at cherche dore," to go through the ceremony, before proceeding into the church itself for the completion of the rite. After these ecclesiastical proceedings came the marriage feast. As a recent writer has remarked,

> One might have expected to find some record of wedding fes-tivities, but the greatest feast in the Stonor Papers is that of the lavish entertainment of worshipful men, priests, and poor people at the funeral of Thomas Stonor.[1]

The *Paston Letters* are equally reticent, and we have no details concerning the feasts which concluded their numerous matri-monial ventures. No doubt there was much good eating and drinking, as contemporary documents will show. Sometimes rich folk, in leaving money by will for the marriages of poor girls, definitely state it is to be spent "towardes theire dynners in the dayes of theire maryages."[2] We also know that Joan Laurence took fourpence with her when she went to Richard Taylor's wedding, possibly as a contribution towards the expenses of the wedding feast.[3]

Whilst neither baptism nor marriage seem to have excited much attention, the impressive nature of medieval funerals shows how strong a hold this final ceremony of the Church had on the minds of all. Nor is this surprising. The parish priests did not fail to preach of the horrors and pains of eternal torment, and the very walls of their churches were often painted with terrifying scenes of torture in hell. The simple parishioners felt a real need of making themselves safe against such a fate. Every time they came to Mass they heard the priest pray for those recently dead, as well as for the whole body of the faithful departed. They naturally longed to ensure their own inclusion among these fortunate beings, when the alternative seemed to be the sufferings and horror of the hell they had been taught to imagine. Hence we can understand and sympathise with the zeal they showed that their end should be fitting, and that everything which might speed their souls to heaven should be done on the most impressive scale. The Church taught them of the supreme importance cf the last moments of life; and, from this, it was a little step to think that the larger the body of

---

[1] *S.L.* p. xliii.   [2] *North Country Wills*, p. 168.   [3] *S.L.* No. 93.

people who could be gathered to pray for their souls as they went out, the better for them.

The funeral services were elaborate, and often the occasion of great ceremony. First came the Vespers Service, or, as it was commonly called, Placebo, because it began with the Antiphon, "Placebo Domino in regione vivorum"—I will please the Lord in the land of the living.[1] This was said during the evening before the day of the funeral. Theoretically, soon after midnight came the next service, known as Matins or Dirige.[2] In practice, however, it usually took place much later in the morning, so that it only slightly preceded the final service of the Mass for the Dead. The greatest care was taken to ensure a large attendance of priests, clerks, and people of all kinds at these services. Often men would leave directions that everyone present at the last rites was to receive a definite reward, which varied according to the status of the several recipients. Thus, for example, Richard Penels, Canon of Exeter, left instructions in his will that every Canon present on the occasion should be given twentypence. Every Vicar was to receive twelvepence, and every chorister threepence.[3]

We are fortunate enough to possess some accounts of the funeral expenses of John Paston, which enable us to understand fairly clearly the procedure and details of these ceremonies. John Paston died in London on the 21st or 22nd of May, 1466, and then after several days his body was brought to Norfolk. It must have been an interesting spectacle, and an illustration of the religious temper of that time, to have seen the corpse being carried along from London to Norwich. A priest was always in attendance, while six poor men walked on either side of the bier carrying torches in their hands. While the body lay at S. Peter's Hungate in Norwich, a solemn dirige was sung there by Friars of the four Orders, and a gathering of 38 priests, 39 boys in surplices, and 26 clerks sang and prayed for the dead man's soul. Not only these, but the Prioress of Carrow, followed by her maid, an anchoress from her lonely cell, as well as 23 sisters from Norman's Hospital, attended this service. Four

---

[1] Psalm cxiv, v. 9 (vulg.).
[2] Beginning "Dirige, Domine, Deus meus," etc., i.e. Lead me O Lord... make thy way plain before my face. Ps. v, v. 8.
[3] *Exeter Regs.* Stafford, p. 420 [1418].

torch-bearers stood about the corpse while the bells of S. Peter's
and of S. Stephen's churches tolled for the dead. After this,
the remains were carried to Bromholm Priory, and a further
great ceremony was held. The details of the preparations made
for this service, and for the reception and entertaining of the
many folk who were present, show the lavish nature of these
funerals. Whether we inspect the lists showing the varied and
numerous people who attended, or the even more varied and
numerous stores of food which were ordered, we get an equally
vivid impression of the whole proceedings. Thus, on the day
John Paston was buried at Bromholm, fourteen ringers were
employed to toll for him, 24 servitors were hired at fourpence
a day to wait on the guests, and 70 other servitors at threepence.
Eighteen barrels of beer, and a large quantity of malt were laid
in; and a runlet of red wine was at hand to serve the needs of
the quality. The extent of the preparations may be gauged by
noticing that two men were kept busy for three days in flaying
the beasts for the feast, whilst it must indeed have "snewed
mete and drynke" in the shape of eggs, bread, fish, poultry, etc.[1]

The funeral of the Lady Katherine Howard, as befitted a
great lady, was on a more sumptuous scale than this, with
129 priests and clerks and 68 children present at her exequies.[2]
The *Stonor Papers* also give us much interesting information,
and include some valuable accounts setting out the details of
the funeral feast after the burial of Thomas Stonor in 1474.[3]
The document runs as follows:

IN PIRTON CHURCH.

[In the Church itself.]

First six altars. Item, the high altar with black ornaments thereto.
Item, candlesticks, censers, basins, silver thereto. Item, [for the]
rector's choir, suits of vestments black and white etc. Item, ornaments for the hearse and for the burial; black cloth to the ground
with a white cloth of gold. Item, a cross with a foot [*i.e.* standing]
on the hearse, silver and gilt. Item, four tapers about the hearse.
Item, two tapers about the burial. Item, black hanging about the
chancel and church. Item, lights for the high altar and other
altars besides. Item, singing wine and singing bread [*i.e.* bread
and wine for the celebration of the Mass].

[1] *P.L.* No. 549.   [2] *Id.* No. LXIV.
[3] *S.L.* No. 138, and see No. 47. The funeral of Thomas Stonor cost
£74. 2s. 5d., which sum must be multiplied by 10 at least to compare with
modern 1914 values.

Meat for poor men at Dirige: Item, after Dirige, bread and cheese for the said poor men. Item, for [priests?] and gentlemen, boiled purtenances of lambs, and veal. Roasted mutton [and] two chickens in a dish.

On the morrow for breakfast: For priests and other honest men. Item, calves heads and boiled beef.

At the dinner on the morrow:
For poor men: Item, umbles [*i.e.* inwards of deer or other animals] for soup, boiled beef,...and roasted pork.
The first course for priests etc.: First...chicken broth, capons, mutton, geese, custard.
The second course: The second soup, hotch-potch of meat and herbs, capons, lamb, pork, veal, roasted pigeons, baked rabbits, pheasants, venison, jelly etc.

Spices.
First a pound of horse-parsley [which was eaten like celery], an ounce of saffron, three pounds of pepper, half a pound cloves, half a pound of mace, a sugar loaf, three pounds of raisins of Corrinth, three pounds of dates, half a pound of ginger, one pound of cynnamon.
Item, four pounds of almonds. Violet-Blue colouring matter, 4*d.* [used for colouring jellies and confectionery]....

[Then follows a list of various details to be remembered in making the final arrangements.]
Item, wooden vessels for the poor men. Item, sitting places for the poor men.
Item, pewter vessels for the gentlemen. Item, a room for them according [to their quality].
Item, spoons and salt-cellars of silver for the most worshipful men.
Item, tablecloths for gentlemen and poor men.
Item, a convenient room for the two butteries for gentlemen and poor men.
Item, salt etc. Item, a vessel for ale. Item, cups, bowls and pots.

[Culinary arrangements.]
Item, a convenient place for the kitchen.
Item, spits, cauldrons, pots, rakes and other necessaries for [the] cooks.
Item, wood and coal.

[Servants.]
Item, Cooks, Butlers, a porter, other servants to serve [the guests] etc.
Item, a man to oversee the said arrangement of the Church.[1]

---

[1] *S.L.* No. 138. I have slightly rearranged some of the items, and am greatly indebted to Mr Kingsford's excellent glossary for the explanation of many terms used in the original memorandum.

Nor had the bereaved finished their labours for the dead when they had laid them to rest with such elaborate ceremony. In the fifteenth century, the offering of daily or frequent masses for the souls of the departed was very common. People were careful to leave money by will so that a priest might be hired to say mass for their souls daily. Sometimes sufficient money was left to ensure this being done in perpetuity, and the growth of chantries all over England is an evidence of the prevalence of this custom. When people were not rich enough to endow a chantry for ever, they arranged that a mass-priest should be hired to sing for them for a number of years. Any collection of medieval wills shows very clearly the widespread nature of this habit.[1] One of the Pastons in 1510 leaves her chaplain ten marks a year for five years to pray for her soul, and the souls of John Hervy, Sir John Paston and John Isley her husbands.[2] Margaret Paston required

an honest secular priest to sing and pray [in Mauteby Church] for my soul, the souls of my father and mother, the soul of the said John Paston late my husband, and for the souls of his ancestors and mine, during the term of seven years next after my decease.[3]

The Pastons followed these customs closely. When William Paston the justice died, his son John and his widow Agnes set aside a rent-charge out of their manor of Swainsthorpe to find a priest to sing for the soul of William in the Chapel of Our Lady the Great in Norwich Cathedral.[4] Besides this, they made arrangements with the vicar of Paston that "masses called certeynes should be performed every Friday for the souls of Wm Paston and Agnes his wife, and the obit of Clement Paston William's father should be kept yearly on the 17th June."[5] A further agreement of much the same nature, also stipulated that the parson should "exhort his parishioners to put up prayers for them every Sunday," and arranged for the celebration of William's obit on the 13th August.[6] Rich people were able to increase their opportunities, as they thought, by making more lavish arrangements. Instead of one mass being

---

[1] E.g. Linc. Diocese Documents, E.E.T.S., pp. 166, 223, 246, 260, 265, 270.
[2] P.L. III. p. 471.   [3] Id. No. 861.
[4] P.L. No. 153, note 2, and No. 555.   [5] Id. No. 39.   [6] Id. No 54

said daily, they could pay for several priests to sing for them. Lady Abergavenny was reported to have "in divers Abbeys in Leicestershire, seven or eight priests singing for her perpetually," by order of her executors, who obtained priests on payment of 200 or 300 marks.

And for the surety that he should sing in the same abbey for ever, they had manors of good value bound to such persons as should please the brethren and [the executors] that the said services should be kept.[1]

Even an entire foundation might be instituted with this object in view. Sir John Fastolf was always anxious to establish a College of Priests at Caister, whose business would have been the daily offering of masses for the souls of the dead. He wished his foundation to consist of

a college of seven priests, whereof one to be master, and of seven poor folk to pray for your [Edward IV] noble estate, and for the soul of the said John Fastolf, and such others as he was beholden to, in perpetuity.[2]

Readers of *King Henry V* will remember his cry:

Five hundred poor I have in yearly pay
Who twice a day their wither'd hands hold up
Toward heaven, to pardon blood; and I have built
Two chantries, where the sad and solemn priests
Sing still for Richard's soul.[3]

Besides all this, there were services at regularly recurring intervals in memory of the dead. People who were not rich enough to pay for daily services in perpetuity, or for a period of years, were sometimes able to provide for a service to be held a month or a year after the death. Special care was taken to ensure a repetition of the three services of Vespers, Matins and Mass for the dead, on the thirtieth day after the decease or burial. This day was known as the thirty-day or the month-mind, and was observed with great solemnity. Dame Elizabeth Browne ordered that at her month-mind there should be said "three trentals [of masses], besides the solemn dirige and mass that is...required for me at that time."[4] In order to be quite sure of having a large and influential gathering at her month-mind, Jane Stonor left orders in her will that every priest

---

[1] *P.L.* No. 290. [2] *Id.* No. 492.
[3] Act IV, scene 1. [4] *P.L.* No. 988.

coming to the month-mind saying dirige and mass was to receive
12*d*., and every poor man acting as a torch-bearer was to have
6*d*.[1] No doubt a great deal of money was spent on this day, and
to some it seemed to be more an occasion for extravagance than
for religion. One of the Stonor's relatives directed that no
month-mind should be kept for him, and that the money thus
saved should be given to the poor.[2]

Then, after a year had gone by, the anniversary of the death
was celebrated by a similar service called the year-mind or
obit. Margaret Paston, for example, directed that her heirs
were to keep her year-day in Mauteby Church for a period of
twelve years. Four tapers, each weighing four pounds, were
to burn "about my hearse when my yearday shall be kept,
as long as they may honestly serve."[3] This making provision
for candles for the month-mind and year-mind seems to have
been very common, and evidently had some ritualistic significance.[4]

The prevailing belief in the efficacy of prayer for the souls of
the dead was at the bottom of all these elaborate services.
Hence it is only natural to find that visible reminders of the
departed were set up in, or near, the church, so that their needs
might not be forgotten. The rich took care to leave money for
the raising of monuments to their memory. These were often
within the church itself, for the bodies of influential people
were then frequently buried in the nave, or chancel, or at the
door of the church. It was often fitting that this should be so,
for in many cases the dead man or woman had been a liberal
benefactor to the church; sometimes restoring the fabric, or
sometimes enriching the church by gifts of vestments or sacred
vessels. William Paston built an aisle to the church of Great
Cressingham, while his son John Paston a few years before his
death had rebuilt the church of S. Peter, Hungate, in Norwich.[5]
Margaret had given vestments to many Norfolk churches, and
a set of service books to Mauteby Church valued at £5. 6s. 8*d*.[6]
One of the Pastons' relatives had spent at least £100 on the

---

[1] *S.L.* p. xxvi, and see No. 47.   [2] *Id.* p. xxvii.
[3] *P.L.* No. 861, and cf. Nos. 396 and 583 for other year-days.
[4] Cutts, p. 315.
[5] *P.L.* No. 549, note 2, p. 269, and see Blomefield, VI. p. 99.
[6] *Id.* No. 861.

choir stalls and other seats in Bromholm Church where John
Paston was buried.[1] Such gifts as these were not uncommon
during the lifetime of well-to-do folk, while contemporary wills
show how universal was the wish of people to bequeath a part
of their goods after death to the glory of God.[2] It is easy to understand how much they valued the privilege of burial within the
holy buildings, and how they loved to think of their monuments
remaining there after they were gone. Their desires were gratified;
for their monuments are often to be found, both in small parish
churches, and in the great cathedrals.

So, after John Paston was dead, and had been buried with all
due ceremonial, his wife showed great anxiety that a fitting
monument should be erected to his memory at Bromholm. Indeed, few things seem to have caused her greater concern than
her son's dilatory methods in carrying out her wishes. The
troubles ensuing on John Paston's death were perhaps excuse
enough for a while; but, when several years elapsed, Margaret
began to get anxious. It was not until September 1471, five
years after his father's death, that Sir John asked his brother
to send some measurements. Hence it would seem that little
had been done up till then. He writes:

I would fain have the measure where my father lies at Bromholm;
both the thickness and compass of the pillar at his head, and from
that the space to the altar and the thickness of that altar and the
imagery of timber work, and what height the arch is to the ground
off the aisle, and how high the ground of the choir is higher than
the ground of the aisle.[3]

It was quite time; for, as Margaret told Sir John, his tardy
action had been noticed and was "a shame, and a thing that is
much spoken of in this country, that your father's gravestone
is not made. For God's love, let it be remembered and purveyed
in haste."[4] Lack of money probably made Sir John hesitate in
proceeding, and several letters from him about this time show
that he was trying to get his mother to pay for the tomb.
Meanwhile the condition of the grave was rapidly becoming
a scandal, and the Prior of Bromholm was at last forced to

[1] *P.L.* No. 818, and see Blomefield, xi. p. 207, for Sir John Fastolf's bene-
factions.
[2] *S.L.* p. xxix; *P.L.* No. 988, and Blomefield, xi. pp. 21, 207 ff.
[3] *P.L.* No. 676.   [4] *Id.* No. 685.

write to the Pastons emphasising what common gossip said about this neglect. He added, "The cloth that lies over the grave is all torn and rotten, and is not worth 2*d*.," and he says he has patched it once or twice.[1] The Prior asked that a new cloth should be sent at once. All this had little effect on Sir John who was so occupied with other affairs that twelve years after his father's death he was still making excuses. Finally the Pastons sold a rich cloth-of-gold covering that had been used at the funeral of John Paston, and devoted the proceeds to erecting the long overdue tomb.[2] Margaret evidently remembered all the trouble she had had over this affair, for in her own will she left instructions as follows:

> I will that my executors purvey a stone of marble to be laid aloft on my grave within a year next after my decease; and upon that stone I will have four scutcheons set at the four corners, whereof etc....And in the midst of the said stone, I will have a scutcheon set of Mauteby's arms alone, and under the same these words written "In God is my trust, etc."[3]

It has already been pointed out that the celebration of a daily mass was the chief duty of every parish priest. No doubt it is true that priests sometimes neglected this duty and only held infrequent services; but, in the households of people having private chapels, in chantries, in collegiate churches, and in cathedrals, day by day the sacrifice of the Mass was offered. Chantry priests were bound by their office to celebrate daily—in many cases it was their sole duty. Yet despite all this, it is clear that daily attendance was not usual outside the higher classes. Contemporary poems and romances show that such people did so, for attendance at Mass is almost part of their daily routine. Lower orders of society were content with attendance on Sundays and generally on the greater festivals. There is little mention of the Mass in the *Paston Letters*, but we should not expect to find so everyday an event dwelt upon except under special circumstances. The wild state of Norfolk in the middle of the fifteenth century made it impossible that the Pastons should not be aware of, and even witness, some of the terrible scenes that from time to time desecrated the churches during

---

[1] *P.L.* No. 765.   [2] *Id*. No. 815.
[3] *Id*. No. 861; cf. *Cely*, p. 108, where also the tomb is erected within a year.

Mass. Some of these will be described at length below and need not be dwelt upon here.[1] The Pastons themselves were devout people, and for many years had kept their own private chaplain and had their own private chapel. This, however, did not prevent their constant attendance at their parish church; and we can gather from the *Letters* that the womenfolk were in the habit of attending on weekdays, as well as on the more important occasions.[2]

There is nothing exceptional in the fact that the Pastons had their private chapel and chaplain, for this was a common practice among wealthy people in fifteenth century England.[3] Not only the nobility, but also many of the lesser county families, and even rich members of the rising merchant class, boasted their own chapels. The plans for new country houses began to include provision for a chapel, and it became evidence of breeding for a man to be able to say that his ancestors had possessed such a privilege. It was a privilege, for every such chapel was under the control of the Bishop of the diocese, and generally he looked with suspicion on attempts to obtain his license to allow the sacraments to be celebrated therein. Anyone could build himself a chamber in which he might gather his family for prayer and devotion; but, unless he had the Bishop's license, he could not have Mass said there. The Bishop's registers afford ample evidence of a widespread desire for this privilege. Care was always taken to see that the rights of the Mother Church of the parish were in no wise infringed. For this reason Bishops ordered folk to attend the parish church on Sundays and on the greater festivals, and to pay all the customary dues and offerings.[4]

The Pastons boasted that they had had their own private chaplain for many years. When Sir John had to prove the gentility of his ancestry to the King's officials, this was one of the strongest points in his case. The court accepted his statements and found that "they showed divers deeds and grants before time of mind, how their ancestors had license to have a

---

[1] See pp. 220–223, and *P.L.* Nos. 179, 201, 434.
[2] *P.L.* No. 59, and cf. Nos. 160, 188.
[3] Cutts, pp. 422–37, and cf. More's protest against this custom. *Works*, 1557, bk I, c. xii. p. 227 ff.
[4] E.g. *Exeter Regs.* Lacy, II. pp. 603, 605, 608, 609, 743, etc.

chaplain and to have divine service within [their house]."[1]
Sir John's grandfather had certainly been in the habit of hearing
Mass in his private chapel, for in 1432-3 he got an indult from
Rome allowing him to have Mass celebrated before daybreak.[2]
All through the *Letters* we are frequently reminded of the
presence of a chaplain in the Paston household, although we
hear little of his religious duties.[3] No mention, however, is
made of the chapel until 1472, when Margaret requested Sir
John to get the license for the same renewed. The Bishop of
Norwich had only granted this for a year, and the time had
nearly elapsed, so

she prays you to get a new license of my Lord [Bishop] of Norwich
that she may have the sacrament in her chapel. I got a license of
him for a year, and it is nigh worn out. You may get it [to last]
for the Bishop's life-[time] if you will.[4]

A few years later, Margaret asked her son to get a license for
her private chapel at Mauteby. Such requests had always to
be accompanied by special reasons, and Margaret explained
"it is far to the church and I am sickly, and the parson is often
out. For all manner of casualties of me and mine, I would have
it granted, if I may."[5] Apparently the Bishop was not very
willing to grant this request, and after a while Margaret became
impatient, and told her son to appeal to a higher authority if
the Bishop remained obdurate. "If you cannot get it of the
Bishop of Norwich, get it of the [Arch]bishop of Canterbury,
for that is most sure for all places."[6] No more is heard of the
matter, so we may suppose that one of these two ecclesiastics
granted her request.

The parish church was a central feature of medieval life, and
many activities group themselves around it. The daily Mass
and the chantries no doubt made a certain impression. This was
reinforced by a continuous succession of festivals at which the
imagination of the people was touched. One of the objects of
the medieval Church was to make the great realities of religion
simple enough to be comprehended by the common people.
This they did largely by dramatic representations, and sym-

---

[1] *P.L.* No. 554.   [2] *C.P.L.* VI. p. 434.
[3] *P.L.* Nos. 58, 59, 697, 702, 732, etc.   [4] *Id.* No. 712.
[5] *Id.* No. 751.   [6] *Id.* No. 755.

bolism, and the use of colour and ritual. The miracle plays were
an outcome of this desire to show vividly in a dramatic form
some of the central truths of the great festivals of the Church.
The ceremony on Ash Wednesday of blessing the ashes and
strewing them on the heads of the parishioners; the series of
dramatic ceremonies in Holy Week beginning with the blessing
and distribution of palms on Palm Sunday; the creeping to
the Cross on Good Friday; the restoration of the Cross from the
Easter sepulchre to its place on the high altar on Easter Day;
the dramatic and spectacular character of the Mass itself:
all these are instances of the way in which the mimetic instinct
was utilised in the service of the Church.

We have spoken so far only of the services of the Church and
of certain semi-dramatic spectacles. Here and there in the
Paston Letters we get brief references to another potent weapon
in the Church's hand—the sermon. It is a matter of some
difficulty to tell what part sermons played in the usual routine
of the parish church. The Bishops certainly tried to insist on
the regular delivery of sermons, but when we recall the lack of
education which characterised so many of the clergy, it is
obvious that very often serious preaching was out of the question.[1] The weakness of the secular clergy in this respect was
greatly emphasised by the coming of the Friars. Preaching was
one of their strongest weapons. "The missionaries of the Pope,"
as they have been called, spread their propaganda by sermons.
Even many of the great churches they built were constructed
with the primary object of providing large preaching halls. Many
of the Friars were artists in words, with the skill and adroitness
that comes of much practice, and their appeal was very powerful.
One of these men flits in and out the pages of the *Paston Letters*
in an amusing way. Father Brackley, of the Greyfriars at
Norwich, was a friend and frequent correspondent of the Pastons.
He was evidently a well-known preacher, and certainly was
not unaware of his abilities in this direction. He relates with
great complacency an example of his readiness and skill. One
Sunday when Justice Yelverton and others were staying at
the Priory in Norwich, it so happened that no preacher was

---

[1] See *The Lollard Bible*, Deanesly, M., pp. 198–202, and Cutts, pp. 214–31.

forthcoming, and Brackley was asked to preach. He readily agreed, and wrote afterwards to the Pastons as follows:

And I preached on the Sunday 1 =fore them, not warned till after meat. And then for lack of Mr Vergeant, or our warden Barnard, I suddenly said the sermon....After the sermon he [Yelverton] said openly to the Prior, [in the] hearing of much folk in the Church "I have heard him often here and elsewhere but this is the best I ever heard him say"...and at evening he drank to me, and made me good cheer.[1]

The parish church was the centre of the social as well as of the religious life of the countryside. Men came there in many cases not only to pray, but also in the hope of transacting business. The parson, as we have seen, was frequently the local agent of the Lord of the Manor, and consequently notices concerning purely secular matters were sometimes given out in church. The Bishops frequently protested against the use of sacred buildings for purely secular purposes. Protests and injunctions notwithstanding, a bewildering variety of social and business details were discussed in the nave of the parish church.[2] It was quite natural that this should be so, for the church was the focus of village life, and any announcement made there at once obtained a wide circulation. Hence when William Paston wished to hold a manor court, he ordered his local representative "to warn the tenants of Bacton tomorrow [Sunday] openly in the church of the said court to be kept on Friday next."[3] Not only were tenants warned to attend manor courts, but in some cases the court itself was held in the church. There are no letters of the Pastons to bear out this point, but Dr Cox writes:

In feudal England the use of churches as courts of justice was almost universally adopted. Manorial courts were not unfrequently held in churches....The Scropton manor rolls, several of which are of Elizabethan date, prove that courts of the manor were held in church.[4]

Local quarrels concerning the ownership of land or cattle were often discussed and settled in church. When Agnes Paston attempted to build a wall which her neighbours thought would

[1] P.L. No. 349, and see p. 249.
[2] Church and Manor, Addy, S. O., c. IX passim, and Myrc, ll. 329–45.
[3] P.L. No. 823, and cf. Scrope, p. 259.
[4] Three Centuries of Derbyshire Annals, Cox, J. C., I. pp. 390–1, and cf. Hist. Sandwich, Boys, p. 365, etc.

prevent their access to certain properties, the wall was broken down while it was only half built. Besides this, Agnes was accosted in church after evensong, when a spirited exchange of views took place—for she was not easily browbeaten. One neighbour who intervened was told "it was no courtesy to meddle in a matter unless he were called to [give] counsel." The quarrel grew more and more heated, until at last, with a final interchange of threats on both sides, the rival parties parted in the churchyard.[1] On another occasion, when Justice Yelverton was attempting to distrain unlawfully upon John Paston's cattle, a servant of the Pastons hastened to the scene. Early in the morning he went to S. Laurence Church, Ipswich, where he met Yelverton's friends and a long and acrimonious dispute took place in the church.[2]

Several other aspects of the religious life of the times present themselves in some of these *Letters*. Besides that side of religion that found its expression within the parish church itself, there was a desire in the hearts of many people to visit churches or places with especially sacred associations. Pilgrimages and pilgrims were well known; and perhaps in few parts of England more so than in Norfolk, which was exceedingly rich in such hallowed spots. The *Paston Letters* contain very many references to pilgrimages made by the Pastons themselves and also by their friends. Almost the first letter written by Margaret Paston shows the simple belief some people had in the efficacy of these pilgrimages to sacred shrines. John Paston was in London recovering from an illness, and his wife in her anxiety had promised

to go on pilgrimage to Walsingham, and to Saint Leonard's [Priory at Norwich] for you. By my troth I never had so sorrowful a time as I had from the moment I knew of your sickness till I learnt of your mending.[3]

There were few more celebrated shrines in all England than that of S. Mary of Walsingham. The *Letters* from time to time report the coming and going of the King or Queen to the holy place,[4] or spread rumours that the Duke of Norfolk or his lady

[1] *P.L.* No. 162.   [2] *Id.* No. 414.
[3] *Id.* No. 36.   [4] *Id.* Nos. 417, 610.

intended to make a pilgrimage there on foot.[1] High and low, all thronged to worship there; for, as Erasmus wrote of it,

Her name [the Virgin Mary] is very famous all over England, and you shall scarce find anybody in that island who thinks his affairs can be prosperous unless he every year makes some present to that lady [who dwells] on the coast...about three miles from the sea.[2]

Nor are the references to Norfolk shrines only. The tomb of S. Thomas at Canterbury still made the most attractive pilgrimage in England, and casual remarks in the *Letters* show how very popular it was. In 1471, Sir John wrote home to his brother and told him that "the King and Queen and many other people are riden and gone to Canterbury." Though this was in September he remarked, "Never so many people [were] seen heretofore on pilgrimage at once, so men say."[3] It must have called up many memories to his brother who, only the year before, in the heat of summer, had gone on foot from Norfolk to Canterbury,[4] "the hooly blisful martir for to seke." Not content with this, John Paston ventured even further, and, in 1473, made a pilgrimage overseas as far as the shrine of S. James of Compostella in N. Spain.[5]

The hold which pilgrimages had on the minds of people is strikingly illustrated by a chance remark of one of Paston's agents. He had been ordered to call on the tenants at Snailwell to collect the rents, but when he did so he found the people were mostly away at Canterbury and elsewhere, and he was forced to return empty handed.[6] People would set out in little bands from their towns and villages, and so ride together for protection. A letter records how "Robert Albon of Yarmouth, with many more...neighbours, this Saturday came home from Canterbury."[7] There is a remarkable example, however, in the *Letters* of the respect that was sometimes paid to pilgrims by even the roughest of men. A band of robbers in Norfolk, about 1450, caused much distress to people living near to Paston village.

[1] *P.L.* Nos. 301, 675, 757, 866, and cf. Nos. 696, 821, 859, 865, 907.
[2] *Colloquies of Erasmus*, trans. by N. Bailey, 1877 edn., p. 241.
[3] *P.L.* No. 676.   [4] *Id.* Nos. 641, 642.
[5] *Id.* No. 727. For details of the great pilgrimages made to this shrine see *Itineraries of Wm Wey*, Roxburgh Club, 1857.
[6] *Id.* No. 561.   [7] *Id.* No. 936.

Once they took captive two pilgrims, a man and a woman. It is difficult to know exactly what took place from Agnes Paston's confused story, but they appear to have robbed the woman and then set her free. The man they led down to their ship, purposing to take him away with them; but then, says Agnes "when they knew he was a pilgrim, they gave him money and set him again on the land."[1]

[1] *P.L.* No. 80.

CHAPTER XV

THE SECULAR CLERGY

Now that we have seen something of the part played by the Church in the life of medieval England, it is time to turn to the clergy of those days. The term "cleric" throughout the middle ages had a very wide significance. It embraced, altogether, seven classes of men; four in Minor Orders and three in Major Orders. Only those in Major Orders, *i.e.* Subdeacons, Deacons and Priests, would be recognised to-day as "clergy." But England in the fifteenth century swarmed with masses of men who were in Minor and Major Orders. Strictly speaking, no one could claim to be in Minor Orders who had not received the "first tonsure" at the hands of the Bishop of the diocese; but in practice it seems probable that men who were sufficiently closely connected with the clergy, in one way or another, often assumed or received the title of cleric; just as nowadays the title of "esquire," which once had a fairly well-defined meaning, is used indiscriminately as a matter of courtesy.[1] Apart from this somewhat uncertain class, we find that doctors, lawyers, scribes, clerks in the King's household and many others were usually in Minor Orders, and therefore came under the legal definition of "cleric," and could claim "benefit of clergy."

If we turn our attention to those in Major Orders, we find that the clergy of medieval England may be divided into two great classes, known as the regular and secular clergy. No real understanding can be gained of the problems and religious life of those days until this is clearly recognised; for these two classes had widely different ideals, and lived widely different lives. The regular clergy are so called because they lived according to a Rule [*regula*], and were always members of a community, and

---

[1] Rashdall, II. pp. 644–5 gives the term "clericus" an even wider meaning and says, "The adoption of the clerical tonsure and dress conferred, so long as the wearer continued celibate, the immunities and privileges of the clerical order," but adds, "The relation between clerkship and minor orders is, however, an obscure subject."

often segregated from the world. The secular clergy spent their lives in the world [*in seculo*] serving as individuals, in parishes, in great churches and in other ways. The ranks of the regulars included the monks and nuns, who were theoretically strictly claustrated; and the orders of Canons Regular, who approximated to the secular clergy in that they often left their cloister and served cures. The Premonstratensian Canons were allowed to do this without first obtaining the permission of either Pope or Bishop. The Austin Canons could only undertake parochial work by permission of these authorities. Then, at a later stage, the Four Orders of Friars were added to the regulars. Although they spent some of their time in the cloister, the Friars were very much in the world from time to time.

Among the secular clergy were the Archbishops, Bishops, Archdeacons, Vicars, parish priests, and many other ecclesiastical officers unknown in modern days.[1] The seculars included men of many varied grades of life; for, although the stipend of the average parish priest was low, there were still many livings and cathedral offices which were well rewarded, and no efficacious method was ever devised throughout the middle ages for preventing the influential man from holding numerous livings at the same time. Hence it is that we find the "poor parson" of Chaucer's time,—whose brother it will be remembered was a ploughman,—side by side with the brother of the Bishop of Hereford, and both accurately described as parsons of parishes. A few years later, however, Thomas de Trillek, the Bishop's brother, was Dean of Hereford, then Dean of S. Paul's, and in 1364 Bishop of Rochester,[2] while we may feel certain from ample contemporary evidence that the "poor parson" lived and died in his humble country parish.

In this chapter we are concerned with the lives and activities of the seculars who formed the bulk of the medieval clergy. They served as vicars, as domestic chaplains, as "capellani" [*i.e.* curates in the modern sense], and as men hired to sing a daily mass, or to serve a cure for an absentee Rector. For the most part they were drawn from comparatively humble families. Year by year fewer men ordained to Major Orders had a sufficient private

[1] *E.g.* Chaucer's Pardoner and Summoner.
[2] *Hereford Reg.* J. de Trillek, Intro. p. ii.

income to support themselves. We can see, for example, from the *Hereford Registers* that, whereas early in the fourteenth century large numbers of men declared before ordination that they had adequate private means, by the middle of the fifteenth century practically no ordinands presented themselves on this ground.[1] The secular clergy in very many parishes by this time were undoubtedly men of the people. Many such men were to be found "willing to accept the lowest possible wages and the smallest possible chance of preferment for the sake of a position which, at the worst, put them far above their father or their brothers."

The pages of the *Paston Letters* reveal very many interesting details concerning the lives of these men. Naturally enough we only find occasional references to the actual services of the Church, or to matters of ecclesiastical importance. These were the priest's daily occupations, and, unless something unusual happened, neither the priest nor his congregation found it necessary to remark upon them. Hence it is not to the *Paston Letters* that we must look for the fullest account of medieval religious life and observance. What they can give us is an intimacy of understanding of the ordinary parish priest, which few other documents can equal. In these letters we can watch him, from day to day, both in and out of church. Too often we are apt to regard the medieval priest solely as an ecclesiastic. The *Paston Letters* modify the tendency, for they show the parish priests in a variety of rôles. We constantly find them doing business for the Pastons, acting as their confidential advisers on purely worldly matters, attending to agricultural affairs, and generally taking an important part in the economic life of the countryside. The following detailed account of the lives and occupations of some Norfolk parsons, as mirrored in the *Paston Letters*, will enable the reader to form an impression of the normal varied activities of the parish priest throughout England.

---

[1] It is impossible to treat this subject fully here. It is hoped to publish later a detailed study of the Episcopal Registers in their bearing on the status of the clergy. An examination of the *Hereford Registers* proves that, between the years 1328–1448, the number of men ordained to the title of their own patrimony shows a steady decrease. For example, the percentage of men so ordained to the total number presented for the order of subdeacon in the years 1328–37 was 60 per cent.; for the years 1378–87 it was 16 per cent.; and in 1428–37 less than 1 per cent.

Undoubtedly in Norfolk many parsons were strongly influenced by the desires, and even orders, of their patrons. Zeal
for their patron's interests is the keynote to the actions of many
of these men; and, no doubt, their devotion was well known
throughout the whole countryside.[1] On one occasion a man was
in great danger of being hanged, and sent a messenger to acquaint
his lord of this. When the messenger had gone as far as he dared
without arousing suspicion, he handed over his message to a
priest, "and bid him fast go [and] give...warning."[2] Equal
confidence was reposed in the parish priest in some cases. Even
so careful a man as Justice Paston did not hesitate to leave
important legal documents in the safe-keeping of the parson of
Cressingham.[3] This, perhaps, was not uncommon, for his grandson Sir John Paston entrusted a bond of £100—a large sum then
—to the care of the Vicar of Sporle.[4] We cannot but assume that
such men as these were trustworthy, and, moreover, were well
known for their probity throughout the countryside. The parson
and the patron probably found each other mutually helpful.
It was clearly convenient for the patron if he could feel sure
that he had someone watching over his interests throughout the
country. The parson, on the other hand, knew that almost all
his hopes of preferment lay in pleasing his patron. To take one
family only, during the fifteenth century the Pastons presented,
or partly presented, to more than twenty different livings in
Norfolk.[5]

At times, however, their fidelity to their patron brought them
into conflict with their parishioners, especially when they acted
to please so mettlesome and haughty a lady as Agnes Paston.
The unfortunate Vicar of Paston "was ravished in [his] wits,
and made full heavily disposed at the great fray that the
[parishioners] made in the time of Mass," as a result of over
zeal in performing her commands. His whole letter shows such
simple and wholehearted trust in his patron, that it must be read
at length, as an excellent example of the light in which the average
fifteenth century priest regarded the local gentry. He writes:

Right worshipful mistress, I recommend me unto you, thanking
you for the great cheer that you made me the last time I was with

---

[1] See below.   [2] *P.L.* No. 75.   [3] *Id.* No. 11.
[4] *Id.* No. 839, and see No. 516.   [5] See Blomefield, *passim.*

you. Mistress, in all your goods and occupations that lieth in my simple power to do, in word, will and deed, I have done my diligence and my power thereto, so I be saved before God, and have owed to your person right hearty love.... Mistress, at the reverence of God, and as ever I may do service that may be pleasing unto you, send me justly word by the bringer of this letter how ye will that I be guided; for it is told me that if I be taken, I may have no other remedy, but [will go] straightway to prison.... Nevertheless as you command me to do, so it be not to my great hurt, I will fulfil it.[1]

The same identification of interests was displayed by William Coting, who was Rector of Titchwell. He writes, "in all goodly haste," one January morning, "for the matter is of substance." The reason for his excitement was only too common in those days; but that it should happen to his patron made it inexcusable in his eyes. "In the grey morning 3 men of my Lord of Norfolk with long spears, carried off 3 good horses from John Poleyn, one of your farmers at Titchwell telling him to treat with my Lord of Norfolk" if he wanted redress. "What am I to do?" asks the outraged parson, eager to set about vindicating his patron's authority, "for such an open wrong unremedied knew I never."[2] An earlier letter shows us that the Rector was conversant with all the details concerning the rents and conditions of the Paston farms within his parish.[3] Sometimes, parsons seem to have been admitted into the councils of the Pastons, and their opinion valued on the most intimate matters. Naturally this was much more so with domestic chaplains, such as Sir T. Howes or Sir James Gloys, who, as we shall see, were as important in council as any member of the family.[4] While the parish priest could not claim such a position there is no doubt he was often consulted; so that when Margaret Paston writes to her husband, reporting what had been talked over at a family council, she specially mentions the Vicar of Paston among those present.[5]

The parish priest may have been actuated in general only by friendship and loyalty to his patron. But in many cases he appears to have been as much a local man of business as a priest. We must allow something for the nature of the documents in trying to form a just estimate of his dual functions, or else the very frequent business allusions, and the very meagre religious

---

[1] *P.L.* No. 434.   [2] *Id.* No. 598.   [3] *Id.* No. 491.
[4] The medieval priest commonly received the courtesy title of 'Sir.'
[5] *Id.* No. 429.

ones, would lead us to suppose that this man had little time for, or interest in, religion. Naturally, however, he would have no need to write often to his patron concerning religious matters, unless some unusual situation arose, for his patron could give but little help in things ecclesiastical. On the other hand, he would be constantly in touch with his patron if he was responsible for the agrarian interests of his parish, as well as the religious ones. We have, for example, the abstract of a letter from the Vicar of Sporle to John Paston, after he had been acting for Paston at a Manor Court. Here there was a dispute concerning the legality of a claim of John Paston's to a piece of land. The Vicar presented Paston's case, put forward his evidences, and generally acted as Paston's bailiff might have done.[1] Other letters from the Vicar of Paston do indeed read very much like those of Richard Calle, and his intimate acquaintance with all the details of leases and with the troubles of the farmers make it clear that he must have spent a great deal of time in attending to the Pastons' affairs. Besides reporting the bare facts, the Vicar gives invaluable advice from his closely studied observation of these tenants, as for example in the case of a certain Henry Warns whom he evidently considered disloyal, and he writes, "Therefore, put no trust in him, because no man can serve two masters."[2]

A paper of Memoranda in the hand of William Paston, dated 18th January, 1479, is full of interest from the light it throws on the relation existing between him and the parson of Melton. He writes:

"Cause one the Steward [of] Colton, a tenant of Marlingford to come to me"; and then, "Cause Sir John Chapman, parson of Our Ladies Church (Melton) send hither the bill of reckoning of Richard Harvey....Cause the parson of Melton come to me at Norwich, for tell [him that] if he comes not hastily, he shall not find me here. Item, pray the parson of Melton to call upon the particular tenants of Melton that have had particular farms from Michaelmas 17 [Ed. IV] till Michaelmas 18, to pay these farms" [rents].[3]

It is clear from this that the parson also acted as William Paston's local agent or bailiff, for all the above-quoted duties would ordinarily be performed by a bailiff, and it is noticeable that William Paston uses much the same form of words to summon

[1] *P.L.* No. 112.   [2] *Id.* No. 741, cf. No. 742.   [3] *Id.* No. 825.

the Steward of Colton and Sir John himself. Evidently, in his mind, there was little difference in the services the two men performed for him. In the same way the Vicar of Stalham was the agent of the Pastons in his parish, and among the collection has survived a letter from him to Margaret Paston giving her "an account of the numbers of her sheep and lambs at Sparham from Drayton and Taverham, and those with the shepherd at Heylesdon."[1]

The impetuous Sir John Fastolf did nearly all his business by means of his own men, or by his faithful chaplain, Sir Thomas Howes. Even he, however, seems to have made use of the local clergy as his agents, and a note to one of his letters hints at this. "Thank the Parson of Hellesden," he writes, "for the three writings of Wiltshire's will and Gorney he sent me by Worcester; but say I prayed him to search for more."[2] Thomas Hert, parson of Hellesdon, was presented to the living by Sir John Fastolf two years before this; and Sir John evidently expected more than priestly offices from him in return.[3]

The fifteenth century saw the sons of peasants and other comparatively humble people able to become parish priests; while, at the same time, the average annual value of most livings was not large. For example, the values of the various livings mentioned in the *Paston Letters*, as given in the return known as the *Valor Ecclesiasticus*, vary from £5. 5s. to £14. 13s. Their average annual value was about £9. We must be careful not to assume that this was the incumbent's actual income, because, on the one hand, he augmented it from outside sources, and, on the other hand, in many cases, he had to provide other clergy to serve the parish chapels, or to assist at the parish church.[4] The Vicar of Paston, to take one case, had a living worth only £6. 15s. 4d.; yet he was assisted by a curate, "Sir Roberde."[5] Little as this seems, there were very many livings worth much less at that time in England, although it must be remembered that there were certain extras the parson would get which were not included in the *Valor* return. Hence the vicar, or even rector, was frequently on an equality with many of his parishioners, both

[1] *P.L.* No. 872, and cf. *Sus. Arch. Trans.* LIV. p. 180.
[2] *Id.* No. 123.   [3] Cf. Scrope, *op. cit.* pp. 258–9.
[4] *E.g. Exeter Regs.* Bronscombe, pp. 253, 334.   [5] *P.L.* No. 160.

socially and financially. These two facts materially influenced the growth of clerical trading; and this century saw many parish priests playing an important part in the agricultural life of their parish. Some of them, either from a natural instinct for cultivating the soil,—which had probably been the life-work of generations of their ancestors,—or because of the possibilities of wealth it offered, were eager agriculturists.[1] One of the most common complaints against the clergy at this period was that their time was occupied in farming and in trading in agricultural produce, to the neglect of their cures. Besides cultivating their own glebe, priests even rented farms to increase their incomes.[2]

The *Paston Letters* deal with this side of the parson's life, more by implication than by direct reference. Nevertheless, there is sufficient evidence to show that in Norfolk, as elsewhere throughout England, the conditions outlined above were common. The fullest information we have comes from a very interesting document, probably drawn up by Margaret Paston in 1478, when the Oxnede living was vacant. In this are set out, at some length, all the details of the Rectory grounds and their value. Adjoining the parsonage house there are

two large gardens with fruit...whereof the fruit is worth yearly 26s. 8d. And there belongs to the said parsonage in free land, arable, pasture and meadow adjoining to the said parsonage, 22 acres or more, whereof every acre is worth 2s.: to let £3. 0s. 4d. And William Paston, when he came first to dwell in the manor of Oxnede, paid to the parson that was then [rector] for the corn growing on the parsonage lands and for the tithings, in corn only, when it was inned into the barn £24.[3]

The parsonage lands were evidently cultivated by the rector himself, for later on the statement says,

if a parson came now and were presented, instituted and inducted, he should have by law, all the crop that is now growing on the parsonage lands, and that was ploughed and sowed at the old parson's costs.[4]

Besides cultivating the parsonage lands, some priests bought or hired other lands. We have a record of one such example, though unfortunately only the very smallest hint of the whole story is given in a brief sentence of Sir James Gloys which says, "William Yelverton has put the parson of Heynford out of his

---

[1] Cf. *Farming Past and Present*, Ernle (Lord), p. 26.
[2] *R.H.S.* 3rd series, Vol. VI. pp. 103-10.   [3] *P.L.* No.819.   [4] *Id.* No. 819.

farm."[1] The Lestrange Accounts also present among the receipts the sum of £4 from Sir Thos. Houghton, parson of Anmer, in payment of rent for the farm of Swanton;[2] and evidence of this kind could be multiplied to show how common it was for parsons to be agriculturists. The parson of Hellesdon farmed on a sufficiently large scale to have his own plough horses,[3] and references to parsons selling grain such as, "Ye owe to the parson of Sent Edmondes Caster for iiij combe malte, and ij combe whete xs,"[4] or paid "To the parson of Crostweyt for 1 qr white vis,"[5] confirm similar evidence in the Lestrange Accounts as to the prevalence of clerical trading in agricultural produce.[6]

All this, however, does not touch the parish priest's main work, which lay in the decent and punctual performance of the services of the Church, and in the celebration and administration of the Sacraments. There is little doubt that the churches were much more the centre of countryside life then than they are now, if for no other reason than that they were not used exclusively for religious purposes. The principal purpose, however, of both church and priest was to enable the Mass to be celebrated daily, although very many people could only attend on Sundays and possibly on the greater feasts.[7]

Such was the turbulent state of England during many years of the fifteenth century, that no priest could be sure of being able to celebrate Mass with that reverent absorption it demanded. The very frequency of the service cheapened it to some extent, especially in the eyes of men inclined to break away from the yoke of the Church; and priests knew by sad experience, that not even when they were before the altar, with the sacred elements exposed, were they safe from interruption, or from the attacks of their enemies. Even when actual violence was not shown, the displeasure of the congregation must have been highly disconcerting to a sensitive priest. The Vicar of Paston confessed as much, reporting the hostility of his parishioners, and said: "the great affray that they made at the time of Mass, ravished my wits, and made me very sorrowfully disposed."[8]

[1] P.L. No. 561.   [2] Arch. xxv. p. 453.   [3] P.L. No. 502.
[4] Id. No. 646.   [5] Id. No. 549.
[6] Arch. xxv. pp. 437, 471, etc., and cf. Vox Clam., Gower, p. 148, and S.L. No. 74.
[7] See Myrc's Liber Festialis, p. 266.   [8] P.L. No. 434.

The presence of a priest, robed in his ceremonial garments and saying the Mass, could not prevent wild and outrageous scenes happening in church, so that even attempts at murder were not unknown. Once while Mass was being celebrated in Birlingham Church on Mid Lent Sunday, 1452, certain lawless men

made an affray upon two of the servants of the reverend Father in God, Bishop of Norwich, the said servants at that time kneeling to see the using of the Mass. There and then, the said fellowship would have killed the said two servants at the priest's back, if they had not been prevented.[1]

This being so, it was not to be expected that the mere precincts of the church would be held sacred by such men, and John Paston and his men were attacked

at the door of the cathedral church of Norwich, with swords, bucklers and daggers drawn, one of them holding the said Paston by both arms at his back as it would seem, purposing to have murdered the said Paston there, if they had not been prevented. [They] also smote one of his servants upon the naked head with a sword, and polluted the sanctuary.[1]

From more detailed accounts given in the petitions to the Chancellors,[2] we can better understand the strange happenings which are briefly alluded to in the *Paston Letters*, of which the above may serve as specimens. It is clear that the desperate bands of men who scoured the countryside, and the scanty control that was exercised, produced scenes in churches which seem almost incredible. While the *Paston Letters* reveal men being attacked while at Mass, or when leaving the church, we have nothing to equal the drastic procedure adopted by a discontented parishioner against his parish priest at Roseland near Falmouth in Cornwall. The dispute arose concerning the parson's claim to mortuaries on the death of his parishioners. In his petition the parson sets forth that the custom of the parish, from time immemorial, was to give him the best garment or the second best beast of a deceased person. This mortuary was denied him in certain cases; and, after he had obtained judgment against the offenders in the Archdeacon's Court, and they still proved obdurate, he was ordered to pronounce an

---

[1] *P.L.* No. 179, cf. No. 201.   [2] See *Chanc. Pro.*

excommunication against them. This he did, but on the Sunday before Christmas Day, they came to church; and, although he

monished and commanded them to go out of the said church so that he might go on with divine service, [they] refused to do this, but kept themselves in the said church to the disturbance of divine service, through which the parishioners went home without Mass, because of their disturbance.

On Christmas Day they appeared again in church well armed, and refused to leave, "but kept themselves in church all day until the hour of noon, through which the first Mass and the second were not celebrated, and the parson lost his offerings that day." Not content with this, they threatened to kill the parson before all the parishioners, and "would have chased the parson out of his chancel by the windows...wherefore the said parson was very glad to escape secretly while others of the parish treated with [them]."[1]

Another unfortunate West Country parson was vested for Mass, but,

before he had said the Gospel of S. John which is called In principio; and in the chancel of the said church [his enemy entered], and commanded the said David [the priest] to take off his vestments and to speak with him. This he was forced to do, and afterwards was made to give up cattle and other goods and to pay £10 within a few days.[2]

An even worse case is recorded, in which the ruffians were not deterred by their hallowed surroundings, nor by the sacred office being performed, from maltreating the officiating priest on the steps of the altar.

Showeth Wm Tyrell, Rector of the church of Winchelsea, and complaineth of Robert Arnold, Roger at Gate, and John Hermit, of this, that on Sunday in the feast of the Nativity of S. John the Baptist, they came to the chapel of S. John in the same parish, with force and arms, and against the peace of our Lord the King, to wit, with swords, bucklers, daggers, bows, arrows, and other kinds of armour, in manner of war, and there, in the same chapel, where the said supplicant was standing at Mass and reading the Gospel, they assaulted him and beat him and wounded him, and ill treated him so that the said supplicant despaired of his life; and they took the book that was before him and the oblations and carried them away.[3]

Such cases must only be regarded as exceptional, but they were a possibility that every parish priest had to face. In the

---

[1] E.g. Chanc. Pro. No. 20, pp. 23-5.   [2] Id. No. 31, pp. 34-5.
[3] Id. No. 92; cf. Redstone, p. 189.

ordinary way, however, we may fancy him daily celebrating Mass in his church, and teaching his simple flock to worship and adore the central mystery of their Faith. Overlaid as it was by formalism and injured by neglect, the Mass was still the service which appealed to all the congregation. The bequests in wills for masses to be said for the souls of the departed, the care taken to ensure obits and certaynes being observed, and the whole system of chantries and chantry priests are sufficient evidence of this. The Pastons shared in this general feeling, and the Parson of Paston bound himself to celebrate Mass every Friday for the souls of William and Agnes Paston, and to exhort his parishioners to offer prayers for them every Sunday, and to celebrate William Paston's obit every year on the 13th August;[1] while, only three years earlier, his predecessor had made arrangements to do very much the same thing.[2]

Although attendance at Mass, at least on Sundays, was almost universal, the majority of people went with no intention of communicating themselves. The ordinary layman only communicated once a year, and this was generally at Easter. Hence William Botoner, wishing to be very emphatic, and writing on the 7th of February, says, "This is the truth, by the blessed Sacrament that I received at Easter,"[3] and Margaret Paston implies as much when, writing of Oxnede Rectory, she says, "And it is an easy cure to keep, for there are not more than 20 persons to be yearly houseled."[4]

Since the parson was so intimately associated with the daily life and pursuits of his parishioners, it is not strange to find him suffering trials and misfortunes similar to theirs. We have already seen that even in church he was not immune from attack, if his enemies were very determined,[5] though sometimes his opponents had the grace to shut him out before doing their worst. When the Duke of Suffolk's men attacked Hellesdon, they spared the Rector the pain of seeing them at their impious work by putting him outside till they had ransacked the church, and bore away all the goods that were left there, both of ours and of the tenants, and left not so much but that

---

[1] *P.L.* No. 54.   [2] *Id.* No. 39, and cf. No. 549.   [3] *Id.* No. 347.
[4] *Id.* No. 819. "Houseled," to receive the sacrament, cf. *Hamlet*, Act I, scene V.   [5] *Id.* Nos. 179, 201.

they [even] stood on the high altar, and ransacked the images, and took away such as they might find.[1]

Probably because of their position and social standing in the parishes, parsons were conspicuous marks for the attacks of bands of the type led by Will Lins, who went

fast about the countryside and accused priests and others of being Scots, and took bribes of them and let them go again. He took last week the Parson of Fritton, and but for my cousin Jermingham the younger, they would have led him forth with them.[2]

Again, another time, Margaret Paston writes that she

is informed that the parson of Brandeston is taken...and led forth and they have rifled his goods, and those of his bailiff, which were left with the parson to keep.[3]

More lawful methods were also adopted against them, and afford interesting evidence concerning their social position. Agnes Paston asks her son John Paston to take the necessary steps to sue the parson of Marlingford for non-performance of an obligation to which he was bound,[4] and many cases could be quoted from the *Chancery Records* of parsons suing and being sued for breach of contract,[5] withholding of money,[6] or refusal to hand on property to the rightful heir.[7] The goods of the parson of Testerton were seized together with those of another man with whom he was associated in wrongdoing, but the distrainer reports: "All those goods, which I have seized of them both, are little money more than £2 or £3 at the most, except the parson's corn."[8]

Many parish priests, as we have seen, were drawn from humble origins, and their newly won position exposed them to many temptations. They had unwonted opportunities, and we cannot be surprised that, in some cases, these opportunities were used for evil. The ignorance and superstition which prevented many from being good priests led some to associate with evil companions. The *Paston Letters* show that Norfolk suffered in common with the rest of England from such men. The parson of Testerton seems to have been arrested for coining, and had evidently joined a very suspicious set of men.[9] Poaching

[1] *P.L.* No. 534.   [2] *Id.* No. 403.   [3] *Id.* No. 516.
[4] *Id.* No. 197.   [5] E.g. *E.C.P.* 27/137.
[6] *Id.* 6/262, 12/141.   [7] *Id.* 10/105, 11/492, 27/50, 33/132.
[8] *P.L.* No. xcix.   [9] *Id.* No. xcix and 905.

and hunting were always weaknesses of the country parson, by means of which he enlivened his vacant hours,[1] but Sir J. Bukk, parson of Stratford, seems to have carried his methods of amusement to extremes when he occupied himself on Sir J. Fastolf's lands and "fished my stanks at Dedham, and helped to break my dam, and destroyed my new mill."[2] More serious offences, however, were all too common, and some parsons were ready to take advantage of the unsettled state of the country-side to descend on defenceless people, and to rob and harass them. The parson of Marlingford had joined such a gang which continually worried the Pastons' tenants, and carried off six cartloads of timber of the Pastons', "bearing bows and glaives about the carts for fear of [the plunder] being taken away."[3]

The conduct of such men must have done incalculable harm to the cause of religion and to the prestige of the parochial clergy. Thos. Denyes, the Coroner of Norfolk, while he was with Edward IV at York, had been obliged to complain of the conduct of a Norfolk man named Twyer. No sooner had Denyes returned from York, than the parson of Snoring, a friend of Twyer's, came to his house one June day, and, after making various accusations against him, carried him off. No more was ever heard of the unfortunate Denyes, until the news that he had been murdered was noised about; and, on the 10th July, Sir J. Tatersall, the bailiff of Walsingham, and the constable took the parson of Snoring and four of his men, and set them in the stocks.[4] John Paston was urged to get a Commission appointed

to sit uppon the parson of Snoring, and on such as were the cause of Thomas Denyes' death, and for many and great horrible robberies. As for the costs thereof, the countryside will pay therefor, for they are sore afraid that unless the said death and the said robbers be chastised, that more folks shall be served in like wise.[5]

The above description will enable the reader to form an impression of the varied activities of the parish priests. It is time to turn to another body of the secular clergy—the domestic chaplains. From the time of the Conquest onwards, they had

[1] *R.H.S.* Vol. VI. p. 119, n. 3, and pp. 97–8, and cf. *Plum. Corr.* p. 22; *A Norfolk Manor*, Davenport, p. 75; and Redstone, pp. 184–5.
[2] *P.L.* Nos. 130–1.   [3] *Id.* No. 865.   [4] *Id.* No. 403.
[5] *Id.* No. 406, and see No. 488 for cases of murder, assault and subsequent perjury by clerics.

been a common figure in the households of the King, and of the great nobles. The practice of employing such men gradually spread until, by the fourteenth and fifteenth centuries, not only great country families, but also the rising merchant classes and the squirearchy found places in their households for such men. There were many reasons encouraging them to do so. In the first place, it was greatly to the convenience of such people that they could have the divine services performed daily within their own houses, thus obviating the necessity of going to the parish church. Many documents might be quoted setting out the various reasons that were put forward when the Bishop's permission to establish a private chapel was being sought.[1] Generally, the inclemency of the weather, together with the distance to the church, or the age and infirmity of the petitioner were urged as considerations calling for the Bishop's indulgence.[2]

Besides performing their religious duties in such chapels, the chaplains filled a variety of other offices in their patrons' houses. This is very strikingly shown in the case of the chapel staff of the Earl of Northumberland. Besides a dean, there were ten other priests, many of whom occupied what seem to be entirely secular offices, such as surveyor of lands, secretary to the Earl, almoner, or master of grammar.[3] In smaller households, the domestic chaplain combined many of these offices in his own person. Hence his usefulness to the ordinary country squire, and it is not surprising that almost every family which could afford it employed its own domestic chaplain.

The *Paston Letters* throw some very striking sidelights on the daily life of these chaplains. Both the Pastons and their friend Sir John Fastolf employed a domestic chaplain. Indeed, when an examination was made touching the gentility of the Paston family, one of the chief pieces of evidence in support of their claim was the fact that, "before time of mind, their ancestors had licence to have a chaplain and have divine service within [their house]."[4]

From time to time various chaplains appear in and out of the pages of the *Paston Letters*, but by far the most interesting

[1] See *Exeter Regs. passim.*   [2] *P.L.* No. 751.
[3] *North. Household Book,* p 323.   [4] *P.L.* No. 554.

and important of them all was Sir James Gloys. He cannot have
come into the service of the Pastons later than 1448, and was
with them continuously till his death in 1473, although for part
of the time he was also Rector of Stokesby. Throughout the
whole period, however, he was the confidential friend and agent
of the Pastons. There can be little doubt that he had not long
been a member of the Paston household before he won the
confidence and approval of Margaret Paston to a marked degree.
This gave him so secure a position that he was able to treat the
younger members of the family with scant respect. The first
time he is mentioned in this correspondence is in terms of
dislike by Edmund Paston, and it seems clear that the chaplain
had been influencing Margaret Paston since Edmund bursts
out angrily, "Unless among us we 'give not him a lift,' I pray
God that we never thrive."[1] Gloys was equally unpopular
among the friends and neighbours of the Pastons, and, once on
his way home from Norwich, "by Wymondham's gate was attacked by Wymondham and two of his men with him and
driven into my mother's place for refuge." Later in the day
Gloys was again assaulted in the street, and Margaret Paston,
fearing what might happen to him, sent him up to London
to her husband.[2]

The passage of years only seems to have increased his hold
over Margaret Paston, and her house must often have been a
very uncomfortable place for those who would not bow to his
ruling. Twenty-four years later, in 1472, young John Paston
speaks of him as "the proud, peevish and evil disposed priest
to us all, Sir James."[3] These very bitter words prepare us for
the vivid sketch he gives of Paston home life further on in his
letter.

Many quarrels are picked to get my brother Edmund and me out
of her house. We go not to bed lightly unchided. All that we do is
ill done, and all that Sir James and Pecock do, is well done....We
fell out before my mother with "Thou proud priest," and "Thou
proud squire," my mother taking his part.[4]

In a later letter he continues,

Sir James is always chopping at me when my mother is present,
with such words as he thinks anger me, and also cause my mother

---

[1] *P.L.* No. 58.   [2] *Id.* No. 59.   [3] *Id.* No. 697.   [4] *Id.* No. 697.

to be displeased with me,...and when he has most unfitting words to me, I smile a little and tell him it is good hearing of these old tales.[1]

Such an unsatisfactory state of affairs was only concluded by the death of Sir James during the next year, and Sir John Paston's advice to his brother, "Beware from henceforth that no such fellow creep in between her and you,"[2] shows the cleavage Sir James had effected between mother and son.

It is not easy from the existing fragments to piece together the whole story of Gloys's life in the Paston household, but enough remains to show how completely Margaret Paston was under his domination. There can be little doubt, too, that her naturally stern cast of mind was hardened by association with this man. When her daughter Margery made her mésalliance with Richard Calle, the Pastons' steward, the spontaneous anger of her mother was evidently fanned by James Gloys. Certainly Calle, who knew the Paston household as well as any man, had no doubt as to who was acting with Margaret Paston against him in this matter, and he says as much in writing to Margery. His assumption was fully justified.[3] When all had done their worst before the Bishop to shake Margery's faith in her lover and had failed, it was Gloys who, on her return home, met her with the news that henceforth she could never enter there again. If further evidence of his supremacy were wanted, the fact that he could dare to support and encourage Margaret Paston's refusal of money to her eldest son, who was nominally head of the family, shows clearly enough his power and sense of security.[4]

The clue to Sir James's continuous hold over Margaret Paston probably lies in her recognition of his business capabilities. Both Margaret Paston and her husband were very careful and hard-working people, and Sir James must have been a great asset in assisting them to manage their manifold affairs. Throughout we have no reference to any spiritual duties performed by Gloys, so we cannot estimate how large a part they played in his daily life, but his zeal and activity on the Pastons' behalf are patent; and, after the death of John Paston, Gloys became invaluable to the widow. One of his earliest letters preserved in this collection, and addressed to John Paston, is an excellent

[1] *P.L.* No. 702.   [2] *Id.* No. 732.   [3] *Id.* No. 609.   [4] *Id.* No. LXXXII.

example of his abilities. In it he sets out at length the condition
of Paston's affairs at Gresham and elsewhere in Norfolk; suggests
the necessary legal actions that ought to be taken; warns him
of the restless state of the countryside, and generally shows a
complete mastery of all the details of the estate.[1] More interesting still, perhaps, are the details he gives of his own activities,
thus affording us an insight into the daily lives and routine of
many men like himself. Among his other duties, he had tried
several times personally to distrain from a defaulting tenant,
but had had to admit defeat, as the man had taken refuge in
his mother's house, and the good woman's curses were too
fearful for Gloys to brave. On another day he rode to a Manor
Court, and tried to arrest a certain man who immediately "set
all the tenants upon me, [who] made a great noise and said
quite plainly [that] I should not have him if he would abide
with them." So Gloys had to leave the Court without his
prisoner, but he was not yet beaten, and informs John Paston
that

I lay in wait upon him on the heath, as he should have come home-
wards, and if I might have met with him I should have had Betts
from him: but he had laid such watch that he had espied us before
he came fully at us...and he took his horse with his spurs and rode
...as fast as he might ride.[2]

Besides all this, the indefatigable man had got Paston's writs
duly attested after considerable trouble; had interviewed (and
probably bribed) many men who were to serve on a jury to
decide a case between the Pastons and a neighbour, and had
been trying to let some of the Paston lands.[3] It is not surprising
that John Paston, who was obliged to spend much of his time
in London, should have been attracted by a man of such ability;
and, no doubt, he felt his Norfolk affairs were safe in Sir James'
hands. When he writes to his wife, he is careful to remind her
to consider the chaplain's advice:

as well for my household, as for the gathering of the revenue of
my "livelode," or grain, or for setting to work my servants, and for
the more politic means of setting and carrying of my malt, and for
all other things necessary to be done.[4]

Whatever his faults may have been, Gloys was not without
courage and was ready to take risks, as he had shown in his

[1] *P.L.* No. 146.   [2] *Id.* No. 146.   [3] *Id.* Nos. 146–7.   [4] *Id.* No. LIX.

attempt to ambush Gonnor.[1] When the dispute between the Duke of Suffolk and John Paston concerning the title to Drayton and Hellesdon was at its height, Sir James showed great courage in riding to Drayton to hold a Court with only one other of the Pastons' adherents. Margaret Paston writes:

Thomas Bond and Sir James Gloys [went] to hold the court in your name, and to claim your title; for I could get none others to keep the court, nor that would go thither but the said Thomas Bond, because I suppose they were afraid of the people that would be there on behalf of the Duke of Suffolk.[2]

Such fears were fully justified, for they were met at the Court by the opposing party supported by 60 men, "some of them having rusty poleaxes and bills." Sir James, however, was not to be daunted, and "did the errands to them, and had the words," and throughout upheld the Paston cause very staunchly.

Sir James was ready to meet the crisis created by the death of John Paston. He seems to have taken charge of the great preparations and ceremonies incident to the burial of his patron. He it is who orders and pays for the mourning garments for the many friends and retainers of the Pastons. He arranges for a sufficiency of "keepers of the torches, of clerks, friars, priests for the dirige at Norwich" etc. The funeral preparations and feasts at Bromholm find him equally active, and he worked unceasingly with Richard Calle the bailiff in making the necessary arrangements for the enormous quantities of food and drink that were required. Even a great part of the account of all this expense he kept himself.[3]

The easy-going ways of Sir John Paston made it more essential than ever that Sir James should continue to act as chaplain and adviser to the family. Sir John recognised this plainly enough, and wrote to his mother shortly after his father's death: "Send a letter to Richard Calle and to Sir James Gloys to come up to London in any wise. For there is no man can do in divers matters that they can do."[4] The reports made by the chaplain now and again show how carefully he was guarding the Paston interests, and also on what very intimate terms he was with them all. When absent in London, the Pastons left their chests at home in the safe keeping of Sir James. Many

[1] P.L. No. 146. See above for details. [2] Id. No. 518.
[3] Id. No. 549. [4] Id. No. LXXI.

of these, we know, contained the most vital evidences, legal documents, money and spare clothes. Sir James was given the keys to guard, and was obviously well acquainted with their contents. John Paston writes from London, "Item, that Mistress Broom send me hither 3 long gowns, and two doublets and a jacket of 'plonket chamlett,' and a murrey bonnet out of my coffer. Sir James has the key."[1]

From all this, in spite of his title of chaplain, Sir James seems to have been more a kind of bailiff than anything else.[2] He frequently worked in conjunction with Richard Calle, the Paston bailiff, although no doubt his clerical office gave him a status more dignified than that of Calle. Besides this, he kept the head of the family in touch with Norfolk affairs by letter, and would sometimes act as amanuensis for Margaret Paston. Yet, despite all his concern with the affairs of the world, he did not entirely forget less material things; for, upon his death, we find Sir John Paston writing eagerly about the books Gloys had left.[3] Perhaps Gloys sometimes refreshed himself after a hard day's business by reading a romance or book of poems.[4] Sir John Paston was an eager book-collector, and possibly had long coveted some items of the chaplain's treasures.

The only other chaplain of whom we have any detailed account is Sir Thomas Howes. In these *Letters*, he is only seen acting as Sir J. Fastolf's agent and chaplain. He too seems to have been chaplain in little but name. Sir John Fastolf set him at Caister, and, throughout the years before Fastolf went to live there himself, Howes carried on all his business. Sir John was always very determined in protecting his own interests; and, no doubt, had discovered that Howes could be relied on as a man of affairs. So Fastolf gave him the living of Castlecombe in Dorset, and from time to time Howes was given other

---

[1] *P.L.* Nos. 670, 678.

[2] Cf. Wyclif, *Two Treatises against Friars*, ed. James, p. 16. "But our Priests ben so busie about worldlie occupation, that they semen better Baylifs or Reves, than ghostlie Priests of Jesu Christ," and cf. Arnold, III. pp. 277, 335, and *Piers Plowman*, c. i. ll. 93 ff., and later Sir T. More's *Works*, 1557, "A Dialogue [against Tyndale etc.], bk I, c. xii. p. 227. "Every mean man must have a priest in his house to wait upon his wife, which no man almost lacketh now, to the contempt of priesthood, in as vile office as his horsekeeper. That is, quoth he, truth indeed and worse too, for they keep hawks and dogs."

[3] *P.L.* Nos. 745-7, 749, 752, 754.   [4] *Id.* No. 690.

livings;[1] but it is clear that he could never have been much else than a local agent of Fastolf. The bad system of those days, which allowed absenteeism and the filling of cures by stipendiary curates, encouraged such an action. The fact that he had a living to bestow, and that Howes was in orders, was sufficient for old Sir John. How could he do better than give it to Sir Thomas, who could thereby live in Norfolk and look after the property, and would also be of little expense to him? It was one of Sir John's ways of rewarding good service. Once, when William Worcester, "who had devoted the best energies of his life to the service of Fastolf,"[2] had complained to his master that he was not receiving the reward his work deserved, Sir John's only reply was that he wished Worcester had been a priest, and then he could have repaid him with a living.[3] When it is remembered that Sir John was a very devout man, as he showed by his efforts to found a College for priests at Caister, and also by other bequests to churches, and yet could think of doing a thing like this, the complaints against the clergy become more explicable. Livings were regarded in too many cases as useful gifts, to be bestowed either for past or prospective services. Almost everything was considered rather than the needs of the parish, and the desirability of getting a fit man. This, as we have seen, led to men so appointed being mere creatures of their patron, painfully anxious to further his interests, because their worldly hopes were almost entirely in his keeping.

Sir Thomas was undoubtedly an able man of business. Throughout the large number of letters in this correspondence which passed between him and his patron, the man's driving force, and the efforts he was continuously making on Fastolf's behalf are conspicuous. To examine fully his daily routine would, to a large extent, only repeat what has been previously done in the case of Sir James Gloys. It is sufficient to say that Fastolf reposed considerable confidence in him, as complete as he ever seems to have given to any man. He delegated considerable power to Howes, but held him strictly answerable for any action that was taken in his master's name. When he once

---

[1] Howes was presented to the living of Castlecombe in Dorset in 1445; to Mauteby, Norfolk, in 1460; to Blofield, Norfolk, in 1460; and to Pulham, Norfolk, in 1465. He died late in 1468.

[2] P.L. Intro. p. clxxiii.   [3] Id. No. 214.

heard that Howes had boasted at Ipswich that he had Fastolf's authority and protection in a certain action, he quickly disabused his agent of any such notion:

> Know for certain, there passed no such warrants under my seal, neither did I command you to labour nor to do things that should be against the law, neither unlawfully against right and truth. And therefore I ought not, nor will not, pay for you.[1]

What his religious duties were, and how he neglected or performed them, we do not know. He was so constantly riding about the countryside attending to the bewildering multiplicity of requests, orders and questions which Fastolf was for ever sending to him from London, that he could have had little time for any spiritual duties. After Fastolf came to live at Caister we know that he "was accustomed, when in health, daily to say certain prayers with his chaplain."[2] There is no definite evidence, however, to show that this chaplain was Howes; and it is more than probable that it was one brought by Fastolf from London, or perhaps the celebrated Greyfriar of Norwich, Dr Brackley.[3] The volume of work to be done certainly did not lessen on Fastolf's arrival, and the continuous litigation and negociating amid which Fastolf seemed happiest, depended chiefly on this so-called chaplain and priest for its continuance.[4]

Howes and Gloys represent the positions held by domestic chaplains favoured by circumstance, and deep in the confidence of their patrons. The ordinary chaplain probably did not receive so much, nor did he occupy himself so deeply with the secular interests of his employers. The work his religious duties entailed was in most cases fairly easily disposed of—the daily saying of the Mass, and the due performance of the other daily offices would seem to be his usual routine duties. We can follow the career of one such chaplain employed by the Pastons. Sir John Still had been engaged by them some time after the death of Sir John Fastolf "to sing for his soul." This he was apparently still doing in 1469, ten years after Sir John's death, and a chance reference also shows us that he was acting as tutor to "lytyll Jack"—whom John Paston the youngest calls "his lytyll

---

[1] *P.L.* No. xxxv, and cf. No. 168.
[2] *Id.* No. 550, II. p. 275.   [3] See pp. 246 ff.
[4] For detailed list of Howe's activities see *e.g. P.L.* Nos. 79, 82, 95, 98, 102, 109, 110, 115, 126–8, 130–3, 141–3, etc.

man."[1] Evidently he had become attached to the family, for we find him remaining with them, although it is frequently mentioned that his wages are in arrears. He was at Caister throughout the siege by the Duke of Norfolk, and bore himself well, for John Paston writes to his brother specially commending Still and another old retainer: "By my troth they are as good men's bodies as any live, and specially Sir John Still and John Pamping. If I were of power to keep them,...by troth they should never depart from me while I lived."[2] His words were not without effect, and the chaplain was still with the Pastons in 1471. These were hard times, however, and every economy had to be exercised. So, despite their regrets, Sir John was told towards the end of that year that he had better get another chapel to serve before Christmas. By this time his wages were over a year in arrears, yet he still looked on Sir John Paston and his family with affection, and was ready to do whatever his patron thought best for him. Whether the Pastons were able to get "the benefice, or free chapel, or some other good service" which they desired for him, we do not know. Two years later, however, we read that "Sir John Paston had promised Still 5 marks in part payment," so he might yet have been with the Pastons, or perhaps it was only that his arrears were being slowly discharged.

Besides their domestic chaplains such as Sir James Gloys, and men who were really chantry priests such as Sir John Still, the Pastons from time to time appointed a priest to serve a chapel they had in Caister Hall. Sir Thomas Howes seems to have held this office for a time; but, after his death in 1468, Sir John Paston made use of the vacancy to further his own ends. At this time he was engaged to Anne Haute, and was anxious to please her friends, who had great influence with the Queen. So he writes to his brother, "So it is now that at the special request of the Queen and other especial good Lords of mine, I have given [the chaplaincy] to the bearer hereof, called Master John Yotton, a chaplain of the Queen's." The zeal of the new chaplain to get this gift is perhaps explained by the fact that he thought the office was worth 100s. a year. Sir John, however, while asking his brother to show every courtesy to

---

[1] *P.L.* No. 585.   [2] *Id.* No. 631.

the new chaplain, remarks that he thinks this is an exaggerated estimate, and adds, "I think it dear enough at 40/- by [the] year. He must have it as it was had before." Certainly the Paston fortunes at this juncture would allow of no augmentation of good Dr Yotton's stipend.[1]

However, Yotton came to Norfolk, and by his gracious behaviour created a favourable impression on Margaret Paston. Although he was formally presented and instituted, it is not likely that he had any intention of residing at Caister, thus exchanging the pleasures of the society about the Queen for that of the Norfolk countryside. No doubt his discovery of the true state of affairs at Caister, where his 100s. had dwindled to 40s., quickened his resolve to return to Court as soon as he could. He kept a tight hold of the office, nevertheless, and nine years later was still in possession, and indeed showed some anxiety as to how "such profits as are growing of [the] chapel at Caister" were accounted for. He even displayed some interest in the fact that, while he was drawing the money, no one was officiating at Caister. But to him, as to so many other clerics at this time, the whole affair was a matter for commonsense arrangement. He wrote to say that he was quite ready "to make a bargain...so that ye might have a priest to sing at Caister."[2] He was dealing with men as hard at driving a bargain as himself, and John Paston advised his brother to come to some arrangement quickly before Yotton "wist what the value were...for I have promised him to send him word this term of the very value of it."[2] Two months later the matter was settled. Dr Yotton by this time had apparently developed "a great conscience in it, because there is no divine service said in the free chapel at Caister."[3] So it was agreed that "Sir J. Brykks, that is now dwelling with a right loving kinsman" of the Pastons, should be appointed; Dr Yotton adding, with a touch of patronage, "that he the rather with your good will would give it to one you owe affection unto."[3]

---

[1] P.L. No. 600.   [2] Id. No. 811.

[3] Id. No. xcii. It seems very probable that Sir J. Still was originally hired to fill the gap caused by Dr Yotton's absence. We have no reference of Yotton ever residing at Caister; and, the year after he received the gift of the chapel, Still is heard of there [No. 608]. We hear no more of Still after 1473 [No. 719]; and in 1478 the chapel had evidently been long neglected, so that Yotton's conscience began to worry him [No. 811].

CHAPTER XVI

THE REGULAR CLERGY

WE have seen the important part played by the parish priest and how he made himself felt in almost every phase of medieval life. His position was indeed analogous to that of the present-day village priest in Italy. While he was well known to all his flock, the duties and necessities of his position made it well-nigh impossible for him to be on friendly terms with many of them. As Lina Duff-Gordon says of the modern Italian priest, "With the exception of the Easter blessing practically the only time that a priest enters a house is when he comes to administer the last sacraments. "È venuto il prete" sounds like a death knell to the family."[1] The village priest in medieval England was forced to exist, as is his brother in modern Italy to some extent, on the offerings and dues to be exacted from his parishioners. Hence there was often a real barrier between the priest and his people; for in Norfolk, as elsewhere, the parish priest was frequently the local rent-collector and land agent for his patron, even if he did not farm out land of his own.[2] If this were not sufficient to alienate him from many of his parishioners, we may be sure that the vigorous collection of all tithes, and the mortuary, and the mass-penny often succeeded in so doing. Many men doubtless would have replied, as the Italian peasants answered, on being asked if the priests did not give to the poor:

Give—give is not in the dictionary of our priests—take, take, take, yes, that word you will see printed in big letters. Why, they often refuse the full burial service, and for everything insist on payment first.[3]

The parish priest's difficulties were not lessened by the presence of the great religious bodies of Regular clergy that existed in England until the Reformation. Although by the fifteenth century the heyday of the monasteries was over, both

---

[1] *Home Life in Italy*, Lina Duff-Gordon, p. 231.   [2] Cf. *Id.* p. 202.
[3] *Id.* pp. 200–1, and cf. Lyndwood, s.v. oblationes.

the older Orders and the Friars exerted an enormous influence
on everyday life. When we remember that the Commons
asserted that about one-third of the wealth of England was in
the hands of the Church, and by far the greater proportion of
this in the hands of the Regulars, even when we have made all
allowances for exaggerations, it is not difficult to appreciate
what power they had. Apart from their economic influence,
however, the Regular clergy had increased the parish priest's
difficulties in many ways. First, they were very often the
appropriators of livings, and therefore had the right to take
all the income and to pay the smallest possible salary to the
priest they put in charge of the cure.[1] Even when the Bishops
insisted on a settled sum being put on one side for the parish
priest, the Regulars tried to cut this down as far as possible.
As a result, the incumbent often received a miserable salary,
and therefore found it absolutely necessary to screw all he could
in the way of tithes, offerings, etc. out of his parishioners.
Secondly, the Regulars impinged upon his spiritual activities,
even within his own parish. This was a special complaint, constantly reiterated against the Friars. Unlike the other Regular
Orders, the Friars were never meant to keep to their cloister.
It was their duty to travel about from place to place, teaching,
helping, and begging their bread as they went. While the monk
was bound only to individual poverty, the friar was pledged
to individual and communal poverty. The practice of the Friars
failed to carry out their theory, and, by the fifteenth century,
they had accumulated enough wealth to construct many magnificent buildings. The problem of evangelical poverty had
caused very great controversy within their ranks, and the
teaching of S. Francis in its strictest form had long been put
on one side by the vast majority of the Franciscans. Contemporary writers, both lay and clerical, show how far the
Four Orders had fallen from their early ideals, and how unscrupulous they had often become in their quest for power.
In this quest, their influence upon the ordinary parish was
considerable, and it is easy to realise how difficult the parish
priest found it to stand against them. These Friars were often
well-trained for their work; they had lived and studied in the

[1] For details, see p. 241.

cloister before going out into the world; often they were in
touch with the greater world and its affairs; and then, coming
to the country parish, brought a breath of unknown and mys-
terious places with them. Trained in every art of appeal, of
gesture, of popular exposition, only too often many of them
were easily able to outdo the parish priest. When they preached
on the village green, the church would be half empty. Instead
of a dreary, and possibly familiar discourse on one of the deadly
sins, the Friar would relate a score of merry tales, or recount
to his gaping audience a sensational miracle that filled them with
wonder and opened their purses as a result. Then he would
quickly collect all he could, by way of alms, or towards the
building funds of his Friary; and so away.

While the homes of the Regulars were familiar landmarks to
the people in all parts of England, in few counties was this
more so than in Norfolk. Religious houses of all kinds had been
settled within its area, and no one could travel very far in
medieval Norfolk without catching sight of the great church,
or the boundary wall of some abbey or priory. Many people
indeed made long journeys to one such Norfolk priory, for the
house of the Austin Friars at Walsingham was second only to
Canterbury in importance among English pilgrimages, and was
famous beyond the seas. At Bromholm Priory, in another part
of Norfolk, a relic of the Holy Cross drew great crowds to
worship and pray before it year by year. Hence it is not strange
that we find very many scattered references to the Regular
clergy in the pages of the *Paston Letters*. The Friars, especially,
were constantly to be seen travelling up and down the country,
and it is a significant fact that it was reported in a news-letter
of 1454 that the Duke of Somerset's spies were going about
disguised as Friars.[1] Few dresses gave a man such freedom as
did the long robe of the Friar. Clothed in this, a man could
make his way into the household of the Duke of Norfolk, or he
could crave a night's lodging of John Paston; while, if either
of these did not suit his purpose, he could win his way to the
fireside of some well-to-do burgess, or even put up with the
discomfort of the poor man's hovel. All grades of society were
affected by the frequent attentions of one or another of the

[1] *P.L.* No. 195.

Four Orders. Consequently, they flit through the pages of the *Paston Letters* from time to time, and in doing so play many rôles. Sometimes we see them holding their services or preaching, at other times acting as private secretaries or messengers, and we even find the worst of them engaged in deceit and robbery.

Not only the Friars, but the other orders of Regulars are seen in these pages. The Pastons themselves originally lived almost under the shadow of the famous priory of Bromholm. Many pilgrims, when they had visited Walsingham, returned home by way of this priory to see the relic of the Holy Cross, and many miracles were reported to have occurred there.[1] Again, the Abbey of S. Benet's at Holm—the oldest religious foundation in Norfolk, whose towers would have been visible from the rising ground at Caister—was frequently in correspondence with Sir John Fastolf and John Paston. No man with Sir John's large landed interests could avoid coming into contact with the monks, for they were always very large landowners themselves, and a constant system of releasing, or exchanging, or letting lands was continuously going on.[2] Part of the proceeds from their estates the Regulars devoted to hospitality, and the monasteries are popularly regarded in our days as having been the inns of the Middle Ages.[3] While this is by no means the whole truth, they did undoubtedly receive both rich and poor, and seldom failed to attribute their poverty to excessive hospitality. The rich man was admitted to the table of the abbot or prior, while inferiors were accommodated in the guest house of the monastery. We find in the *Paston Letters* that in 1475 the Duchess of York stayed at the Abbey of S. Benet's, and brought with her all her household. She seemed to be in no hurry to move, for current rumour had it that she meant to remain there for some time "if she liked the air."[4] The religious houses sometimes became a shelter for the oppressed, and when Robert Ledham's gang was terrorising Norfolk in 1452-3, several of his victims, "for salvation of their lives," withdrew to some such safe refuge. Hence we find one man staying at

---

[1] *P.L.* No. 80.   [2] *E.g.* see Nos. 17, 213.

[3] See *Eng. Monastic Life*, Gasquet, pp. 30–2, and cf. Jusserand, pp. 119–26.

[4] *P.L.* No. 761, and see Nos. 9, 277.

S. Benet's, while others went to "fortresses and good towns."[1]
Besides entertaining people coming to the monastery for such
diverse reasons as these, the Abbot would invite his friends to dine
occasionally, or would ask a neighbouring squire to come and
discuss a business matter over a friendly meal. When the living
of Stokesby fell vacant, and there seemed to be some doubt
as to who should be the new parson, the Abbot of S. Benet's
wrote to John Paston, and asked him to dinner, "trusting that
our communication had in the said [matters] shall cause peace
and pleasure to all parties."[2] The Pastons were on friendly
terms with this monastery, and many years after the above
letter was written the Abbot took one of the Paston servants
into his employment, and told Sir John Paston that he would
not fail him while he lived, and that if he could do anything
for him, or for any servant of his, he would do it faithfully.[3]
William Worcester, an old servant of Sir John Fastolf and
John Paston, seems to have been received there at one time,
probably because of this friendship between his masters and
the Abbot; but he evidently fell on evil days, and grumbles to
Margaret Paston that the new Abbot has deprived him of the
chamber which once was his.[4]

All their varied hospitality undoubtedly pressed on the
revenues of these houses, and only their enormous possessions
enabled them to do what they did. This hospitality, their other
great expenses, and, we must add, (wherever the documents are
sufficiently full to tell a complete tale), their not infrequent
mismanagement[5] made it continually necessary for the Regulars
to seek for more and more lands, or fresh sources of revenue.
The *Paston Letters* occasionally give us glimpses of this side of
monastic life, although by now these sources were running dry.
Here and there, as at Walsingham, we find that a monastery is
selling land in order to raise money[6]; while, as Lords of the
Manor, the Prior and Convent became entitled to all the

---

[1] *P.L.* No. 201.   [2] *Id.* No. 230.   [3] *Id.* No. 646.   [4] *Id.* No. 582.

[5] See for example Bp Goldwell's visitation of the Norfolk religious houses
in 1492. Out of the 36 houses visited, complaints of mismanagement and
consequent dilapidation were made in 14 cases and in 13 cases the brethren
complained that they were not shown the accounts. *Visitation, Diocese
Norwich*, ed. Jessopp, A., [C.S.], 1888.

[6] *P.L.* No. 212-3 and cf. No. 17.

customary dues arising from the manors. So we find the Abbey of S. Benet's owning a mill, and no doubt profiting considerably from the fact that the law of the manor required all tenants to grind their corn at the Lord's mill. Here also, as elsewhere in records of the Middle Ages, we are constantly reminded that the Regulars always had a possible source of revenue in the advowsons of rectories they were able to get into their own hands. A monastery could get permission from the Pope and from the Bishop of the diocese to "appropriate" a Rectory. It was then free to use the greater part of the income from this source for monastic instead of for parochial purposes.

The church at Paston, being very near the Priory of Bromholm, had long been appropriated to that foundation by the fifteenth century, and it is therefore a Vicar, and not a Rector, of Paston who is a friend of the family. This change impoverished the incumbent at Paston, for after the appropriation had taken place his portion in money was only declared at twenty shillings. The Priory of Bromholm, however, received therefrom an income of £10. 6s. 8d. besides 52 acres of land.[1] Probably, as in most cases, in addition to this sum the Vicar was given the proceeds of the altarage, oblations, mortuaries and personal tithes, as well as all small tithes. Almost everything came under the heading of "small tithes," except the tithes of grain. These were usually strictly secured by the appropriators, leaving the Vicar with the tithes of such things as calves, chickens, lambs, foals, pigs, geese, wool, milk, pasturage, wood, fish, etc. In some cases, the amount gleaned from the greater tithes by the Regulars may not have been very large, but it was most often entirely unearned by them, and in the aggregate came to a very considerable sum. The comparative figures of the richer Norfolk parishes only are given in the return made in 1291, but from these we can see that in 33 cases of appropriated livings the Vicars received only £204. 2s. 4d., while the total value of the livings was £1002. 4s. 2d. In other words, the average income received by each of these Vicars was £6. 3s. 8d., while each monastery or priory received on an average £24. 3s. 8d.[2] It is

[1] Blomefield, VIII. pp. 128-9, and cf. I. pp. 452-3 for fuller details of a Norfolk appropriation. *Id.* II. p. 97, shows that the Prior at once leased out the original parsonage and croft.

[2] *Taxatio Ecclesiastica P. Nicholai*, Pub. Records, 1802, pp. 78-90.

difficult to estimate exactly how many rectories had been appropriated in Norfolk. A careful examination of the *Taxatio
Ecclesiastica* of Pope Nicholas of 1291 gives a total of 697 livings
in the county, of which 193, or 28 per cent. were appropriated.
Even if we accept the more moderate figure of the *Victoria
County History*, we see that 25 per cent. were in the hands of the
Regulars as early as 1291, and during the next two centuries
a few more rectories were appropriated. The division of the
moneys accruing to the livings seems to have been roughly in
the proportion given above. A return known as the *Norwich
Domesday Book* helps us here, and from it the figures in various
deaneries have been worked out as fully as the information there
given will allow. The deanery of Bromholm, for example, yields
eight cases in which the values of both rectory and vicarage
are given, and we find that they amounted to £117. 6s. 8d.,
and £29. 6s. 9d. respectively. Six vicarages in the deanery of
Cranwich yield almost exactly the same proportion.[1]

Perhaps the most interesting of the devices used at this time
was the issuing of Letters of Fraternity. The receipt of such a
letter enabled the holder named therein to participate in all
the divine blessings and favours showered down upon the particular monastery issuing the letter, and upon all their Order,
and also to benefit by the prayers and masses said by the
monastery. These privileges naturally were only bestowed on
those who showed by their lives, or by their gifts, that they
were in closest sympathy with Holy Church and all its work.
The Pastons were evidently favourably viewed in this connection, for we know that both William Paston[2] and his wife
Agnes[3] were associated with religious orders by such letters,
and that one of their grandsons received a letter of fraternity
from the prior provincial of the Franciscans in 1475.[4] The
tremendous value a credulous person of those times must have
set on such a letter, is best seen from the terms in which the
Abbot of Bury addresses William Paston.

William, by divine permission Abbot of the exempt monastery of
S. Edmund, and the Prior and Convent of the same place, to the

---

[1] These results have been obtained by gathering together the figures of
the *Norwich Domesday Book*, as quoted by Blomefield, *passim*, in his
account of the several parishes in these two deaneries.
   [2] *P.L.* No. 13.   [3] *Ib.* No. 557.   [4] Blomefield, VI. p. 487.

honourable man William Paston, health and eternal felicity after death, by the suffrages of prayer. For the devotion which you have to God, and to our monastery, in which the most glorious King and martyr S. Edmund corporally and uncorruptibly resteth; we receive you with the affection of sincere charity, and wish to reward you with a return of spiritual benefits; and believing that it will be acceptable to God and to the Saints, we kindly admit, by these presents, your honourable person into the fraternity of our chapter. We, moreover, grant to you, equally in life and in death, as far as the mercy of God permits, a perpetual participation in all masses, psalms, prayers, fasts, abstinences, holy watchings, alms, labours, and all other spiritual benefits which the Lord hath ordained to be performed by our brethren appointed, or that shall be appointed in our said monastery. We also add, and of special grace grant, that when the day of your death shall be made public in our Chapter-house, with the representation of those who were present, that your name shall be inserted in our Martyrology, to be repeated in every succeeding year; and that your name shall be sent to all monasteries of our religion, and to many other holy places established in England, to be eternally praised in the devout prayers of the holy fathers who dwell therein. And other things for the health of thy devout soul shall be fulfilled, which have been accustomed to be done for the brothers and sisters of our aforesaid chapter; and for all other friends who have gone the way of all flesh in past times.

In testimony of which grant we have caused our seal to be placed to these presents. Given in our aforesaid Monastery on the Feast of S. Ambrose, Bishop and Confessor, 1429.[1]

Besides such methods, the Regulars could always depend on the gifts of the faithful, though to a diminishing extent. Contemporary wills give us numerous instances of this, for there is an almost monotonous reiteration of, "I leave to the four orders of the Friars at...," or "I leave to the prior of...." We may look at the wills of some members of the Paston family to illustrate this. When John Paston died, he was buried at Bromholm, and in his will left 40s. to the Prior, and 6s. 8d. each to nine monks, and 1s. 8d. to a less fortunate monk. Besides this, he ordered that a dole of £5. 13s. 4d. should be paid to the priory. At Norwich, each of the four orders received £2, while the nuns of "Normandys" [i.e. Norman's Hospital] were given 4d. each.[2] His wife, in later years, left bequests to each of the four orders, both in Norwich and Yarmouth, besides numerous bequests to certain nunneries and other religious foundations.[3]

---

[1] *History of the Abbey of S. Edmund's Bury*, Yates, W., p. 156. Cf. *P. P.* c. xiii. 8.   [2] *P.L.* No. 549.   [3] *Id.* No. 861.

Old Agnes Paston was also a generous supporter of the White-friars of Norwich. She had been given a letter of fraternity by them, and expressly states this as a reason for leaving money to help them pay off their debts. She and her husband also left silver vessels to be sold by the Whitefriars, so that they might be able to repair their library.[1]

It was not necessary for the Regulars to wait for the death of such benefactors, before they could hope for rich gifts. When Henry VI recovered from his serious illness in 1455, he at once sent his almoner to Canterbury to make a King's offering there, as a token of his gratitude.[2] The Pastons, during the life-time of John Paston, certainly gave money to help the famous priory at Walsingham, and received a letter of thanks, "for that you do so much for Our Lady's house at Walsingham."[3] Another member of the Paston family spent the very large sum of £100 on the erection of new quire-stalls at Bromholm Priory.[4] Probably every religious house had its own special friends, and the Prior and Convent of Bromholm seem to have regarded the Pastons in this light. Since they lived so near to the priory, and were very influential in that part of Norfolk, this is not very remarkable. So we constantly find the Pastons occupied about the affairs of the priory,[5] and there is a very interesting letter from the Prior to John Paston. The monks were re-building their dormitory, and for this purpose required eight beams for the principals, not less than eleven feet long. Such fine timber was difficult to obtain in Norfolk, and the Prior asked for John Paston's assistance in an application to the Duchy of Lancaster to supply the timber.[6]

The monasteries, besides receiving goods and gifts for themselves, were sometimes made guardians or trustees of valuables. Both the Pastons and Sir John Fastolf made use of religious houses in this way. No doubt the feeling of security and continuity these places presented to people at that time, was largely responsible for this. Sir John Fastolf evidently trusted the Regulars; for, although he was not a very trusting man as a rule, at the time of his death the Abbot of S. Benet's Hulme

---

[1] P.L. Nos. 557, 880.   [2] Id. No. 226.   [3] Id. No. 50.
[4] Id. No. 818.   [5] E.g. Id. Nos. 14, 63, 368.
[6] Id. No. 856, and cf. No. 46 for similar want of timber.

had charge of over £2000 of the knight's money in gold and silver. Besides this, the Abbey stored large quantities of gold and silver vessels left in their keeping. Moreover Sir John had deposited a very great deal of plate in London, with the Abbot of Bermondsey.[1] Small sums of money were sometimes left in the safe keeping of an Abbot, and drawn on when required. When Clement Paston had some money free, he asked his brother to deposit it in this way. He writes, "Brother, I pray you deliver the money that I would have to some prior of some abbey, [or] to some master of some college, to be delivered when I can espy any land to be purchased."[2]

This trust in the competence of the Regulars to guard treasure was not always well founded, as an interesting incident recorded in the *Paston Letters* shows. The executors of William Paston had a dispute with the Prior and Convent of Norwich concerning the sum necessary to be paid in order that mass might be said perpetually for William Paston. As an earnest of their intention to devote a goodly sum to this purpose, the executors deposited "a coffer with a great substance of money" with the Prior. Years elapsed, and the convent continued to offer up masses for the repose of the soul of William Paston, always hoping that a definite agreement would soon be made. During this time, however, although the chest remained the same to outward view, it was gradually being emptied of its contents by an unknown hand. When the monks at last opened the chest, they found they were guarding an empty box![3]

As we have already noticed, the Friars were the most energetic religious force at this time. Their extraordinary energy and perseverance made them well known throughout the country, and Norfolk was no exception. We get a very fair impression of their ceaseless industry from the pages of the *Paston Letters*, for we meet them on every hand and in the most diverse rôles. They are to be seen acting as secretaries, chaplains and confidential advisers, or delivering stirring sermons at Paul's Cross in London, or occupied in learning and the administration of the affairs of their Order. Within their ranks, we find men of the most diverse talents: the Doctor of Divinity, fresh from oratorical triumphs, is found coming back to his

[1] *P.L.* No. 335.   [2] *Id.* No. 395.   [3] *Id.* No. 893.

cloister and mixing there with other Friars, who had no kinship
with him except the kinship of their common calling. The type
of man the Four Orders sometimes enrolled may be seen from
Chaucer's picture of the Friar in the *Canterbury Tales*.

Fortunately, the *Paston Letters* have preserved another full
length portrait of a Friar, and here the naïveté of the man is
at once typical and revealing. John Brackley, a Franciscan of
Norwich, was received into that Order while he was still a young
man. His father was a lyster or dyer of Norwich, and a great
benefactor of the Franciscans; so that, when he died, his body
was buried in their church. No doubt it was largely through
his influence that his son joined the Order, and the old man
had little cause to regret his action; for, step by step, his son
rose to academic distinction, and became a famous preacher
and a Doctor of Divinity. Most of the details of his life have
not survived. Blomefield, the Norfolk historian, says that "he
was an intimate friend and chaplain to Sir John Fastolf, whom
he attended to his death; became a great friend to the Pastons,
was tutor to Sir John Paston, and chaplain to Judge Paston."[1]
It is difficult to determine his exact relation from time to time,
although we know he was very intimate with the Pastons and
Sir J. Fastolf. Whatever these relations may have been, Friar
Brackley had no doubt of his own value to those he served.
Without question he laboured unceasingly for his patrons,
and consequently felt very strongly that the labourer was
worthy of his hire. He even carried this doctrine further, and
recommended a brother Friar to the liberality of the Pastons,
pointing out to them that the man had been constantly by his
side during a two years' sickness. "Several times, but for his
care, I should have been dead" he writes; and it is obvious that
he feels this man's friendly devotion should be vicariously rewarded by the Pastons whom he had often served.

Few readers will fail to form a very clear impression of this
man after reading his letters. Friar Brackley is a capital example
of the dictum "le style, c'est l'homme"; for his letters, with
their curious admixture of English, dog-Latin, texts from the
Scriptures, boastings and worldly affairs, exactly describe the

---

[1] Blomefield, IV. p. 115.

man. The following passage is given in the original spelling, and will illustrate some of the peculiarities of his letter-style:

Ryte reverent mayster and most trusty frend in erthe, as lowly as I kan or may, I recomaunde me, &c., Syr, in feyth I was sore aferd that ye had a gret lettyng that ye come not on Wednys day to met, &c., Be myn feythe, and ye had be here, ye schuld haf had ryte good chere, &c., and hafe faryd ryte wele after your pleser, &c., with more, &c.....The Lord Skalys is to my Lord Prince, &c., [Edward, Prince of Wales] to wayte on hym, &c. He seyth, per Deum Sanctum, as we sey here, he schal be amrel [*i.e.* admiral] or he schal ly there by, &c. Be my feyth, here is a coysy werd [unsettled world]. Walsham of Chauncery, that never made lesyng, told me that Bokkyng was with my Lord Chanceler this terme, but I askyd not how many tymys, &c.

As I haf wrytyn to yow oftyn byfor this, Facite vobis amicos de mammona iniquitatis, q'de. T.T., JH., et J.W., cum ceteris Magistri Fastolf fallacibus famulis magnam gerunt apud vos invidiam, quod excelleritis eos in bonis, &c. Judas non dormit, &c....Ideo sic in Psalmo: Spera in Domino et fac bonitatem et pasceris in divitiis ejus et delectare in Domino, et dabit tibi petitiones cordis tui. Et aliter: Jacta cogitatum tuum in Domino et ipse te enutriet. Utinam, inquit Apostolus, abscindantur qui vos conturbant, &c. Et alibi: Cavete vos a malis et importunis hominibus. Precor gratiosum Deum qui vos et me creavit et suo pretioso sanguine nos redemit, vos vestros et vestra gratiose conservet in prosperis et gratiosius dirigat in agendis.

Scriptum Walsham, feria quarta in nocte cum magna festinatione &c. Utinam iste mundus malignus transiret et concupiscentia ejus.

Vester ad vota promptissimus,
Frater J. Brackley,
Minorum minimus.[1]

It is clear from the above, as well as from many other letters written by Brackley, that he was on very intimate terms with the Pastons. Throughout the litigation which followed upon Fastolf's death, the Friar stood loyally by the family. He seems to have been at Caister some time before Sir John's decease, and certainly was there during the last days. While there, he was unwearied in agreeing with his master when he spoke well of John Paston. Brackley wrote to him a few days before Fastolf's death and urged him to come to Caister, saying, "It is high time; he draweth fast homeward, and is right low brought, and sore weakened and [en]feebled, &c....Every day

---

[1] *P.L.* No. 341, and cf. Nos. 349, 356, 996.

this five days he sayeth, 'God send me soon my good cousin Paston, for I hold him a faithful man, and even one man.' Cui ego, 'that is sooth,' &c. Et ille, 'Show me not the meat, show me the man.' "[1] After the death of Fastolf, Brackley never wavered in his support of the Pastons when they asserted that the will they produced was the last and true will of Sir John. Even on his death-bed, when he was questioned specifically on this matter, Brackley adhered positively to his former statements.

So faithful a friend was frequently of great service to the Pastons. He was often trusted by them to get the necessary evidence and documents, so that they might proceed with their many law cases, and was guardian of their money and goods from time to time.[2] His activities on their behalf did not cease here, for, when a some-time servant of the Pastons and of Sir J. Fastolf was causing anxiety to the family, Brackley wrote in the harshest terms of him, and did all he could to render his work abortive.[3]

In the midst of his purely secular pursuits, Brackley never entirely forgot his priestly office, and was never happier than when engaged in his favourite business of preaching. The Friars were always celebrated for their preachers, and evidently Brackley was well known even among the best, for Blomefield notes that he became a famous preacher, besides which we find his oratory mentioned in several of the *Paston Letters*. As became so famous a man, he had a hearty contempt for those weaker than himself at the art. He is derisive at the expense of one such man, whom he terms "a lewde doctor of Ludgate," and who had recently preached at Paul's Cross. It was a poor sermon, says Brackley, "and he had little thanks as he was worthy, and for his ignorant demeaning, his brethren [are] had in the less favour at London."[4] Brackley himself no doubt showed what should have been done when he preached from the same place a year or two later. Unfortunately his sermon does not survive for our delectation and instruction; but a Whitsunday sermon, preached by him in the Greyfriars' Church at Norwich, is still to be read. In the course of this sermon, Brackley

[1] *P.L.* No. 331.   [3] *Id.* No. 408, and Nos. XLVII and LXIII.
[2] *Id.* No. 331.   [4] *Id.* No. 341.

states that the requirements of a good preacher are "Connyng, boldnesse, and langags." Perhaps Brackley had all three of these things, though it must be confessed that to the modern reader, his sermon is curiously disappointing. True, it is only the skeleton of his discourse which we can read, and we must therefore imagine for ourselves the enthusiasm and oratory of the Friar, which gave life to these seemingly dead sentences, and also seek elsewhere for the wealth of anecdote and reminiscence with which he kept the attention of his audience. His notes show that strong tendency to divide and subdivide the various parts of the argument which is one of the characteristics of the medieval sermon, and they breathe more of the schoolman than of the eager evangelist. A short extract will give a taste of his quality:

Friends...There be three manner of joys, the one empty, another half full, the third is a full joy. The first is plenty of worldly goods; the second is ghostly grace; the third is everlasting bliss. The first joy, that is affluence of temporal goods, is called a vain joy, for if a man were set at a board with delicate meats and drinks, and he saw a cauldron boiling before him with pitch and brimstone, in the which he should be thrown naked, as soon as he had dined, if he should joy much in his delicious meats, it should be but a vain joy...."Semiplenum gaudium est quando quis in praesenti gaudet et tunc cogitans de futuris dolet, ut in quodam libro Graeco, 'Quidam Rex Graeciae,'" &c. Here you may see but half a joy; who should joy in this world, if he remembered him the pains of the other world? ...Therefore let us joy in hope of everlasting joy and bliss. "Gaudete, quia nomina vestra scripta sunt in caelo," ut gaudium vestrum sit plenum. A full joy is in heaven....Ideo, fratres, variis linguis loquens [precor] ut gaudium vestrum sit plenum vel habeatis gaudium sempiternum.[1]

[1] *P.L.* No. 372, and see also p. 208 for another example of Brackley's preaching.

CHAPTER XVII

THE LIFE OF THE COUNTRYSIDE

AGRICULTURE was an essential occupation in the fifteenth century, for almost the whole of the food required by the people was home-grown. Hence the land is the inseparable background of the history of these times. On it worked and sweated the labourers and the husbandmen, who won from the soil the means of livelihood for themselves and the wealth which enabled the landowners to buy food and to hire men for their own purposes. The Pastons, in common with others of their class, were largely dependent on their lands for both revenue and food. The Feudal system of land tenures was disappearing, and money was becoming an increasingly important factor in the life of the countryside. It was no longer the custom that every man should pay for his holding by doing so many days' work on his Lord's demesne. Many men at this time paid a fixed rent for their land, and with this money the Lord could hire other men to cultivate his own fields. Money was thus important to the small tenant so that he might pay his rent, and it was essential to the Lord so that he might hire labour to produce his own food-stuffs. Both needed some money also to purchase whatever necessaries, or luxuries, the land could not produce.

Since men like John Paston were largely dependent for ready money on the revenues arising from their lands, it is not strange to find them in sore straits when these revenues were not forthcoming. Even great lords were often in financial difficulties, and we find the Duke of Buckingham quite unable to pay a debt because, as he says, "the season of the year has not yet grown," and therefore, presumably, the rents had not yet been collected.[1] The Pastons were frequently in want of ready money, and there are many references to their poverty from time to

---

[1] *P.L.* No. 49. See No. 184 for debt of £437 owed by Duke of York to Sir J. Fastolf: originally borrowed for six months, the debt was only partially paid up nearly 10 years later! See also *Town Life*, I. 258 n. 1, 261.

time, even though they were the owners of extensive manors. Margaret once had to tell her husband that, unless he came home soon, she would be obliged to borrow money as she had only four shillings.[1] A few years later, her son Sir John was stranded in London in even worse plight. His brother thus reports of him: "As for my brother,...so God help me, he hath not at this season a penny in his purse, nor knows where to get any."[2]

During the next few years the family seems to have been in sore straits for ready money from time to time. Sir John in London is constantly appealing for aid, while his mother in Norfolk is having to borrow,[3] or to sell woodlands,[4] or to distrain upon tenants who had not paid their rents. A letter from Norfolk to Sir John shows how closely the Pastons were looking to their debts, and also illustrates how the land-owner was dependent on the good or bad seasons as much as the actual tiller of the soil. John Paston writes to his brother, "I have spoken with Barker [one of their agents], and he hath no money, nor none can get till harvest, when he may distrain the crop upon the ground. He says there is not owing more than five marks."[5] The closest attention was needed if the landowner was to get a good return for his land, and the Pastons had to take every possible step to get their lands let at a fair price, and also to see that their rents were regularly paid. Naturally, therefore, the topics of land and rent and distraints are very frequent in the letters, so much so that the original editor omitted much information under this head as matter "relating to...business about Paston's farms and tenants"! Sufficient has been left, however, to show the many difficulties that were continuously arising. Sometimes the agents of the Pastons had to report that they were obliged to let the land for what they could get, and that it would be useless to insist on its full value. When farmers were never sure how the varying phases of local faction quarrels or the greater struggles of the nobles might affect their holdings, they were loth to pay very high prices. Richard Calle, the bailiff, is forced to write to his master:

Please you that you remember the bill I sent you at Hallowmass for the place and lands at Beyton which Cheseman had...for five

[1] *P.L.* No. XLVI.   [2] *Id.* No. LXXIV.   [3] *Id.* No. 681.
[4] *Id.* No. 686.   [5] *Id.* No. 697.

marks [66/8]. There will no man have it above 46/8 for Albaster and I have done as much thereto as we can, but we cannot go above that. And yet we cannot let it so for this year without they have it for five or six years.[1]

By this time so many landowners were anxious to let their lands that men were able to bargain with them, and prices were to a certain extent competitive.[2] Repairs were a constant source of drain on the revenues of an estate, so that the landlords tried to foist this burden on the tenant and the tenant on the landlord. The result was endless disputes as to where the liability lay. Richard Calle exposes the whole question in writing to his master, for he says he can only let a farm if Paston will "bear all charges of the reparations and fencing about the place, which should be great cost."[3] When it was expressly agreed the tenant should bear the costs of repairs the price of land per acre was consequently less. For instance, a man offers 6d. an acre if he is to do repairs, where formerly he had paid 7d. or 8d. and the landlord had done the repairs. When rent day came, however, some men would dispute the collector's demand because of repairs they had done, for which they claimed payment.[4]

Landowners were forced at times to take strong measures in order to get their rents. Most commonly they distrained on the household goods, or agricultural implements, of the debtor. Paston's agents were continuously at work on his various properties distraining for rent. John Russe wrote to his master and said:

As to Skilly, farmer of Cowhaw, we entered there and said we would have payment for the half year past and surety for the half year coming, or else we would distrain, and put him out of possession, and put in a new farmer.

Evidently they terrified the farmer, who pointed out that his harvest was not yet in (June 1st) and promised to find some of the money within 14 days.[5] Threats were not always sufficient, and sometimes beasts or ploughs had to be seized. A ludicrous touch is given in a report by James Gloys, who says he tried

---

[1] *P.L.* No. 135.
[2] See *A Norfolk Manor*, Davenport, p. 78, for similar occurrences on another Norfolk estate.
[3] *P.L.* No. 136.   [4] *Id.* No. 647.   [5] *Id.* No. 284.

to distrain upon a tenant several times; but, he adds, "I could never do it, unless I would have distrained him in his mother's house, and this I durst not for her cursing."[1]

Often in these troubled times the wretched tenant could not know to whom his rent was due, for though one man might be owner *de jure*, another was possessor *de facto*.[2] Accordingly, no sooner did the tenant offer to make payment to one man, than the other would appear and forbid him to do any such thing under pain of being obliged to pay up again. When Lord Molynes took possession of Gresham[3] he wrote to the tenants saying, "The money that you pay to my wellbeloved servant John Partridge, I will be your warrant as for your discharge, and [will] save you harmless against all those that would grieve you."[4] This was all very well if the men of Lord Molynes were present to give protection to the tenants, but it often happened that the rival claimant would sweep down on the unprotected farms, and drive off cattle to be kept as a pledge until the money should be forthcoming.[5] We must not exaggerate these occasional troubles, however, for on most manors men seem to have held their farms and paid their rents without much quarrelling.

On every manor there still existed the ancient institution of the Manor Court, or Halmote. These courts were held several times a year by the Lord of the Manor, or by his agent, and were originally an integral part of the system of Feudal tenures. In their heyday these courts controlled almost every phase in the lives of the manorial tenantry. The powers of the Court were very wide, and in most matters the Lord was, theoretically at least, very despotic. It was at the Manor Court that all kinds of fines were determined and paid. Here the father paid a fine to his Lord when his son went to the University, or when his daughter was married outside the manor, or when he himself wished to live outside. Here every offence against the law and custom of the manor was punished. The man who left the highway before his house in bad repair, or allowed his cattle to stray, or sent too many beasts to pasture on the common, or cut wood or undergrowth without permission; all these were dealt with at this court. When a man died, his son appeared

[1] *P.L.* No. 146.   [2] *Id.* No. 841.   [3] See pp. 5 ff.
[4] *Id.* No. 65.   [5] *Id.* Nos. 205, 408, 500.

at this court and paid homage to the Lord before he might take up his father's lands, together with a fine for such "relief." In short, there is scarcely any side of rural life which was not directly affected by the Manor Courts. Not only did they settle and exact every kind of money payment, but here also was interpreted "the custom of the Manor," and that unwritten law which depended on tradition and use, and stretched back into antiquity, "when the mind of man remembereth not to the contrary."

Unfortunately we cannot reproduce in full the proceedings at one of the many Manor Courts held by the Pastons. The details in most extant Rolls are very similar, and the extracts from a Court Roll of 1444–5, which are here given, will illustrate the many-sided workings of these institutions:

Standon Manor Court. 23rd Year of Henry VI. 1444–1445.

Staundon, the great Court held thereon Wednesday next after the Feast of S. Michael, in the 23rd year of the reign of King Henry the Sixth, after the Conquest.

Hugh Dutton, Thomas Gerveys, Wm Bramley, Thomas Martyn, John Voxe, Thomas Amyson, Nicholas Bromlegh, Richard Chesterton, Ralph Hykoc, John Wylkys, Wm Byshoppe, John Darold, jurors, who come and present the lord of Rugge 8^d; the tenants of the lands and tenements of John Couper, of Rugge 4^d; the Lord of Weston 6^d; Walter Stafford de la Dale 8^d; John Knightley 4^d; the Prior of Ronton for his lands in Walford 8^d; Roger Swynestede, John Fletcher, freeman, who owe suit, and have made default this day; therefore they are in mercy[1] 2^d.

And they present that John Voxe 1^d, unjustly felled two ash trees worth 4^d in his close, which he holds of the lord, according to the custom of the manor. It is ordered that the price aforesaid be levied to the use of the Lord.

And they present that Thomas Amyson 2^d, entered on the lord's pool in front of the mill, and there unjustly fished, and took fish there without the lord's license; therefore he is in mercy. . . .

And they present that Thomas Martyn unjustly entered upon the demesne land of the lord at Shortewode, and there unjustly broke the lord's hedge, on the Feast of the Invention of the Cross, . . . and there his six oxen and three steers unjustly commoned and consumed the pastures there; which said Thomas, present in court, thereupon put himself upon his charter granted of ancient time by the lord

---

[1] *I.e.* will be amerced.

for his justification, or otherwise he throws himself upon the lord's grace by the pledge of Thomas Gerveyse....

And they present that Thomas Endon, late of Ashton, is dead, who held of the lord by knight's service, one tenement in Ashton aforesaid,...therefore it is ordered that one heriot be taken from the aforesaid tenure; and moreover it is ordered that a distress be levied before the next court upon the lands and tenements lately belonging to the said Thomas, sufficient as well for the homage due to the said lord as to satisfy the lord for his relief for the land and tenements aforesaid, saving the right &c....

To this court came Hugh Dutton, and claimed to hold of the lord in the right of Joan his wife, daughter of William Boydell, the moiety of the lands and tenements lately belonging to the said William in Oneley, at the yearly rent of 2/6 at the Feast of S. Martin, suit of court twice a year and by knight's service; and he did fealty to the lord and is admitted tenant.

And they present that Thomas Ameson still allows the hall with [the chamber on] the north side to be in ruin and unroofed; the sheep pen to be badly roofed, and the timber thereof at the east end to be utterly destroyed, and the stable to be nearly fallen down for two feet, and the new grange to be not fully roofed, and the bake-house to be wholly open....

To this court came Philip Snokstone, miller, and took of the lord the water mill there, with the pasture of the same, the dams and their appurtenances, and one half a virgate of land, with one rood of land called "Hulleyerde" late in the tenure of Thomas Martyn...to hold to him and his assigns for the term of 20 years next following, and fully to be completed according to the custom of the manour, rendering therefore to the lord yearly 56/6, at two terms of the year.... And so there is an increase of 3/2 of rent. And the aforesaid Philip to find the repairs of the said mill and messuage and the damages of the same with their appurtenances, from year to year during the said term....And he did fealty to the lord.[1]

Manor Courts were held several times a year, and the *Paston Letters* make many allusions to them. Some of the letters give us vivid pictures of these courts which the formal rolls can never give. Just as disputes between contending landlords affected the tenant when he was called upon to pay his rent, so, when he went to the Manor Court, he found a similar difficulty in knowing what to do, if, as sometimes happened, the rival claimants were both present. We have a good account of one of these quarrels written down soon after it occurred. John Paston was involved in a dispute over some lands which he claimed by virtue of holding the wardship of a youth. So he

[1] *Hist. of Standon*, Salt, E., pp. 88–91.

sent his agents to hold a Court and to assert his rights. Here is their report:

We were at Cowhaw, having Bartholomew Elis with us, and there was Long Bernard sitting to hold a Court. And we at the first "Noy" [oyez?] [came in[to]] the Court, and Bartholomew having [spoken in] these terms to Bernard saying, "Sir, forasmuch as the King has granted by these letters patent the wardship with the profits of the lands of T. Fastolf during his nonage to John Paston and T[homas] H[owes], wherefore I am come as their steward, by their commandment, upon their possession to keep court and leet. Wherefore I charge you by the virtue hereof to cease and keep neither court not leet, for you have no authority." Quoth Bernard, "I will keep both court and leet, and ye shall none keep here, for there is no man hath so great authority." Then quoth Bartholomew, "I shall sit by you and take a recognizance as ye do." "Nay" quoth Bernard, "I will suffer you to sit, but not to write." "Well" quoth Bartholomew, "then forcibly you put us from our possession, which I doubt not but shall be remembered [against] you another day" &c. "But Sirs" quoth he, "you that be tenants to this manor, we charge you that you do neither suit nor service, nor pay any rents or 'ferms' but to the use of John Paston and T[homas Howes]; for if you do, you shall pay it again." And thus we departed, and Bernard kept court and leet.[1]

It is easy to imagine the feelings of the wretched tenants left in Court to face this dilemma, and wondering how to please both parties! Perhaps the most dramatic event connected with Manor Courts recorded in these letters was the appearance of Sir John's brother at Saxthorpe. Sir John had made over certain rights in the manor of Saxthorpe to two men; and, through some misunderstanding, they thought it included the right to hold a Manor Court. So they sent their Steward to hold the Court. When young John Paston learnt what was happening, he hurried thither, followed by a single attendant. On entering, he at once interrupted the proceedings and said that Gurney, the Steward, had no right to hold a Court. Paston describes the scene to his brother as follows:

I charged the tenants that they should proceed no further in their Court upon pain of that might follow it, and they stopped for a season. But they saw that I was not able to make my part good, and so they proceeded further. And I saw that, and sat me down by the Steward, and blotted his book with my finger as he wrote, so that all the tenants affirmed that the Court was interrupted by

[1] *P.L.* No. 219.

me as in your right, and I required them to record that there was
no peaceable Court kept, and so they said they would.[1]

John Paston's vigorous action must have caused a great sensa-
tion amongst those who were present, as they watched him
leaning over the Steward and defacing each word as it was
written down.

A more humorous account is given of a Manor Court held
by the Duke of Suffolk at Hellesdon in 1478. As an eyewitness
tells us, the Duke was full of spleen against Paston, and by

his bearing there that day there was never no man that played
Herod in Corpus Christi play better and more agreeable to his
pageant than he did.[2] But you shall understand that it was afternoon, and the weather hot, and he so feeble for sickness that his
legs would not bear him, but there were two men had great pain
to keep him on his feet, and there you were judged. Some said
"Slay"; some said "Put him in prison." And forth came my Lord
and he would meet you with a spear, and have none other amends
for the trouble that you have put him to but your heart's blood, and
that he will get with his own hands.[3]

Evidently, among the many spectacles which enlivened medieval
life, the chance of an amusing or a dramatic half-hour at the
Manor Court was not to be overlooked!

We must not lose sight of the men themselves by considering
only the administrative side of country life. Rents and leases,
manor courts and immemorial customs, only give us one side
of the picture. Men had certainly become freer than they were
in the preceding centuries. Yet, if Hodge was no longer "ad-
scriptus glebae" as once he had been, he was still held a partial
captive by the economic necessity which conditioned all his
movements.[4] The small tenant-farmer was almost equally tied
to his land, and these two great classes toiled on from day to
day, and so won a living from the soil. Generally speaking, the
energies of the tenant-farmer were fully occupied in growing
sufficient food for his own needs, and a surplus whereby to get
money for his rent and for necessary purchases.[5] The good

---

[1] *P.L.* No. 688.   [2] Cf. Chaucer, *C.T.*   [3] *P.L.* No. 817.
[4] For discussion of the condition and status of the agricultural labourer,
see Rogers, *Work*, p. 326; Cunningham, *Growth of English Industry*, pp.
439 ff.
[5] A few great landowners like Sir J. Fastolf had, in addition to their
lands, sufficient resources at their command to make agriculture something
more than a bare means of livelihood.

wife was her own baker, brewer, weaver and dyer.[1] Her husband
and his friends were also continuously engaged in their various
farming occupations, and, as a result, could supply most of the
simple needs of their households. If the land was fertile, the
farmer was in a strong position. He grew his corn and other
crops on his arable land; his cattle fed on the commons or in
his untilled fields; his dairy supplied him with milk, butter and
cheese, while his oxen and sheep ensured him a certain supply
of meat. When he wanted wood to mend his barns, or to burn
on the hearth, he found it near at hand on the edge of the woods
and forests which he was usually allowed to make use of, either
by agreement with, or by payment to, his overlord.[2] The thatch
for his house he gathered from the reeds growing in mere or
river, or from the long straw stubble of his fields. The rough
daub and wattle outbuildings, and the houses of the poorer
labourers were easily repaired by recoating them with clay; or,
if more difficult repairs were necessary, the local carpenter was
called in. Both carpenter and blacksmith were essential units
of the medieval country community. The repair of plough-
shares, wheelbarrows, mattocks, scythes and the like on the
one hand, and on the other hand the making or reparation of
carts, hurdles, vats, or the building of the framework of a new
house or grange, gave full employment to these two men. Otherwise the farmer and his family and their servants were very
independent. During the long winter months, when there was
little farm work to be done, they mended the broken harness,
repaired hoes and rakes, cut shingles or new ox-yokes, made
new hurdles for the fields, and chopped up the spare pieces of
wood to burn in the house.

Agriculture was still in a very rudimentary state. Little progress had been made in the science of farming, and at this time
roots, clovers and many grasses were unknown in England.
The chief crops were wheat, oats, barley, rye, peas, beans and
vetches. As there were no root crops and no clover, it was
impossible to cultivate land on any system of rotation of crops,
as we understand it. The only method the medieval farmer

[1] See pp. 52 ff.
[2] For fines for cutting wood, etc. without permission, see Manor Rolls,
Hone, *op. cit.*, pp. 149, 152, 171, 189.

could adopt was to allow a field to lie fallow every second or
third year. Ploughing took place at various times. In the
autumn, the ground was ploughed for wheat. Oats and peas had
to be sown by Easter, so that the ploughs were busy again soon
after Christmas. When this was done, it was time to begin to
plough the land for the barley crop. Frequently oxen and horses
worked together in a plough-team, though oxen by themselves
were more generally used for this purpose. The varied work
of the farm made it necessary not to use horses for ploughing
if possible, but to keep them for carting manure, taking corn
to the mill and other work of this nature. When his horses
were too outworn to be used in London, Sir J. Fastolf sent them
home to Norfolk to work on his farms there.[1]

When the seed was sown, weeding, ditching, fencing, and a
thousand other minor operations kept the farm hands busy.
Here and there in the *Paston Letters* we get glimpses of this
continuous activity. Sir J. Fastolf, for example, asks John
Paston to see that the stream which runs between the Mauteby
and Caister lands is cleared out, because it has become overgrown
with weeds. This is in May, when no doubt farm work was
not so busy as it had been throughout the Spring. Again, about
Christmas time, John Paston writes and tells his wife to get
certain work done on ditches and hedges. The thrifty squire
probably thought his men would be idle, but did not consider
all the circumstances fully enough, for his wife replies that his
orders cannot be carried out. She writes:

Jenny was here to-day and told me that you desired that I should
[order to be made] a ditch at Hellesdon. The season is not [good]
for to make any new ditches, nor to repair any old until after Christmas, as it is told me.[2]

Then at last came the harvest. Even to-day, with every
mechanical advantage, harvesting is a time which taxes all the
energies of the farm to the full, and the medieval harvest was
certainly equally strenuous. Everyone was working at the
highest pitch to gather the crop, and apparently great crowds
would work together, and go from field to field reaping, binding
and carrying, all working in a body[3]. When all was safely in

---

[1] *P.L.* No. 123.   [2] *Id.* No. LII.
[3] See *Hist. Hawstead*, Cullam, pp. 212–24, and *R.H.S.* 1918, pp. 28–58.

the barns, there was much rejoicing and feasting. There is little wonder that the harvest brought so much rejoicing, for men saw in the fulness of the crops the possibility of living throughout the coming winter. Agricultural life in those days was a thing of strange contrasts. Hunger and satiety were both equally well known to all these people. The rude plenty of the autumn was only too often followed by semi-starvation. Piers Plowman tells the common experience of many thousands when he naïvely relates how he is struggling to exist during the last months before the harvest:

> I have no penny, quoth Piers, pullets for to buy,
> Neither goose nor griskin; but two green cheeses,
> A few curds and cream, and a cake of oats,
> And bread for my bairns of beans and of peases.
> And yet I say, by my soul, I have no salt bacon;
> Not a cockney, by Christ, collops to make.
> But I have leek-plants, parsley and shallots,
> Onions and pot herbs and cherries, half red...
> By this livelihood we must live till Lammas-time,
> And by that I hope to have harvest in my croft,
> Then may I dight my dinner as me dearly liketh.[1]

[1] *P.P.* B. VI. ll. 282 ff. "Cockney," egg; "collops," ? eggs and bacon.

APPENDIXES

I. BOOKS OF THE PASTON FAMILY

MSS

Romances

The Death of Arthur beginning at Cassabelaun.
Guy of Warwick.
Richard Cœur de Lion.
The Meeting of the Duke and the Emperor.

Book of the Seven Sages.
[Sir Gawaine and] the Grene Knight.
Palatyse and Scitacus.

By Chaucer

The Parliament of Birds.
Troilus.
Legend of Ladies [Legend of Good Women?].

By Lydgate

Siege of Thebes.
Temple of Glass.

"Chaucerian"

La belle dame sans Merci.

Lydgate

de Regimine Principum.

Ballads

Guy and Colbronde.
[The Horse the Sheep and] the Goose.

In French

"2 French books."

Religious and Didactic

...of the Meeds of the Mass.
Lamentation of Childe Ypotis [i.e. Epictetus].
The Abbey of the Holy Ghost.

A prayer to the Vernicle.
Life of S. Christopher.
Disputation between Hope and Despair.

Classics

de Senectute.
de Amicitia.
de Sapientia.

de Othea.
de Arte Amandi.
A nominale.

Historical, etc.

Chronicle...to Edward III.
A book of new Statutes from Ed. III.
Chronicles of Jerusalem.
Fastolfe's jornes in France.
Book of Knighthood.
Treatise on War.
Rules of Chivalry.

Heraldic

The old book of blazonings of arms.
The new book portrayed and blazoned.
A copy of blazonings of arms, and the names to be found by letter [i.e. alphabetically].
A book of arms portrayed, in paper.

Printed Books

The Game and Play of Chess. [First English edition printed by Caxton at Bruges, not before 1475. Second edition at Westminster, not before 1480.]

Other books mentioned, but ownership uncertain

A Bible [price not more than 5 marks].
L'arbre de Bataille [mentioned by Duke Norf. A copy known to be among Sir J. Howard's books in 1480].

Vitas Patrum	valued at	2s.
S. Thomas de Veritatibus	,,	10s.
"Hugucio and Papie"	,,	20s.
3 books of sophistry	,,	1s. 8d.
1 song book	,,	1s. 8d.
1 psalter	,,	6s. 8d.
1 primer	,,	2s. [and also one recorded belonging to Sir T. Tuddenham, No. 140]
Books in coffer	,,	1s. 8d.
Many small books	,,	10s.[1]

II. LIST OF JOURNEYS

A. FORTY-SIX JOURNEYS, EACH REPRESENTING ONE DAY'S TRAVEL

MILES	FROM	TO	SOURCE OF INFORMATION
51	Birmingham	Daintree	Owen and Blakeway, *History Shrewsbury*, vol. i. 279.
51	Daventry	S. Albans	*Id.*
50	Babraham	London	*Archaeologia*, xxv. 463. Lestrange Accounts.
47	Walsingham	W. Dereham	F. A. Gasquet, *Collectanea Anglo-Premonstratensia*, i.196.
45	Salisbury	? } in 2	*Id.* iii. vi.
45	?	Exeter} days	*Id.* iii. vi.
45	Brandon	Barkway	*Arch.* xxv. 464.
44	Colchester	Tilbury	*Coll. Ang. Pre.* iii. vi.
42	Rochester	Dover	*Howard Household Books*, ii.186.
42	,,	,,	*Id.*
41	Beccles	Ipswich	*Coll. Ang. Pre.* iii. vi.
41	Colchester	Thetford	*Howard*, ii. 222.
41	Ware	Newmarket	*Arch.* xxv. 439.
41	,,	,,	*Id.*
41	,,	,,	Hillen, *History King's Lynn*, i. 156.

[1] See *P.L.* Nos. 140, 191, 370, 568, 592, 596, 632, 690, 696, 697, 739, 869, 954.

MILES	FROM	TO	SOURCE OF INFORMATION
41	Ware	Newmarket	*Arch.* xxv. 567.
41	Lynn	Newmarket	Hillen, i. 156.
38	Walsingham	Thetford	*Howard,* ii. 448.
35	Newmarket	Huntingdon	*Arch.* xxv. 431.
35	Newmarket	Castleacre	*Id.*
35	Barkway	London	*Id.* 464
35	,,	,,	Grace Book B, 94.
35	,,	,,	*Id.* 68.
35	,,	,,	*Arch.* xxv. 430.
35	Honiton	Sherburne	*Coll. Ang. Pre.* i. 194.
34	Gloucester	Bristol	*Id.*
31	Swineshead	Lincoln	*Howard,* i. 227.
30	Leyston	Langley	*Coll. Ang. Pre.* i. 195.
30	Shrewsbury	Wolverhampton	Owen and Blakeway, i. 279.
30	Cambridge	Ware	Grace Book B, 93.
29	Kendall	Burgh	*Coll. Ang. Pre.* i. 193.
28	Arundel	Lewes	*Id.* i. 195.
28	,,	,,	*Id.* iii. vi.
27	Cambridge	Southeyre	*Arch.* xxv. 557.
26	Ipswich	Leyston	*Coll. Ang. Pre.* i. 195.
26	Rochester	Canterbury	Wylie, *Hist. Henry IV,* i. 95.
26	,,	,,	*Id.*
26	,,	,,	*Howard,* ii. 219.
26	,,	,,	*Id.* 218.
26	,,	,,	*Coll. Ang. Pre.* iii. vi.
25	Bristol	Glastonbury	*Id.* i. 194.
25	Brandon	Lynn	*Howard,* i. 227.
25	Stoke	Chelmsford	,, ii. 217.
25	Colchester	Chelmsford	,, ii. 221.
25	Lavenham	Stoke	,, ii. 450.
22	Spalding	Swineshead	*Coll. Ang. Pre.* i. 194.

1602

1602 miles in 46 journeys = 34·8 miles per day.

B. FIVE CONTINUOUS JOURNEYS

MILES	FROM	TO	DAYS	SOURCE OF INFORMATION
175	Torre Abbey	London	4	*Coll. Ang. Pre.* iii. vii.
170	Exeter	London	4	*Shillingford Papers,* 3, 6, 61, 67.
153	Shrewsbury	London	4	Owen and Blakeway, i. 279.
131	Weymouth	London	4	5 *Hist. MSS. Report,* 578.
100	King's Lynn	London	2½	Hillen, i. 156.

729   18½

= 39·4 miles per day.

III. COLLATION OF EDITIONS AND
THE ORIGINAL LETTERS

(I) THE ORIGINALS OF THE *PASTON LETTERS*

Many of the originals are now in the British Museum, and are distributed as follows:

(a) Volumes I and II of Fenn's original edition (see (III) below) were purchased in 1933 and now form Add. MSS. 43,488–91.[1]

(b) Volumes III and IV were purchased in 1896 and now form Add. MSS. 34,888–9.

(c) Volume V (published posthumously) came to the Museum in 1866 and is to be found in Add. MSS. 27,443–4.

(d) The letters which were formerly part of the collection of Sir Thomas Phillipps were bought in 1919 and now form Add. MSS. 39,848–9. They chiefly concern Sir John Fastolf, and contain matter not printed by Gairdner.

(e) There are a number of other letters in Add. MSS. 33,597 and Add. MS. 28,212.

(f) A considerable number of letters and documents are to be seen at Oxford chiefly in the Bodleian Library and at Magdalen College.[2]

(g) Five letters are preserved in the library of Pembroke College, Cambridge. For these, see 5 *Hist. MSS. Report*, pp. 484 ff.

(II) PURPOSE OF THIS APPENDIX

The following pages will enable the reader to trace 1094 out of the 1098 originals of this correspondence.[3] The references in Gairdner's editions only state that the document is among the "Paston MSS.; B.M. or from Fenn's original edition". The lists which follow will enable the reader to examine any letter without the initial difficulty of searching through many folios and even volumes before reaching it.

---

[1] On the vicissitudes of the Letters, see Gairdner (1904). I. 1–23, and for the history of Volumes I and II, see *Friends of the National Libraries. Annual Report, 1933–34*, pp. 18–22.

[2] For the material in Magdalen College, see 4 *Hist. MSS. Report*, pp. 461 ff.

[3] I have been unable to trace Nos. 38, 284, 852 and 982.

(III) EDITIONS OF THE *PASTON LETTERS*

1. *Original Letters Written during the Reigns of Henry VI, Edward IV, and Richard III. By various Persons of Rank or Consequence...with notes....* By J. Fenn. 5 vols. London, 1787–1823.
2. New edition.... By A. Ramsay. London, 1840–1.
3. *The Paston Letters, 1422–1509.* Edited by J. Gairdner. New edition. 3 vols. London, 1872–5.
4. New edition. By J. Gairdner. 3 vols. Westminster, 1896.
5. New edition by J. Gairdner, Introduction and Supplement. 4 vols. Westminster, 1901.
6. New and complete Library edition. Edited with notes and an Introduction by J. Gairdner. 6 volumes. (Limited impression.) London, 1904.

Selections

7. *The Paston Letters; a selection.* Edited by M. D. Jones. Cambridge, 1909.
8. *Selections from the Paston Letters.* Edited by A. D. Greenwood. London, 1920.
9. *Selections from the Paston Letters.* Edited by A. H. R. Ball. London, 1949.
10. *The Paston Letters: a selection.* 2 vols. Revised edition by J. Warrington. London, 1956.
11. *The Paston Letters:* selected and edited by N. Davis. Oxford, 1958.
12. *The Paston Letters: a selection in modern spelling.* Edited by N. Davis. London, 1963.

(IV) COLLATION OF THE VARIOUS MODERN EDITIONS

Modern readers of the *Paston Letters* will probably make use of one of the various editions of Dr James Gairdner, as enumerated above. His original edition of 1872–5 (No. 3), and the edition of 1896 (No. 4) are identical. In 1901 he re-issued his work in four volumes (No. 5) instead of three, collecting the original prefaces to each of the three volumes into an introductory volume, and also printing there the full text of letters which were either given in abstract, or merely catalogued in the two earlier editions. Finally in 1904, he published a definitive edition in six volumes (No. 6), of which volume one forms the introduction. In the following tables, this edition (No. 6) has been collated with that of 1901 (No. 5).

Readers of the two earlier editions (Nos. 3 and 4) will find all the references to the 1901 (No. 5) edition, except those in Roman numerals, will apply to their editions.

1904 (No. 6)	1901 (No. 5)	Original to be found in	1904 (No. 6)	1901 (No. 5)	Original to be found in
1	1	Add. MS. 27,443, f. 74	48	963	Chancery Roll, Duchy
2	1	„ 34,889, f. 141			Lancaster, 22 Henry
3	II	„ „ f. 142			VI. Y. 2 c. No. 79
4	2	Add. Chart. 17,225	49	964	Douce Charters, No. 18,
5	3	„ „ 17,243			Bod. Lib. Oxf.
6	4	Add. MS. 27,443,	50	VIII	Add. MS. 34,888, f. 19
		ff. 75–77	51	37	„ „ f. 9
7	III	Add. MS. 34,889, f. 213	52	38	?
8	IV	„ 34,888, f. 1	53	39	Add. Chart. 14,571
9	959	Bod. Lib. Oxf. Chart.	54	40	Add. MS. 27,443, f. 94
		730	55	41	„ „ f. 95
10	5	Add. MS. 27,443, f. 78	56	42	„ „ f. 96
11	6	„ „ f. 79	57	IX	„ 34,888, f. 10
12	7	„ „ f. 80	58	43	„ 43,488, f. 6
13	8	„ „ ff. 81, 82	59	965	Tanner MS. 95, f. 82
14	960	Bod. Lib. Oxf. Chart.	60	44	Add. MS. 34,888, f. 12
		731	61	45	„ 27,443, f. 97
15	9	Add. MS. 27,443, f. 83	62	46	„ 34,888, f. 13
16	10	„ „ f. 84	63	47	„ „ f. 14
17	11	„ „ f. 85	64	48	„ „ f. 15
18	12	„ „ f. 86	65	49	„ 43,488, f. 8
19	13	Add. Chart. 17,226	66	50	„ „ f. 9
20	14	Add. MS. 27,443, f. 87	67	51	Add. Chart. 14,819
21	15	„ „ f. 88	68	52	Add. MS. 27,443, f. 98
22	16	Add. Chart. 17,227	69	53	„ „ f. 99
23	17	„ „ 14,313	70	54	Add. Chart. 17,235
24	18	„ „ 17,228	71	966	MSS. Hickling, 130, 140,
25	19	Add. MS. 34,888, f. 3			Mag. Coll. Oxf.
26	20	„ 39,848, f. 1	72	967	MSS. Hickling, 71, 74, 75,
27	21	Add. Chart. 17,237			89, 104, Mag. Coll. Oxf.
28	22	„ „ 17,229–31	73	55	Add. Chart. 17,236
29	V	Add. MS. 34,888, f. 4	74	X	Add. MS. 34,889, f. 178
30	VI	„ 34,889, f. 140	75	56	„ 34,888, f. 18
31	23	Mentioned by Fenn only	76	57	„ 27,443, f. 100
32	24	Add. Chart. 17,232	77	59	„ 39,848, f. 2
33	961	Add. MS. 27,446, f. 113	78	60	„ 43,488, f. 7
34	25	„ 43,488, f. 4	79	61	„ 43,491, f. 5
35	26	„ 27,443, f. 89	80	XI	„ 34,889, f. 143
36	27	„ 43,488, f. 5	81	XII	„ 34,888, f. 57
37	28	„ 27,443, f. 90	82	62	„ „ f. 23
38	29	„ 34,888, f. 7	83	992	„ „ ff. 24–5
39	VII	MS. LC. II, 230, f. 1	84	63	„ „ f. 28
		Pemb. Coll. Camb.	85	64	„ 27,443, f. 101
40	30	Add. Chart. 14,598	86	65	„ 43,488, f. 52
41	31	„ „ 17,233	87	66	„ 27,443, f. 102
42	32	R. Parl. v. 59	88	67	„ 34,888, f. 29
43	962	Bod. Lib. Oxf. Chart.	89	XIII	„ 34,889, f. 164
		740	90	68	„ 43,491, f. 7
44	33	Add. Chart. 17,234	91	69	„ 27,443, f. 103
45	34	Add. MS. 27,443, f. 91	92	XIV	Palmer's Foundation and
46	35	„ „ f. 93			Antiquity of Great
47	36	„ 34,888, f. 8			Yarmouthe, p. 61

1904 (No. 6)	1901 (No. 5)	Original to be found in	1904 (No. 6)	1901 (No. 5)	Original to be found in
93	70	Add. MS. 34,888, f. 33	148	119	Douce MS. 393, f. 92
94	71	„ „ f. 34	149	120	Add. MS. 43,488, f. 26
95	XV	„ „ f. 32	150	121	Douce MS. 393, f. 93
96	993	„ „ f. 30	151	122	Add. MS. 34,888, f. 51
97	72	„ 28,212, f. 21	152	XIX	„ 34,889, f. 160
98	73	„ 43,488, f. 22	153	123	„ 39,848, f. 9
99	74	„ 27,443, f. 104	154	124	„ 34,888, f. 52
100	75	„ 34,888, f. 35	155	125	„ 27,443, f. 117
101	76	„ „ ff. 36–9	156	126	Original sold 2 March,
102	77	Add. Chart. 17,240			1870
103	78	Add. MS. 27,443, f. 105	157	127	Add. Chart. 17,238
104	79	„ 39,848, f. 3	158	128	Add. MS. 39,848, f. 10
105	80	„ 34,888, f. 40	159	129	„ „ f. 11
106	81	„ 43,488, f. 11	160	130	„ 34,888, f. 53
107	82	„ 39,848, f. 4	161	131	„ 39,848, f. 12
108	83	Douce MS. 393, f. 100	162	132	„ 27,443, f. 118
109	84	Add. MS. 34,888, f. 41	163	XX	„ 34,888, f. 168
110	85	Douce MS. 393, f. 99	164	133	„ 39,848, f. 13
111	XXII	MS. LC. 11, 230, f. 6 Pemb. Coll. Camb.	165	XXI	„ 34,889, f. 150
			166	137	„ 27,443, f. 121
112	86	Douce MS. 393, f. 101	167	138	„ 34,888, f. 61
113	87	„ „ f. 102	168	139	„ 27,443, f. 122
114	88	Add. MS. 27,443, f. 106	169	140	„ 34,888, f. 62
115	89	Douce MS. 393, f. 103	170	XXIII	„ „ f. 63
116	90	Add. MS. 27,443, f. 107	171	141	„ 39,848, f. 14
117	91	„ 43,488, f. 12	172	XXIV	„ 34,889, f. 230
118	XVI	„ 34,888, f. 164	173	142	„ 39,848, f. 15
119	92	„ 27,443, f. 108	174	143	„ „ f. 16
120	93	„ 43,488, f. 13	175	144	„ 27,444, f. 1
121	94	„ „ f. 14	176	145	„ „ f. 2
122	95	„ 39,848, f. 5	177	XXV	„ 34,889, f. 158
123	96	„ 43,488, f. 43	178	146	„ 27,444, f. 3
124	97	„ 34,888, f. 42	179	147	„ „ f. 4
125	98	„ 43,488, f. 15	180	148	„ 34,888, f. 64
126	99	„ 43,491, f. 1	181	XXVI	„ 34,889, f. 169
127	XVII	„ 34,888, f. 73	182	XXVII	„ 34,888, f. 55
128	100	„ 27,443, f. 109	183	149	„ „ f. 65
129	101	„ „ f. 110	184	150	„ 27,444, f. 5
130	102	„ 39,848, f. 6	185	151	„ „ f. 6
131	103	„ 34,888, f. 43	186	152	„ 39,848, f. 17
132	104	Douce MS. 393, f. 88	187	153	„ 34,888, f. 66
133	105	Add. MS. 37,443, f. 111	188	154	„ 39,848, f. 18
134	106	„ „ f. 112	189	155	„ 27,444, f. 7
135	107	Add. Chart. 17,239	190	156	„ „ f. 8
136	108	Add. MS. 27,443, f. 113	191	157	„ 34,888, f. 67
137	109	„ 39,848, f. 7	192	158	„ „ ff. 68–9
138	110	„ „ f. 8	193	159	„ „ f. 70
139	111	„ 34,888, f. 44	194	160	„ 27,444, f. 9
140	112	„ 27,443, f. 114	195	161	„ „ f. 10
141	XVIII	„ 34,888, f. 45	196	162	„ 34,888, f. 71
142	113	„ „ ff. 47–8	197	163	„ „ f. 72
143	114	„ 43,488, f. 17	198	164	„ 27,444, f. 11
144	115	„ 34,888, f. 49	199	165	„ „ f. 12
145	116	„ 27,443, f. 115	200	166	Note by Gairdner
146	117	„ 34,888, f. 50	201	167	Add. MS. 34,888, f. 74
147	118	„ 27,443, f. 116	202	168	„ 39,848, f. 19

1904 (No. 6)	1901 (No. 5)	Original to be found in	1904 (No. 6)	1901 (No. 5)	Original to be found in
203	169	Add. MS. 39,848, f. 20	258	214	Add. MS. 34,888, f. 105
204	170	„ „ f. 21	259	215	„ „ f. 106
205	171	„ 34,888, f. 75	260	216	„ ,. f. 107
206	172	„ „ f. 78	261	217	„ 39,848, f. 22
207	XXVIII	„ „ f. 76	262	218	„ 34,888, f. 108
208	XXIX	„ „ f. 79	263	219	„ 27,444, f. 27
209	XXX	„ „ f. 60	264	220	„ 39,848, f. 23
210	173	„ „ f. 82	265	221	„ 27,444, f. 28
211	174	„ 27,444, {f. 13 / f. 14	266	222	„ 34,888, f. 109
			267	223	„ „ f. 110
212	175	„ „ f. 15	268	224	„ 27,444, f. 29
213	176	„ „ f. 16	269	225	„ „ f. 30
214	177	„ „ f. 17	270	226	„ 43,488, f. 21
215	XXXI	„ 34,888, f. 83	271	227	„ 39,848, f. 24
216	178	„ „ f. 84	272	228	„ 34,888, f. 111
217	179	„ 27,444, f. 18	273	229	„ 27,444, f. 31
218	180	Add. Chart. 17,241	274	230	„ 34,888, f. 112
219	181	Add. MS. 27,444, f. 19	275	231	„ 39,848, f. 25
220	XXXII	„ 33,597, f. 1	276	232	„ 27,444, f. 32
221	182	„ 34,888, f. 85	277	233	„ „ f. 33
222	183	„ „ f. 86	278	234	„ 34,888, f. 113
223	184	Add. Chart. 17,242	279	235	„ 39,848, f. 26
224	185	Add. MS. 34,888, f. 87	280	236	„ 27,444, f. 34
225	186	„ 27,444, f. 20	281	237	„ 39,848, f. 27
226	187	„ 43,488, f. 18	282	238	„ 34,888, f. 114
227	188	„ 34,888, f. 88	283	239	Chancery Miscellanea, 37, File 111, 4-11
228	189	„ „ f. 89			
229	190	„ 27,444, f. 21	284	240	Add. MS. 39,848, f. 28
230	191	„ 34,888, f. 90	285	241	„ 43,488, f. 27
231	XXXIII	„ 34,889, f. 225	286	242	„ 39,848, f. 29
232	192	„ 27,444, f. 22	287	243	„ 43,488, f. 28
233	193	„ „ f. 23	288	244	„ „ f. 25
234	194	Douce MS. 393, f. 82	289	245	„ 39,848, f. 30
235	195	Egerton MS. 914	290	246	„ 27,444, f. 35
236	196	Add. MS. 34,888, f. 91	291	247	„ 34,888, f. 115
237	197	„ „ f. 92	292	248	„ 39,848, f. 31
238	198	„ 27,444, f. 24	293	XXXVII	„ 34,889, f. 171
239	199	„ 34,888, f. 93	294	249	„ 34,888, f. 116
240	200	„ 27,444, f. 25	295	250	„ „ f. 117
241	201	Add. Chart. 16,545	296	251	„ „ f. 118
242	202	Add. MS. 34,888, f. 97	297	252	„ „ f. 119
243	203	„ „ f. 98	298	968	Bod. Lib. Oxf. MSS. Misc. 30,742, f. 66
244	XXXIV	„ „ f. 94			
245	204	„ 27,444, f. 26	299	253	Add. MS. 43,488, f. 29
246	205	„ 34,888, f. 99	300	254	„ 34,888, f. 120
247	206	„ 43,488, f. 20	301	255	„ 27,444, f. 36
248	207	„ 34,888, f. 100	302	256	„ 34,888, f. 121
249	208	„ 43,488, f. 37	303	257	„ 43,491, f. 2
250	209	„ 34,888, f. 101	304	258	„ 39,848, f. 32
251	XXXV	„ „ f. 102	305	259	„ 27,444, f. 37
252	210	„ „ f. 104	306	260	„ 34,888, f. 122
253	XXXVI	„ 34,889, f. 217	307	261	„ 39,848, f. 33
254	211	„ 43,488, f. 19	308	262	„ 28,212, f. 26
255	LXXIX	„ 33,597, f. 5	309	263	Add. MSS. 34,888, ff. 123-4 and 27,444, f. 38
256	212	„ 43,488, f. 24			
257	213	„ „ f. 23			

1904 (No. 6)	1901 (No. 5)	Original to be found in	1904 (No. 6)	1901 (No. 5)	Original to be found in
310	264	Add. MSS. 34,888, ff. 125-6 and 27,444, ff. 39-41	362	311	Add. MS. 43,491, f. 3
			363	312	„ 34,888, f. 135
			364	313	„ 43,488, f. 40
311	265	Note by Gairdner	365	314	„ 39,848, f. 45
312	266	Add. MS. 39,848, f. 34	366	315	„ 43,488, f. 41
313	969	„ 43,490, f. 41	367	CXLI	„ 34,889, f. 163
314	267	„ 34,888, f. 127	368	316	„ 39,848, f. 46
315	268	„ 27,444, f. 42	369	317	„ 43,488, f. 42
316	269	„ „ f. 43	370	318	„ „ f. 46
317	270	„ 39,848, f. 35	371	319	„ 27,444, f. 57
318	271	„ „ f. 36	372	320	„ 39,848, f. 47
319	272	MS. in private hands	373	321	Add. Chart. 17,246
320	273	Add. MS. 27,444, f. 44	374	322	Add. MS. 34,888, f. 136
321	274	„ 43,488, f. 31	375	323	„ „ f. 137
322	275	„ 39,848, f. 37	376	324	„ 39,848, f. 48
323	276	„ „ f. 38	377	325	„ 43,488, f. 47
324	277	„ 34,888, f. 128	378	326	„ 27,444, f. 58
325	278	„ 27,444, f. 45	379	327	„ „ f. 59
326	279	„ 43,488, f. 32	380	328	„ 39,848, f. 49
327	280	„ 34,888, f. 129	381	329	„ 43,488, f. 33
328	XXXVIII	„ 34,889, f. 173	382	330	„ „ f. 53
329	XXXIX	„ 35,251, f. 24	383	331	„ 34,888, f. 139
330	281	„ 27,444, ff. 46-47	384	970	„ „ f. 138
			385	332	„ 27,444, ff. 60-66 and 39,849, f. 1
331	282	„ 43,488, f. 34			
332	283	„ 34,888, f. 130			
333	284	?	386	333	„ 22,927
334	285	Add. MS. 43,488, f. 35	387	334	Modern copy among MSS. at Narford
335	286	„ 39,848, f. 39			
336	287	„ „ f. 40	388	335	Add. Chart. 17,247
337	288	„ „ f. 41	389	336	Archæologia, XXI. p. 252
338	289	„ 27,444, ff. 48-9	390	337	Add. MS. 27,444, f. 67
			391	338	„ 34,888, f. 140
339	996	„ 34,889, f. 104	392	971	Bod. Lib. Oxf. Chart. 725
340	290	„ 43,488, f. 45			
341	291	„ 27,444, f. 50	393	339	Add. MS. 34,888, f. 141
342	292	„ 43,488, f. 36	394	340	„ 27,444, f. 68
343	293	„ 27,444, f. 51	395	341	„ 34,888, f. 142
344	294	„ 34,888, f, 131	396	342	„ 43,488, f. 48
345	295	„ 27,444, f. 52	397	343	„ 27,444, f. 69
346	296	„ „ f. 53	398	344	„ „ f. 70
347	297	„ „ f. 54	399	345	„ 43,488, f. 49
348	298	„ 43,488, f. 10	400	346	„ 43,491, f. 4
349	299	„ 39,848, f. 42	401	347	„ 27,444, f. 71
350	300	„ „ f. 43	402	348	„ „ f. 72
351	301	„ 43,488, f. 44	403	349	„ „ f. 73
352	302	Add. Chart. 17,244	404	XLII	„ 34,888, f. 161
353	XL	Add. MS. 34,889, f. 170	405	XLIII	„ „ f. 143
354	303	„ 27,444, f. 55	406	350	„ 27,444, f. 74
355	304	„ 34,888, f. 132	407	351	„ 34,888, f. 146
356	305	„ „ f. 133	408	352	„ 27,444, f. 75
357	306	„ 27,444, f. 56	409	XLIV	„ 34,888, f. 147
358	307	Add. Chart. 17,245	410	353	„ „ f. 149
359	308	Add. MS. 39,848, f. 44	411	972	„ 27,446, ff. 114-115
360	309	„ 34,888, f. 134			
361	310	„ 43,488, f. 39	412	973	„ 34,888, f. 150

1904 (No. 6)	1901 (No. 5)	Original to be found in	1904 (No. 6)	1901 (No. 5)	Original to be found in
413	974	Mag. Coll. Oxf. Index of Deeds, Southwark, No. 50a	467	401	Add. MS. 43,489, f. 9
			468	402	„ 34,888, f. 184
			469	403	„ „ f. 185
414	354	Add. MS. 27,444, f. 76	470	404	„ 43,489, f. 10
415	355	„ 34,888, f. 151	471	405	„ 34,888, f. 186
416	997	„ „ f. 152	472	406	„ „ f. 187
417	XLV	„ „ f. 158	473	407	Patent Roll, 1 Ed. IV, Part 3, No. 13
418	356	„ 27,444, f. 77			
419	357	„ 43,491, f. 6	474	L	Add. MS. 34,888, f. 181
420	358	„ 27,444, f. 78	475	408	„ 27,444, f. 102
421	359	„ „ f. 79	476	409	„ 34,888, f. 188
422	360	„ „ ff. 80–1	477	410	„ „ ff. 189–90
423	361	„ 34,888, f. 155	478	411	„ „ f. 191
424	362	„ 27,444, f. 82	479	412	„ „ f. 192
425	363	„ 34,888, f. 156	480	413	„ 43,491, f. 8
426	364	„ „ f. 157	481	414	„ 27,444, f. 103
427	365	„ 27,444, f. 83	482	415	„ 34,888, f. 193
428	366	„ „ f. 84	483	416	„ 43,489, f. 11
429	XLVIII	„ 34,889, f. 156	484	417	N.A. vol. IV, p. 26
430	367	„ 43,488, f. 55	485	418	Add. MS. 27,444, f. 104
431	368	„ 34,888, f. 172	486	419	„ 34,888, f. 194
432	369	„ „ f. 173	487	420	„ 27,444, f. 105
433	370	„ „ f. 174	488	421	„ 34,888, f. 195
434	371	„ 27,444, f. 85	489	422	„ 27,444, f. 106
435	XLVI	„ 34,889, f. 199	490	423	„ 34,888, f. 196
436	372	„ 34,888, f. 171	491	424	„ „ f. 197
437	XLVII	„ „ f. 166	492	425	„ 27,444, f. 107
438	373	„ „ f. 169	493	426	„ „ f. 108
439	374	„ „ f. 170	494	427	„ „ f. 109
440	375	„ 27,444, f. 86	495	428	„ 34,888, f. 198
441	376	„ „ f. 87	496	429	„ „ f. 199
442	377	„ „ f. 88	497	134	„ 27,443, f. 119
443	378	„ „ f. 89	498	135	„ 34,888, f. 54
444	379	„ „ f. 90	499	136	„ 27,443, f. 120
445	380	„ „ f. 91	500	430	„ 27,444, f. 110
446	381	„ „ f. 92	501	432	„ 34,888, f. 200
447	382	„ „ f. 93	502	433	„ „ f. 201
448	383	„ „ f. 94	503	434	„ „ f. 202
449	384	„ 43,489, f. 6	504	435	„ 27,444, f. 111
450	385	„ „ f. 4	505	436	„ „ f. 112
451	386	„ „ f. 5	506	437	„ „ f. 113
452	387	„ 34,888, f. 177	507	438	„ „ f. 114
453	388	„ 27,444, f. 95	508	439	„ „ f. 115
454	XLIX	„ 34,888, f. 175	509	440	„ 34,888, f. 203
455	389	„ „ f. 178	510	441	„ 43,490, f. 40
456	390	Douce MS. 393, f. 85	511	442	„ 34,888, f. 204
457	391	Add. MS. 43,489, f. 7	512	443	„ 43,489, f. 13
458	392	„ 34,888, f. 179	513	444	„ 34,888, f. 205
459	393	„ 27,444, f. 96	514	445	„ 43,489, f. 14
460	394	„ 43,489, f. 8	515	446	„ 34,888, f. 206
461	395	„ 27,444, f. 97	516	447	„ 27,444, f. 116
462	396	„ „ f. 98	517	448	„ „ f. 117
463	397	„ 34,888, f. 180	518	449	„ 34,888, f. 207
464	398	„ 27,444, f. 99	519	450	„ 39,848, ff. 50–3
465	399	„ „ f. 100	520	451	Note by Gairdner
466	400	„ „ f. 101	521	452	Add. MS. 34,888, f. 208

1904 (No. 6)	1901 (No. 5)	Original to be found in	1904 (No. 6)	1901 (No. 5)	Original to be found in
522	453	Add. MS. 34,888, f. 209	572	494	Add. MS. 27,444, ff.132–6
523	454	„ „ f. 210	573	LVII	MS. LC II 230, f. 4 in Pemb. Coll. Camb.
524	455	„ 27,444, f. 118	574	496	Add. MS. 34, 889,f. 14
525	456	„ 34,888, f. 211	575	LIX	„ „ f. 15–16
526	457	„ 27,444, f. 119	576	497	„ „ f. 25
527	458	„ 34,888, f. 212	577	498	„ 27,444, f. 137
528	459	„ 43,489, f. 19	578	499	„ „ f. 138
529	460	„ „ f. 16	579	500	„ „ f. 139
530	461	„ 27,444, ff.120–1	580	501	„ „ f. 140
531	462	„ 43,489, f. 17	581	502	„ „ f. 141
532	463	„ „ f. 7	582	503	„ 34,889, f. 26
533	464	„ „ f. 18	583	504	„ „ f. 27
534	LI	„ 34,889, f. 182	584	505	„ „ f. 28
535	LIII	„ „ f. 183	585	506	„ 27,444, f. 142
536	465	„ 34,888, f. 213	586	LX	„ 34,889, f. 190
537	466	„ „ f. 214	587	507	„ 27,444, f. 143
538	467	„ 27,444, f. 122	588	508	„ „ f. 144
539	975	„ 27,446, f. 116	589	509	MS. Top. Norfolk, c. 4
540	468	„ 27,444, f. 124	590	510	Add. MS. 27,444, f. 145
541	469	Tanner MS. 106, f. 35b	591	LXI	„ 34,889, f. 9
542	470	Add. MS. 27,444, f. 125	592	511	„ 27,444, f. 146
543	471	„ 39,848, f. 55	593	512	„ 34,889, f. 29
544	472	„ 34,888, f. 215	594	513	„ „ f. 30
545	473	„ 27,444, f. 126	595	514	„ 27,444, f. 147
546	474	„ 34,888, f. 216	596	515	„ „ f. 148
547	475	Add. Chart. 14,514	597	516	„ „ f. 149
548	476	Add. MS. 34,888, f. 217	598	517	„ „ f. 150
549	477	„ „ f. 218	599	518	„ 27,445, f. 1
550	478	„ „ f. 219	600	519	„ „ f. 2
551	479	„ „ f. 220	601	520	„ „ f. 4
552	480	„ „ f. 221	602	521	„ „ f. 3
553	LII	„ 34,889, f. 198	603	522	„ „ f. 5
554	481	„ 27,444, f. 127	604	523	„ 34,889, f. 31
555	482	„ 34,889, f. 1	605	524	Note by Gairdner
556	483	„ 43,489, f. 21	606	525	Add. MS. 27,450, f. 1
557	LV	„ 34,889, f. 2	607	526	„ 34,889, f. 32
558	484	„ „ f. 5	608	527	„ 27,445, f. 6
559	485	„ „ f. 6	609	528	„ 34,889, f. 33
560	486	„ 43,489, f. 22	610	529	„ 27,445, f. 8
561	487	„ 27,444, ff. 128–9	611	530	„ „ f. 9
562	976	„ 27,446, f. 117	612	LXII	MS. LC. II. 230, f. 5 Pemb. Coll. Camb.
563	977	„ „ f. 118	613	531	Add. MS. 34,889, f. 34
564	LVI	„ 34,889, f. 7	614	532	„ „ f. 35
565	488	MS. Top. Norfolk, c. 4	615	978	Bod. Lib. Oxf. Chart. 738–9
566	489	Bod. Lib. Oxf. Chart. 734	616	533	Add. MS. 27,445, f. 10
567	490	Add. MS. 34,889, f. 8	617	534	„ 34,889, f. 36–7
568	491	„ 27,444, f. 130	618	535	„ 27,445, f. 11
569	492	Bod. Lib. Oxf. Chart. 726–7	619	536	„ 34,889, f. 40
570	LVIII	Add. MS. 33,597, f. 6	620	LXIII	„ 33,597, f. 2
571	493	„ 34,889, ff. 12–13	621	537	Note by Gairdner
			622	LXIV	Add. MS. 34,889, f. 38

1904 (No. 6)	1901 (No. 5)	Original to be found in
623	LXV	Add. MS. 34,889, f. 208
624	LXVI	„ „ f. 223
625	538	„ „ f. 41
626	539	„ „ f. 42
627	540	„ 27,445, f. 12
628	541	„ 43,489, f. 15
629	LXVII	„ 34,889, f. 99
630	542	„ 27,445, f. 13
631	543	., 34,889, f. 43
632	544	„ 27,445, f. 15
633	545	„ „ f. 14
634	546	„ „ f. 16
635	547	„ „ f. 17
636	548	„ „ f. 18
637	549	Blomefield's Norfolk, VI. 483
638	979	MS. Mag. Coll. Oxf.
639	550	Add. MS. 27,450, f. 91
640	551	Mag. Coll. Oxf. Index of Deeds. Norfolk and Suffolk. No. 34
641	552	N.A. IV. p. 34
642	553	Add. MS. 27,445, f. 19
643	554	N.A. IV. p. 32
644	555	Add. MS. 27,445, f. 20
645	556	„ „ f. 7
646	557	N.A. IV. p. 16
647	558	Add. MS. 34,889, ff. 44–5
648	559	Add. Roll. 17,258
649	560	Add. MS. 34,889, f. 46
650	561	„ 27,445, f. 21
651	562	„ „ f. 22
652	563	„ 34,889, f. 47
653	564	„ 27,445, f. 23
654	565	„ „ f. 24
655	566	„ „ f. 25
656	LXVIII	„ 34,889, f. 226
657	567	„ „ f. 50
658	LXIX	„ „ f. 51
659	LXX	„ 33,597, f. 3
660	568	„ 34,889, f. 55
661	569	„ „ f. 56
662	570	„ „ f. 57
663	571	„ 27,445, f. 26
664	LXXI	„ 33,597, f. 8
665	572	N.A. IV. p. 29
666	573	Add. MS. 34,889, f. 58
667	574	„ 39,848, f. 56
668	LXXII	„ 34,889, f. 59
669	LXXIII	„ „ f. 61
670	575	„ 27,445, f. 27
671	576	„ 34,889, f. 63
672	980	4 Hist. MSS. p. 461a
673	LXXIV	Add. MS. 34,889, f. 196
674	LXXV	„ 35,251, f. 25

1904 (No. 6)	1901 (No. 5)	Original to be found in
675	577	Mag. Coll. Oxf. Index of Deeds, Norfolk and Suffolk. No. 47
676	578	Add. MS. 27,445, f. 28
677	579	Mag. Coll. Oxf. Index of Deeds. Norfolk and Suffolk. No. 47 (12)
678	580	Add. MS. 27,445, f. 29
679	LIV	„ 34,889, f. 166
680	581	MS. Bod. Lib. Oxf.
681	582	Fenn. iv. 280
682	583	Add. MS. 34,889, f. 65
683	584	Original missing
684	585	Add. MS. 43,491, f. 11
685	586	Add. Chart. 17,248
686	587	Add. MS. 43,489, f. 33
687	588	„ 43,490, f. 43
688	589	„ 34,889, f. 66
689	590	4 Hist. MSS. p. 461a
690	591	Add. MS. 27,445, f. 30
691	592	„ 34,889, ff. 67–8
692	593	„ „ f. 69
693	594	„ 27,445, f. 31
694	595	„ 34,889, f. 72
695	596	„ 43,491, ff. 12–13
696	597	„ 27,445, f. 32
697	598	„ „ f. 33
698	599	N.A. IV. p. 30
699	LXXVI	Add. MS. 34,889, f. 186
700	LXXVII	„ 33,597, f. 4
701	LXXX	„ 34,889, ff. 20£-z
702	LXXXI	„ „ f. 127
703	600	„ „ f. 73
704	601	„ „ f. 74
705	602	„ „ f. 75
706	603	„ „ f. 76
707	604	„ „ f. 76
708	605	Add. Chart. 18,249
709	606	Add. MS. 43,489, f. 35
710	607	„ 34,889, f. 77
711	LXXVIII	„ „ f. 70
712	608	„ 27,445, f. 34
713	609	„ 34,889, ff. 78–9
714	610	„ 43,489, f. 29
715	611	„ „ f. 31
716	612	„ 34,889, ff. 80–1
717	613	„ 27,445, f. 35
718	614	„ 43,489, f. 30
719	615	„ „ f. 37
720	616	„ 34,889, f. 82
721	617	„ „ ff. 83–4
722	618	„ „ f. 85
723	619	„ „ ff. 86–7
724	620	„ „ f. 88
725	621	„ „ ff. 89–90

1904 (No. 6)	1901 (No. 5)	Original to be found in	1904 (No. 6)	1901 (No. 5)	Original to be found in
726	622	Add. MS. 34,889, ff. 91–2	769	663	Add. MS. 43,489, f. 41
727	623	„ 27,445, f. 36	770	664	„ „ f. 42
728	624	„ „ f. 36	771	665	„ „ f. 43
729	625	„ 34,889, f. 93	772	666	„ 27,445, f. 43
730	626	„ 43,489, f. 32	773	667	Mag. Coll. Oxf. Index of
731	627	Coll. of Arms. Brooke's			Deeds. Norfolk and
		Aspilogia, i. 35			Suffolk. No. 30
732	628	Add. MS. 34,889, f. 94	774	668	Add. MS. 43,489, f. 44
733	629	„ „ ff. 95–6	775	669	„ „ f. 45
734	630	„ 39,848, f. 50	776	670	„ 27,445, f. 45
735	631	„ 34,889, f. 97	777	671	„ 39,848, f. 57
736	632	„ 43,491, f. 10	778	672	„ 34,889, f. 111
737	633	„ 27,445, f. 37	779	673	Mag. Coll. Oxf. Index of
738	634	Add. Chart. 14,526			Deeds. Norfolk and
739	635	4 Hist. MSS. p. 461b			Suffolk. No. 5
740	636	Add. MS. 34,889, f. 98	780	674	Add. MS. 27,445, f. 46
741	LXXXII	„ „	781	675	„ 43,491, f. 16
		ff. 192–3	782	676	„ 43,489, f. 47
742	637	„ 43,491, f. 14	783	677	„ 34,889, f. 112
743	638	„ 43,489, f. 36	784	678	„ 27,445, f. 47
744	639	MS. Titchwell, 120, Mag.	785	679	„ „ f. 48
		Coll. Oxf.	786	680	„ „ f. 49
745	640	MS. Titchwell, 199, Mag.	787	681	„ „ f. 50
		Coll. Oxf.	788	682	„ „ f. 51
746	641	Add. MS. 34,889, f. 101	789 {	LXXXV	Add. MSS. 34,889, f. 130
747	642	„ „ f. 102		683	and 27,445, f. 52
748	643	„ 27,445, f. 38	790	684	Add. MS. 27,445, f. 53
749	644	Add. Chart. 17,249	791	685	„ „ f. 54
750	645	Mag. Coll. Oxf. Index	792	LXXXVI	„ 34,889, f. 211
		of Deeds. Norfolk and	793	686	„ 27,445, f. 55
		Suffolk. Nos. 11, 17,	794	LXXXIV	„ 34,889, f. 116
		28, 29, 36 and 61	795	687	„ 43,491, f. 17
751	646	Add. MS. 27,445, f. 39	796	688	„ 34,889, f. 120
752	647	„ „ f. 40	797	689	„ „ f. 121
753	648	„ 43,491, f. 15	798	690	„ 43,489, f. 49
754	649	Add. Chart. 17,250	799	691	Mag. Coll. Oxf. Index of
755	650	4 Hist. MSS. p. 461b			Deeds. Norfolk and
756	651	Add. MS. 27,445, ff. 41–			Suffolk. No. 38
		2 and f. 44	800	692	Add. MS. 43,491, f. 9
757	652	Mag. Coll. Oxf. Index	801	693	„ 27,445, f. 56
		of Deeds. Norfolk	802	694	„ „ f. 57
		and Suffolk. No. 4	803	695	„ „ f. 58
758	653	Copied by Fenn from	804	696	„ 43,489, f. 50
		Narford collection	805	697	„ 27,445, f. 59
759	654	Add. MS. 43,489, f. 44	806	698	„ 39,848, f. 58
760	655	„ 34,889, f. 104	807	699	Mag. Coll. Oxf. Index of
761	LXXXIII	„ „ f. 206			Deeds. Norfolk and
762	656	„ „ ff. 105–6			Suffolk. No. 63
763	657	4 Hist. MSS. p. 461b	808	700	Add. MS. 43,489, f. 51
764	658	„ „ „	809	701	„ „ f. 52
765	659	„ „ „	810	702	„ 27,445, f. 60
766	660	Add. MS. 34,889, f. 107	811	LXXXVII	„ 34,889, f. 108
767	661	Mag. Coll. Oxf. Index	812	703	„ 43,491, f. 18
		of Deeds. Norfolk	813	704	„ „ f. 19
		and Suffolk, no. 50	814	705	„ 27,445, f. 61
768	662	MS. Bod. Lib. Oxf.	815	706	„ „ f. 62

1904 (No. 6)	1901 (No. 5)	Original to be found in	1904 (No. 6)	1901 (No. 5)	Original to be found in
816	707	Add. MS. 27,445, f. 63	865	754	Add. MS. 27,445, f. 87
817	708	„ „ f. 64	866	755	„ 43,490, f. 156
818	709	Mag. Coll. Oxf. Index of Deeds. Southwark. No. 17a	867	756	„ 27,445, f. 88
			868	757	„ 34,889, f. 129
			869	xc	„ „ f. 215
819	710	Add. MS. 27,445, f. 65	870	58	„ 34,888, f. 22
820	711	„ „ f. 66	871	758	„ 27,445, f. 89
821	712	„ „ f. 67	872	759	Mag. Coll. Oxf. Index of Deeds. Norfolk and Suffolk. Nos. 13, 36
822	713	4 Hist. MSS. p. 462a			
823	714	Add. MS. 43,489, f. 38			
824	715	„ 27,445, f. 68	873	760	Add. MS. 27,445, f. 90
825	716	„ „ f. 69	874	761	„ 43,490, f. 16
826	717	„ 43,489, f. 55	875	762	„ 27,455, f. 91
827	718	Note by Gairdner	876	763	„ „ f. 92
828	719	Add. MS. 39,848, f. 59	877	764	„ 43,490, f. 17
829	720	„ 27,445, f. 70	878	765	„ 27,445, f. 93
830	721	„ 43,490, f. 4	879	766	MS. Bod. Lib. Oxf.
831	722	„ 27,445, f. 71	880	767	Add. MS. 27,445, f. 94
832	723	„ 43,490, f. 6	881	768	„ 43,490, f. 18
833	724	„ „ f. 7	882	769	„ 27,445, f. 95
834	725	„ „ f. 8	883	770	„ „ f. 96
835	726	Mag. Coll. Oxf. Index of Deeds. Norfolk. No. 67	884	771	„ 43,491, f. 20
			885	772	„ 27,445, f. 97
836	727	Add. MS. 43,490, f. 9	886	773	„ „ f. 98
837	LXXXVIII	„ 34,889, f. 125	887	774	„ „ f. 99
838	728	„ 27,445, f. 72	888	775	„ „ f. 100
839	729	„ 43,490, f. 10	889	776	„ 43,490, f. 20
840	730	Close Roll, 13 Ed. IV, m. 5	890	777	„ 27,445, f. 101
			891	778	„ „ f. 102
841	731	Add. MS. 43,490, f. 5	892	779	„ „ f. 103
842	732	„ 27,445, f. 73	893	xci	„ 34,889, f. 188
843	733	„ „ f. 74	894	780	„ 27,445, f. 104
844	734	„ „ f. 75	895	781	„ „ f. 105
845	735	Early Chancery Proceedings, vol. i. p. xc	896	782	„ 43,490, f. 22
			897	783	„ „ f. 23
846	736	Add. MS. 43,490, f. 11	898	784	„ „ f. 24
847	737	„ „ f. 44	899	785	„ „ f. 25
848	LXXXIX	„ 34,889, f. 122	900	786	„ „ f. 21
849	738	Add. Chart. 14,973	901	787	„ „ f. 26
850	739	Add. MS. 27,445, f. 76	902	788	„ „ f. 27
851	740	„ „ f. 77	903	789	„ 27,445, f. 106
852	741	„ „ f. 78	904	790	„ „ f. 107
853	742	„ „ f. 79	905	791	„ „ f. 108
854	743	„ „ f. 80	906	792	„ 43,491, f. 21
855	744	„ „ f. 81	907	793	„ 27,445, f. 109
856	745	„ „ f. 82	908	794	„ 43,491, f. 22
857	746	„ „ f. 83	909	795	„ 27,445, f. 110
858	747	„ 43,490, f. 13	910	796	„ „ f. 111
859	748	Mag. Coll. Oxf. Index of Deeds. Norfolk and Suffolk. No. 33	911	797	„ 43,491, f. 23
			912	798	„ 43,490, f. 31
			913	799	„ 27,445, f. 112
860	749	Add. MS. 43,490, f. 14	914	800	„ „ f. 32
861	750	„ „ f. 15	915	801	„ 27,445, f. 113
862	751	„ 27,445, f. 84	916	802	„ 27,446, f. 1
863	752	„ „ f. 85	917	803	„ „ f. 2
864	753	„ „ f. 86	918	804	„ 43,490, f. 33

1904 (No. 6)	1901 (No. 5)	Original to be found in	1904 (No. 6)	1901 (No. 5)	Original to be found in
919	805	Add. MS. 27,446, f. 3	975	859	Add. MS. 27,446, f. 47
920	806	„ „ f. 4	976	860	Add. Chart. 17,252
921	807	„ „ f. 5	977	981	Add. MS. 27,446, f. 119
922	808	„ „ f. 6	978	861	Add. Chart. 17,253
923	809	„ 43,490, f. 34	979	862	Add. MS. 27,446, f. 48
924	810	„ 27,446, f. 7	980	863	„ „ f. 49
925	811	„ „ f. 8	981	864	„ „ f. 50
926	812	„ „ f. 9	982	865	„ „ f. 51
927	xcii	„ 34,889, f. 152	983	866	„ „ f. 52
928	813	„ 27,446, f. 10	984	xciv	„ 34,889, f. 220
929	814	„ „ f. 11	985	867	Add. Chart. 17,256
930	815	„ 43,490, f. 35	986	868	Add. MS. 27,446, f. 53
931	816	„ 27,446, f. 12	987	869	„ 43,491, f. 26
932	817	„ „ f. 13	988	870	„ „ f. 27
933	818	„ 43,491, f. 24	989	871	„ 27,446, f. 54
934	819	„ 27,446, f. 14	990	872	„ „ f. 55
935	820	„ „ f. 15	991	873	„ „ f. 56
936	821	„ 43,491, f. 25	992	874	Printed by Fenn from a copy
937	822	„ 27,446, f. 16	993	875	Add. MS. 43,490, f. 42
938	823	„ „ f. 17	994	876	„ „ f. 48
939	824	„ „ f. 18	995	877	MS. Bod. Lib. Oxf.
940	825	„ „ f. 19	996	878	N.A. iv. p. 36
941	826	„ „ f. 20	997	879	Add. MS. 43,490, f. 49
942	827	„ 43,489, f. 25	998	880	Add. Chart. 17,257
934	828	Add. Chart. 17,251	999	881	Add. MS. 43,490, f. 52
944	829	Add. MS. 27,446, f. 22	1000	882	„ 27,446, f. 59
945	830	„ „ f. 23	1001	883	„ 43,490, f. 50
946	831	„ „ f. 24	1002	884	„ „ f. 53
947	832	„ „ f. 21	1003	885	„ 27,446, f. 60
948	833	„ „ f. 25	1004	886	„ „ f. 61
949	xciii	„ 34,889, f. 133	1005	xcv	„ 34,889, f. 228
950	834	„ 27,446, f. 26	1006	887	„ 43,490, f. 51
951	835	„ 27,451, f. 2	1007	888	„ 27,446, f. 62
952	836	„ 27,446, f. 27	1008	889	„ 43,490, f. 54
953	837	„ „ f. 28	1009	890	„ „ f. 55
954	838	„ „ f. 29	1010	891	N.A. iv. p. 24
955	839	„ „ f. 30	1011	xcvi	Add. MS. 34,889, f. 176
956	840	„ 43,490, f. 38	1012	892	Douce MS. 393, f. 78
957	841	„ 27,446, f. 32	1013	893	Add. MS. 27,446, f. 63
958	842	„ „ f. 31	1014	894	„ „ f. 64
959	843	„ „ f. 33	1015	895	„ „ f. 65
960	844	„ „ f. 34	1016	xcvii	„ 34,889, f. 135
961	845	„ „ f. 35	1017	896	„ 27,446, f. 66
962	846	„ 43,490, f. 39	1018	897	„ „ f. 67
963	847	„ 27,446, f. 36	1019	898	„ „ f. 68
964	848	„ „ ff. 37–8	1020	899	„ „ f. 69
965	849	„ „ f. 39	1021	900	Douce MS. 393, f. 84
966	850	„ „ f. 40	1022	xcviii	Add. MS. 34,889, f. 48
967	851	„ „ f. 41	1023	901	„ 27,446, f. 70
968	852	?	1024	902	„ „ f. 71
969	853	Add. MS. 27,446, f. 42	1025	903	„ „ f. 72
970	854	„ „ f. 43	1026	904	„ „ f. 73
971	855	„ „ f. 44	1027	xcix	„ 34,889, f. 139
972	856	„ 34,889, f. 134	1028	905	„ 27,446, f. 74
973	857	„ 27,446, f. 45	1029	906	„ „ f. 75
974	858	„ „ f. 46			

1904 (No. 6)	1901 (No. 5)	Original to be found in	1904 (No. 6)	1901 (No. 5)	Original to be found in
1030	907	Add. MS. 27,446, f. 76	1059	936	Add. MS. 27,446, f. 96
1031	908	„ 43,490, f. 12	1060	937	„ „ f. 97
1032	909	Douce MS. 393, f. 79	1061	932	„ „ f. 92
1033	910	Add. MS. 34,889, f. 137	1062	938	„ „ f. 98
1034	911	Douce MS. 393, f. 81	1063	941	N.A. p. 20
1035	912	„ „ f. 80	1064	934	Add. MS. 27,446, f. 94
1036	913	Add. MS. 27,446, f. 77	1065	942	Douce MS. 393, f. 87
1037	914	Douce MS. 393, f. 83	1066	943	N.A. iv. pp. 37–8
1038	915	Add. MS. 27,446, f. 78	1067	944	Add. MS. 27,446, f. 100
1039	916	„ „ f. 79	1068	945	„ „ f. 101
1040	917	„ „ f. 80	1069	946	„ „ f. 102
1041	918	„ „ f. 81	1070	947	„ „ f. 103
1042	919	„ „ f. 82	1071	939	„ „ f. 99
1043	920	„ „ f. 83	1072	940	Douce MS. 393, f. 86
1044	CI	MS. LC. II, 230, f. 7 Pemb. Coll. Camb.	1073	948	Add. MS. 34,889, f. 138
1045	921	Add. MS. 27,446, f. 84	1074	949	„ 27,446, f. 104
1046	922	„ „ f. 85	1075	950	„ „ f. 105
1047	923	„ „ f. 86	1076	951	„ „ f. 106
1048	924	„ „ f. 87	1077	952	„ „ f. 107
1049	925	Bod. Lib. Oxf. Chart. 729	1078	953	„ „ f. 108
1050	926	Add. MS. 27,446, f. 88	1079	954	Add. Chart. 17,255
1051	927	Douce MS. 393, f. 90	1080	CII	Add. MS. 34,889, f. 231
1052	928	„ „ f. 89	1081	CIII	„ 33,597, f. 10
1053	929	Add. MS. 27,446, f. 89	1082	CIV	„ 34,889, f. 148
1054	930	„ „ f. 90	1083	CV	„ „ f. 181
1055	931	„ „ f. 91	1084	982	?
1056	933	„ „ f. 93	1085	955	Add. MS. 27,446, f. 109
1057	c	„ 33,597, f. 9	1086	956	„ „ f.110
1058	935	„ 27,446, f. 95	1087	957	„ „ f. 111
			1088	958	„ „ f. 112

Wills			Wills		
1	983	Reg. Dioces. Norvic. Hyrning, f. 51b	5	987	Norw. Archdeaconry Reg. vol. i. f. 76a
2	984	Reg. Luffenham, f. 29	6	988	Reg. Milles, f. 12
3	985	Norwich Episcop. Reg. 16	7		Reg. Horne, f. 12
4	986	Norw. Archdeaconry Reg. vol. i. f, 29b	8		Reg. Norvic. Rix, f. 107
			9		Reg. Benet, f. 29

IV. LETTERS IN THE ORIGINAL SPELLING

A LOVE LETTER[1]

Ryght reverent and wurschypfull, and my ryght welebeloved Voluntyne, I recomande me unto yowe, ffull hertely desyring to here of yowr welefare, wheche I beseche Almyghty God long for to preserve un to Hys plesur, and yowr herts desyre. And yf it please yowe to here of my welefar, I am not in good heele of body, nor of herte, nor schall be tyll I her ffrom yowe:

> For there wottys no creature what peyn that I endure,
> And for to be deede, I dare it not dyscure.

And my lady my moder hath labored the mater to my ffadur full delygently, but sche can no mor gete then ye knowe of, for the wheche God knowyth I am full sory. But yf that ye loffe me, as I tryste verely that ye do, ye will not leffe me therefor; for if that ye hade not halfe the lyvelode that ye hafe, for to do the grettest labur that any woman on lyve myght, I wold not forsake yowe.

> And yf ye commande me to kepe me true wherever I go,
> I wyse I will do all my myght yowe to love and never no mo.
>> And yf my freends say, that I do amys,
>> Thei schal not me let so for to do,
> Myne herte me bydds ever more to love yowe
>> Truly over all erthely thing,
>> And yf thei be never so wroth,
> I tryst it schall be better in tyme commyng.

No more to yowe at this tyme, but the Holy Trinite hafe yowe in kepyng. And I besech you that this bill be not seyn of none erthely creatur safe only your selffe, &c.

And thys letter was indyte at Topcroft, with full hevy herte, &c.

By your own,

MARGERY BREWS.

MEDIEVAL MATCH-MAKING[2]

Trusty and weel be loved cosyn, I comaunde me to zow, desyryng to here of zowre weelfare and good spede in zowre matere, the qwech I prey God send zow to his plesaunce and to zoure hertys ease.

Cosyn, I lete zow wete that Scrope hath be in this cuntre

[1] *P.L.* No. 783.   [2] *P.L.* No. 71.

to se my cosyn zoure suotyr, and he hath spoken with my cosyn
zoure moder, and sche desyreth of hym that he schuld schewe
zow the endentures mad between the knyght that hath his
dowter and hym, whethir that Skrop, if he were maried and
fortuned to have children, if tho children schuld enheryte his
lond, or his dowter, the wheche is maried.

Cosyn, for this cause take gode hede to his endentures, for he
is glad to schewe zow hem, or whom ze wol a sygne with zow;
and he seith to me he is the last in the tayle of his lyflode, the
qweche is CCCL. marke and better, as Watkyn Shipdam seith, for
he hath take a compt of his liflode dyvers tymes; and Scrop
seith to me if he be maried, and have a sone an eyre, his dowter
that is maried schal have of his liflode L. marke and no more;
and therfore, cosyn, me seemeth he were good for my cosyn
zowre sustyr, with[out] that ye myght gete her a bethyr. And
if ze can gete a better, I wold avyse zow to labour it in as schort
tyme as ze may goodly, for sche was never in so gret sorow
as sche is now a dayes, for sche may not speke with no man,
ho so ever come, ne not may se ne speke with my man, ne with
servauntes of hir moderys but that sche bereth her an hand
otherwyse than she menyth. And sche hath sen Esterne the
most part be betyn onys in the weke or twyes, and some tyme
twyes on o day, and hir hed broken in to or thre places. Wherfor,
cosyn, sche hath sent to me by Frere Newton in gret
counsell, and preyeth me that I wold send to zow a letter of hir
hevynes, and prey zow to be hir good brothyr, as hir trost is
in zow; and sche seith, if ze may se be his evydences that his
childern and hire may enheryten, and sche to have resonable
joynture, sche hath herd so meche of his birth and his condicions,
that and ze will sche will have hym, whethyr that hir moder
wil or wil not, not withstandyng it is tolde hir his persone is
symple, for sche seyth men shull have the more deyute of hire
if sche rewle hire to hym as sche awte to do.

Cosyn, it is told me ther is a goodly man in yowre Inne, of
the qweche the fader deyed litte, and if ze thynk that he were
better for hir than Scroop, it wold be laboured, and yif Scroop
a goodly answere that he be not put of tyl ze be sure of a bettyr;
for he seid whan he was with me, but if he have some counfort-
able answer of zow, he wil no more laboure in this mater be
cause he myght not se my cosyn zoure sustyr, and he seyth he
myght a see hire and sche had be bettyr than she is; and that
causeth hym to demyr that hir moder was not weel willyng, and
so have I sent my cosyn zowre moder word. Wherfore, cosyn,
thynk on this mateer, for sorow oftyn tyme causeth women to
be set hem otherwyse then thei schulde do, and if sche where

in that case, I wot weel ze wold be sory. Cosyn, I prey zow brenne this letter, that zowre men ne non other man se it; for and my cosyn zowre moder knew that I had sent yow this letter, sche shuld never love me. No more I wrighte to zow at this tyme, but Holy Gost have zow in kepyng. Wretyn in hast, on Seynt Peterys day, be candel lyght.

Be youre Cosyn,

ELIZABETH CLERE.

THE OBEDIENT SON[1]

Ryght worschful Syr, in the most lowly wyse, I comaund me to yowr good faderhod, besechyng yow of yowre blyssyng. Mut it plese yowr faderhod to remembre and concydre the peyn and hevynesse that it hath ben to me syn yowr departyng owt of thys contre, here abydyng tyl the tyme it please yow to schewe me grace, and tyl the tyme that by reporte my demenyng be to yowr plesyng; besechyng yow to concydre that I may not, ner have noo mene to seke to yow as I ought to do, and savyng under thys forme, whych I besech yow be not take to no dysplesur, ner am not of power to do any thynge in thys contre for worschyp or profyht of yow, ner ease of yowr tenantys whych myght and scholde be to yowr pleasyng. Wherfor I besech yow of yowr faderly pyte to tendre the more thys symple wryghtyng, as I schal owt of dowght her after doo that schal please yow to the uttermost of my power and labor; and if ther be any servyce that I may do if it please yow to comaund me, or if y maye understonde it, I wyl be as glad to do it as any thyng erthely, if it wer any thyng that myght be to yowr pleasyng. And no mor, but Allmyghty God have yow in kepyng.

Wretyn the v. day of Marche.

By your older sone,

JOHN PASTON.

[1] *P.L.* No. 323.

INDEX

Note. John Paston, and his two sons John, are referred to as
John I, John II, John III respectively.

Printed in the United States
55015LVS00001B/100-117